[bad__]
[news_]

HELLIONS BY ZEB WELLS VOL. 1. Contains material originally published in magazine form as HELLIONS (2020) #1-4. First printing 2020. ISBN 978-1-302-92558-1. Published by MARVEL WORLDWIDE, INC., a subsidiary of MARVEL ENTERTAINMENT, LLC. OFFICE OF PUBLICATION: 1290 Avenue of the Americas, New York, NY 10104. © 2020 MARVEL No similarity between any of the names, characters, persons, and/or institutions in this magazine with those of any living or dead person or institution is intended, and any such similarity which may exist is purely coincidental. **Printed in Canada.** KEVIN FEIGE, Chief Creative Officer; DAN BUCKLEY, President, Marvel Entertainment; JOHN NEE, Publisher; JOE QUESADA, EVP & Creative Director; TOM BREVOORT, SVP of Publishing; DAVID BOGART, Associate Publisher & SVP of Talent Affairs; Publishing & Partnership; DAVID GABRIEL, VP of Print & Digital Publishing; JEFF YOUNGQUIST, VP of Production & Special Projects; DAN CARR, Executive Director of Publishing Technology; ALEX MORALES, Director of Publishing Operations; DAN EDINGTON, Managing Editor; RICKEY PURDIN, Director of Talent Relations; SUSAN CRESPI, Production Manager; STAN LEE, Chairman Emeritus. For information regarding advertising in Marvel Comics or on Marvel.com, please contact Vit DeBellis, Custom Solutions & Integrated Advertising Manager, at vdebellis@marvel.com. For Marvel subscription inquiries, please call 888-511-5480. **Manufactured between 9/30/2020 and 10/27/2020 by SOLISCO PRINTERS, SCOTT, QC, CANADA.**

10 9 8 7 6 5 4 3 2 1

HELLIONS

Writer: Zeb Wells
Artist: Stephen Segovia
Color Artist: David Curiel
Letterers: VC's Cory Petit (#1–2)
& Ariana Maher (#3-4)

Cover Art: Stephen Segovia
& Rain Beredo

Head of X: Jonathan Hickman
Design: Tom Muller
Assistant Editors: Annalise Bissa
& Lauren Amaro
Editor: Jordan D. White

Collection Editor: Jennifer Grünwald
Assistant Managing Editor: Maia Loy
Assistant Managing Editor: Lisa Montalbano
Editor, Special Projects: Mark D. Beazley
VP Production & Special Projects: Jeff Youngquist
SVP Print, Sales & Marketing: David Gabriel
Editor in Chief: C.B. Cebulski

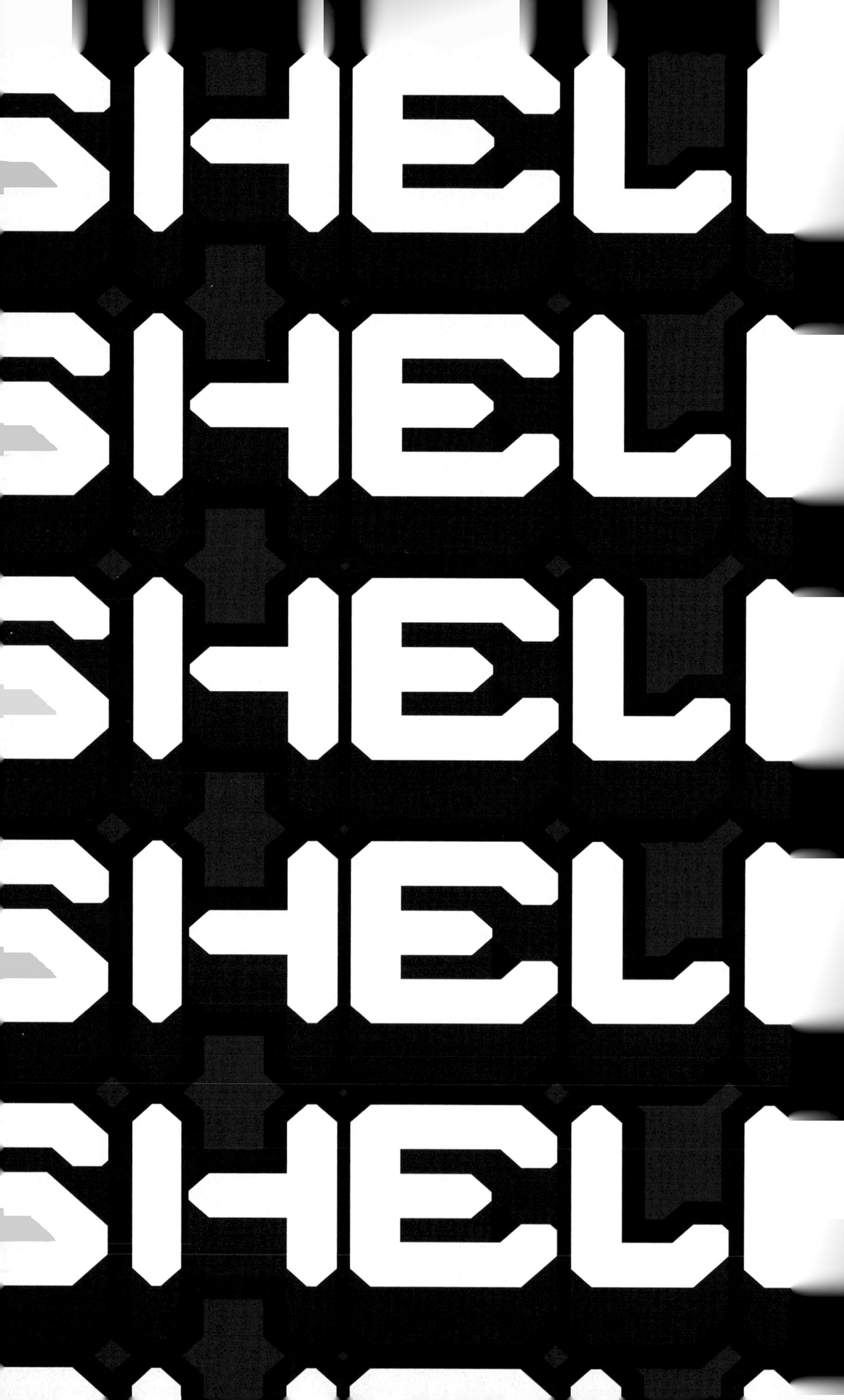

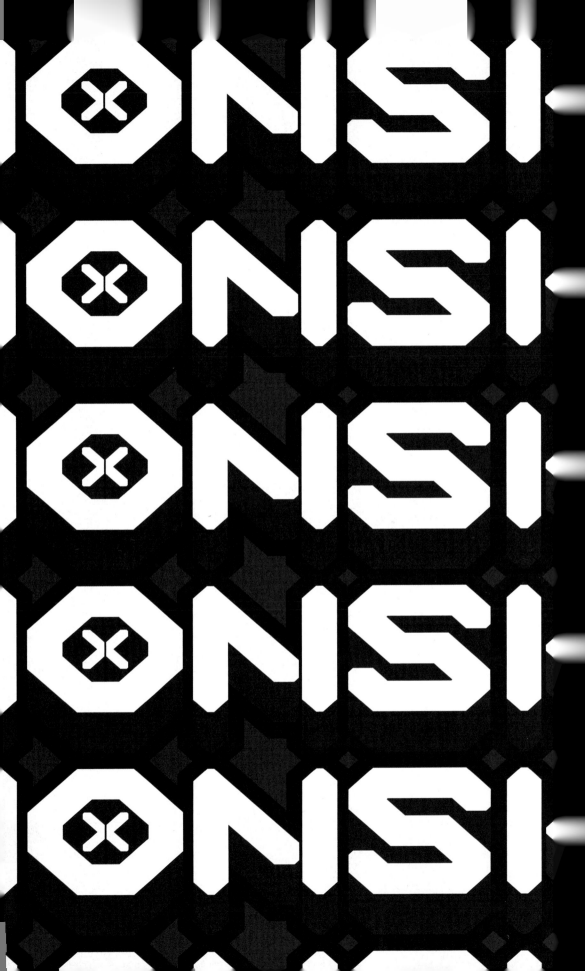

[dawn_of_x]

[bad__]
[news_]

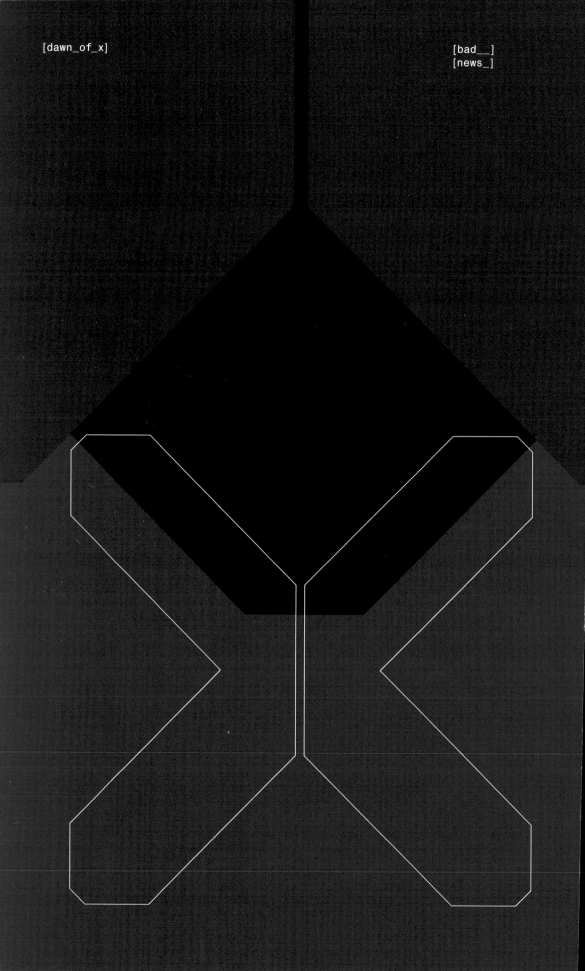

[hell_[0.1]
[ions_[0.1]

It is folly to create an Eden, if one
has no use for snakes.

-NIGHTCRAWLER

[hell_[0.X]
[ions_[0.X]

[hell_[0.1].....]
[ions_[0.1].....]

[Hellions_alpha.]

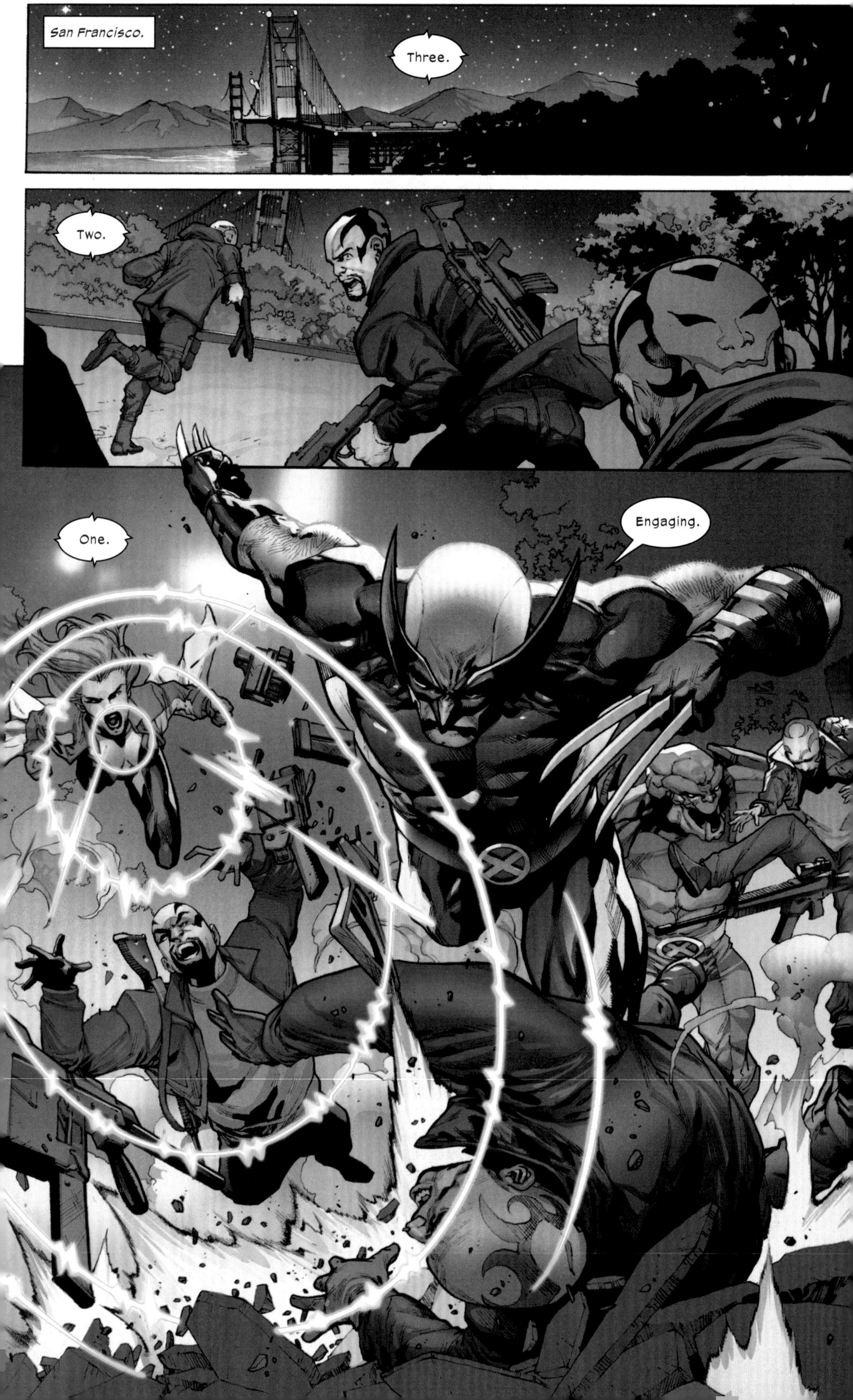
San Francisco.
Three.
Two.
One.
Engaging.

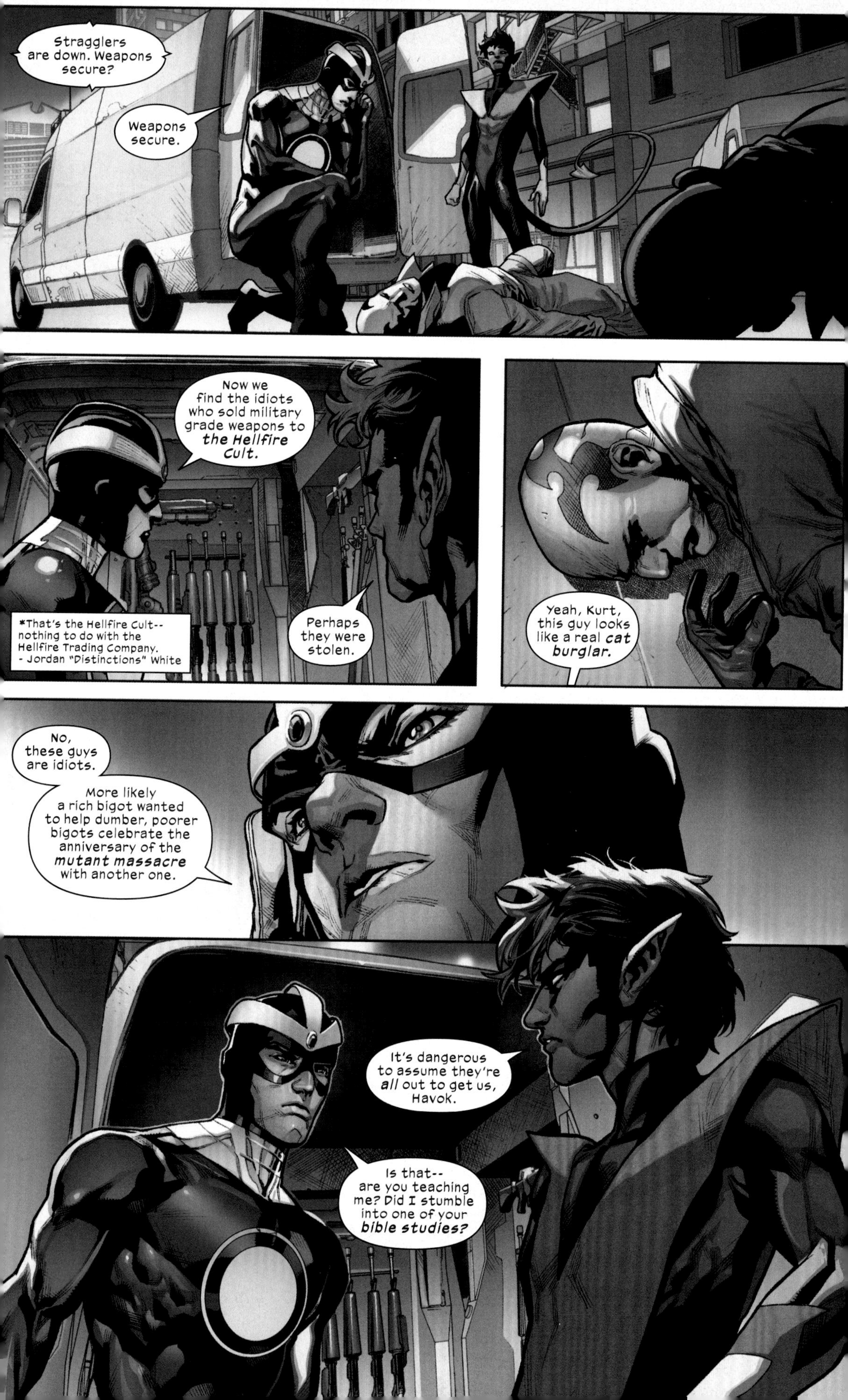
Stragglers are down. Weapons secure?
Weapons secure.
Now we find the idiots who sold military grade weapons to the Hellfire Cult.
*That's the Hellfire Cult--nothing to do with the Hellfire Trading Company. - Jordan "Distinctions" White
Perhaps they were stolen.
Yeah, Kurt, this guy looks like a real cat burglar.
No, these guys are idiots.
More likely a rich bigot wanted to help dumber, poorer bigots celebrate the anniversary of the mutant massacre with another one.
It's dangerous to assume they're all out to get us, Havok.
Is that--are you teaching me? Did I stumble into one of your bible studies?

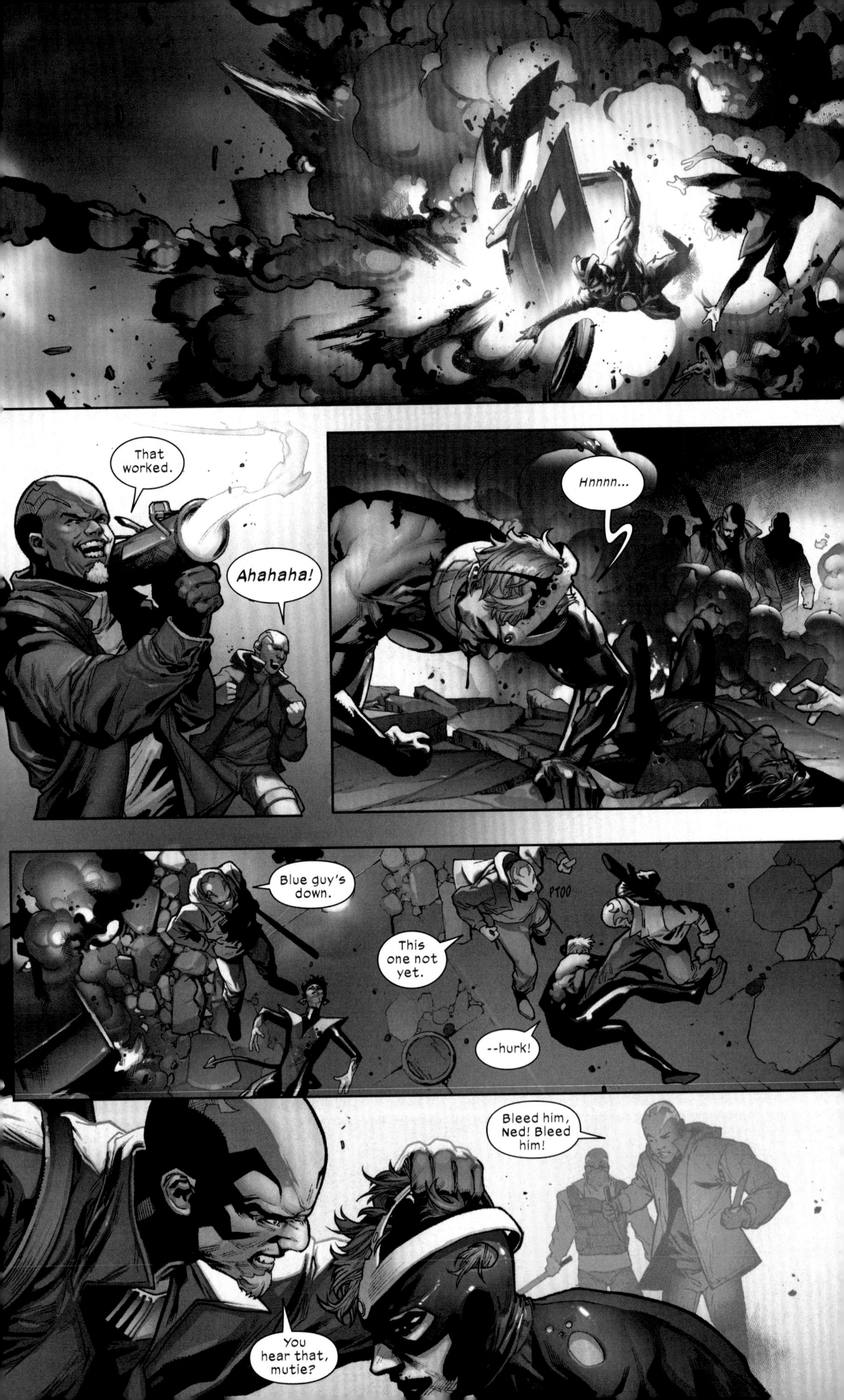
That worked.
Ahahaha!
Hnnnn...
Blue guy's down.
PTOO
This one not yet.
--hurk!
Bleed him, Ned! Bleed him!
You hear that, mutie?

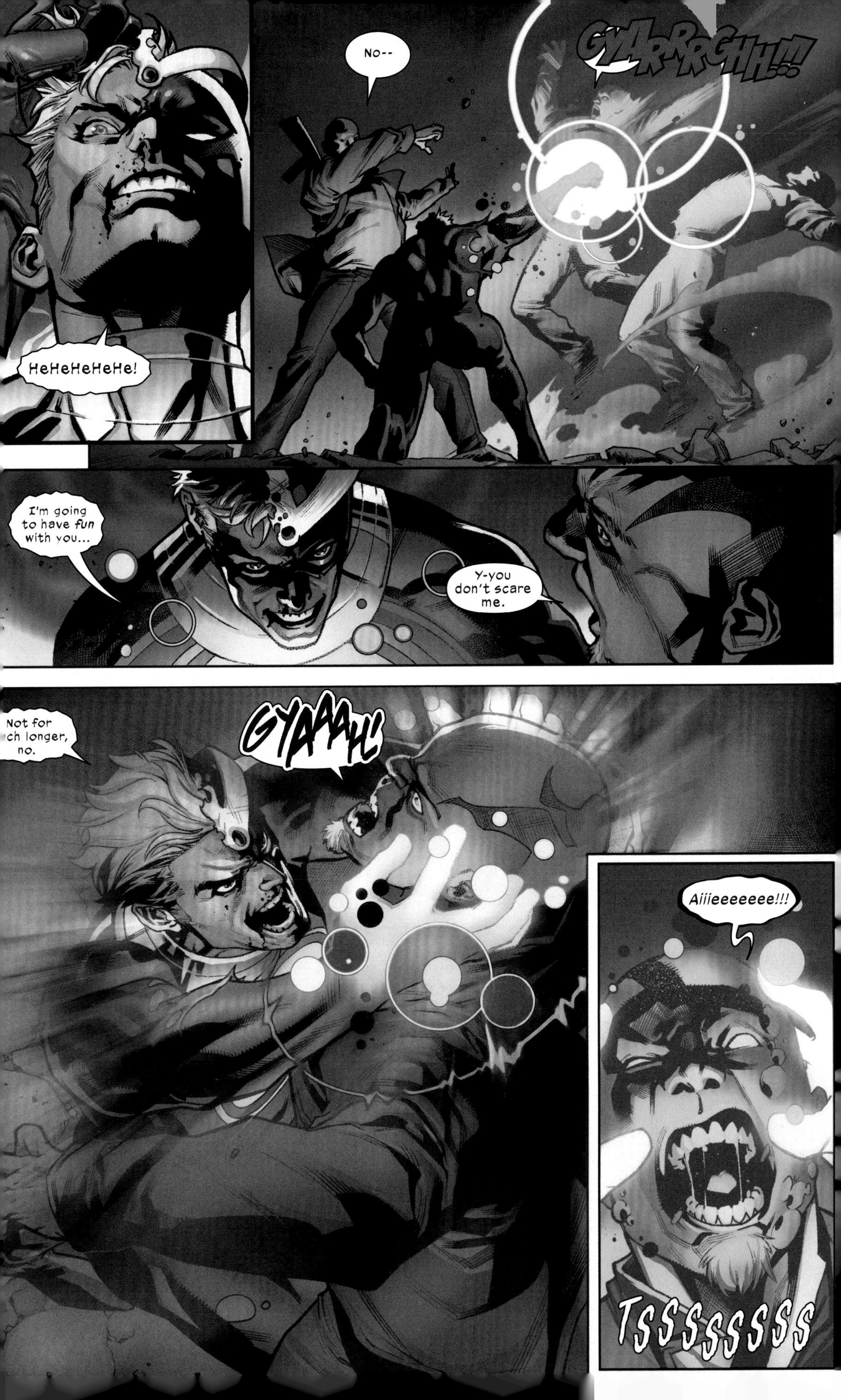
HeHeHeHeHe!
No--
GYARRRGHH!!!
I'm going to have fun with you...
Y-you don't scare me.
Not for ch longer, no.
GYAAAH!
Aiiieeeeeee!!!
TSSSSSSSS

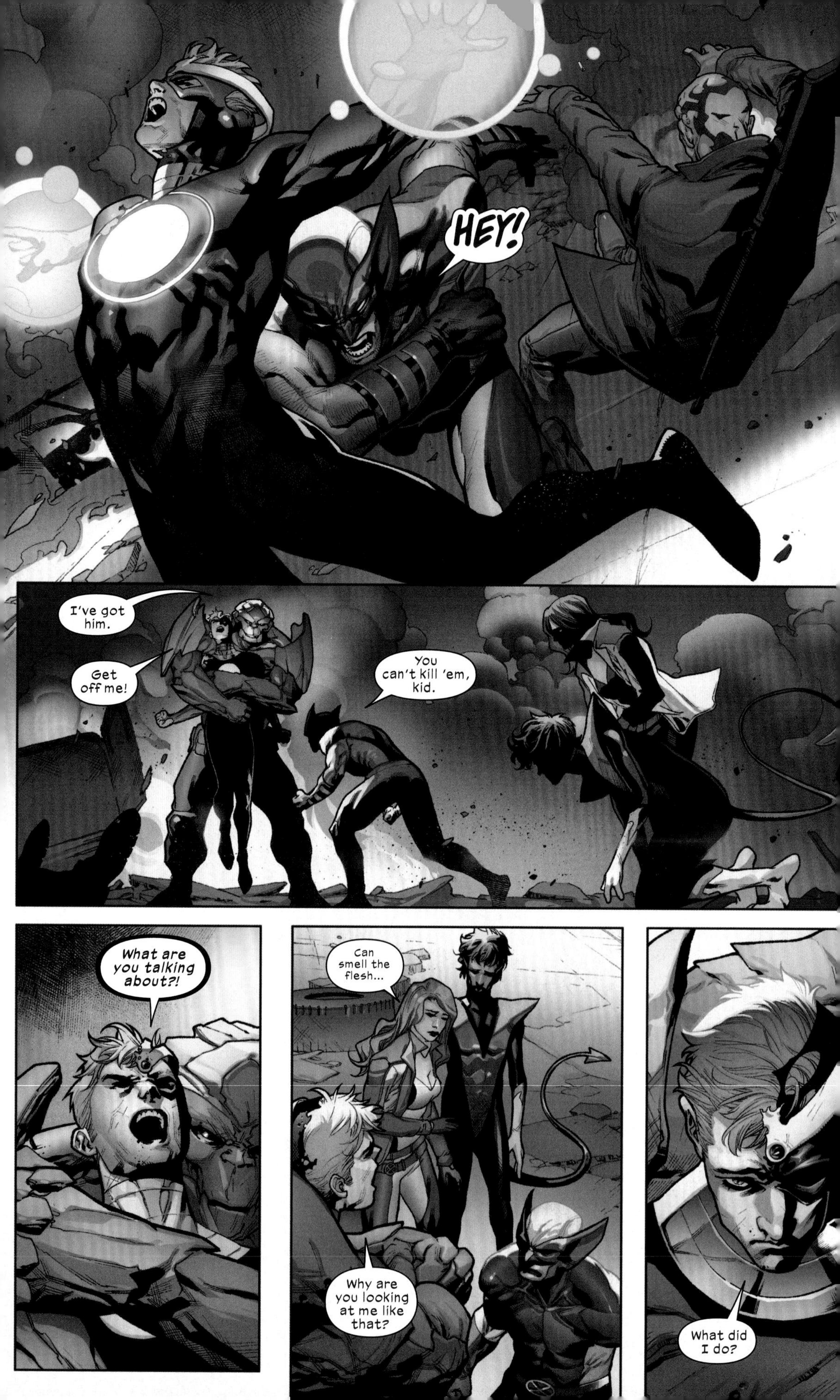
HEY!
I've got him.
Get off me!
You can't kill 'em, kid.
What are you talking about?!
Can smell the flesh...
Why are you looking at me like that?
What did I do?

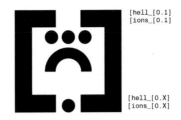

[hell_[0.1]
[ions_[0.1]

[hell_[0.X]
[ions_[0.X]

WELCOME HOME

The island-nation of Krakoa offers a home -- and a fresh start -- for all mutants.

Easier said than done.

Havok

Orphan-Maker

Nanny

Wild Child

Empath

Scalphunter

Mr. Sinister

Psylocke

[hell_[0.1]...]
[ions_[0.1]...]

[.wreaking....]

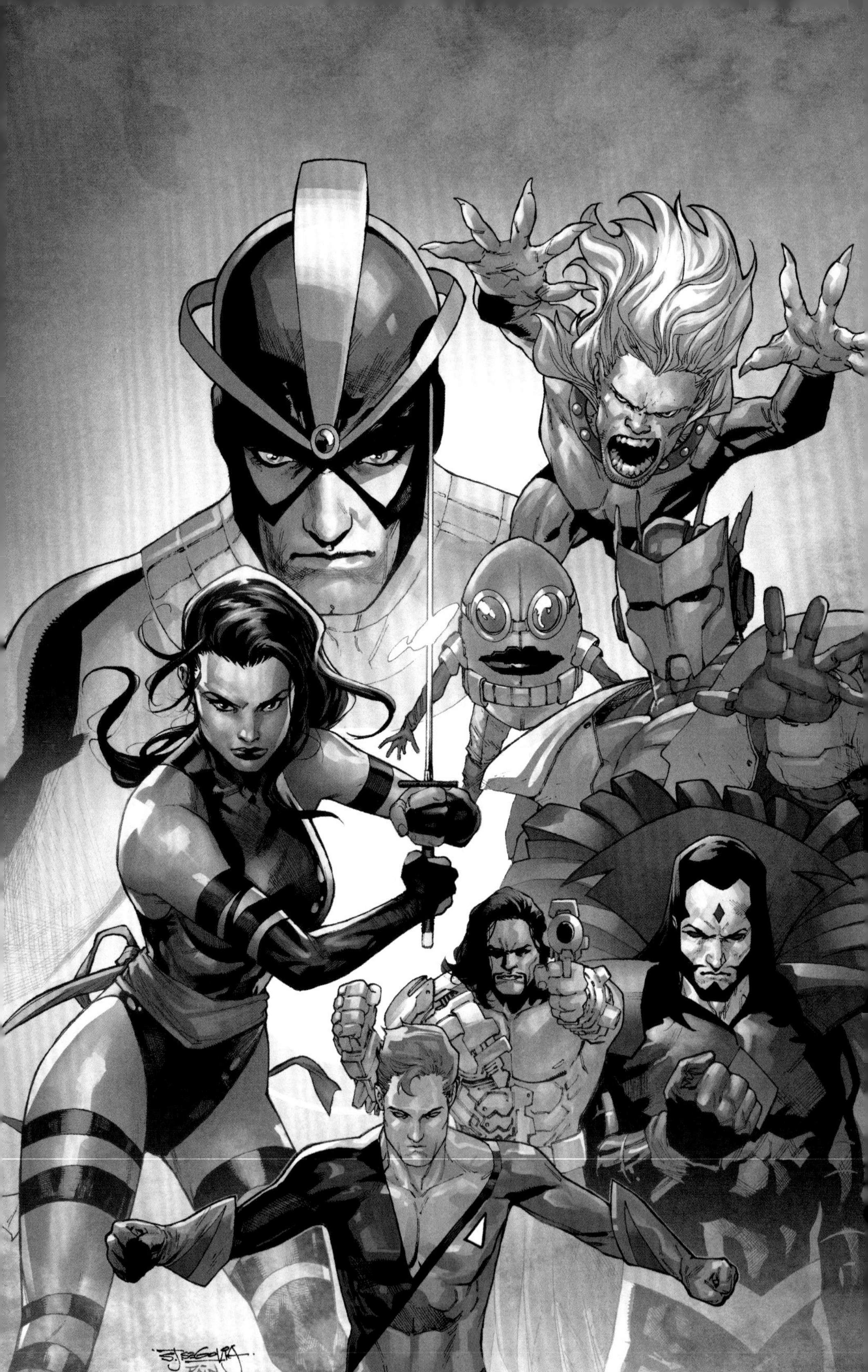

Let Them Be Snakes

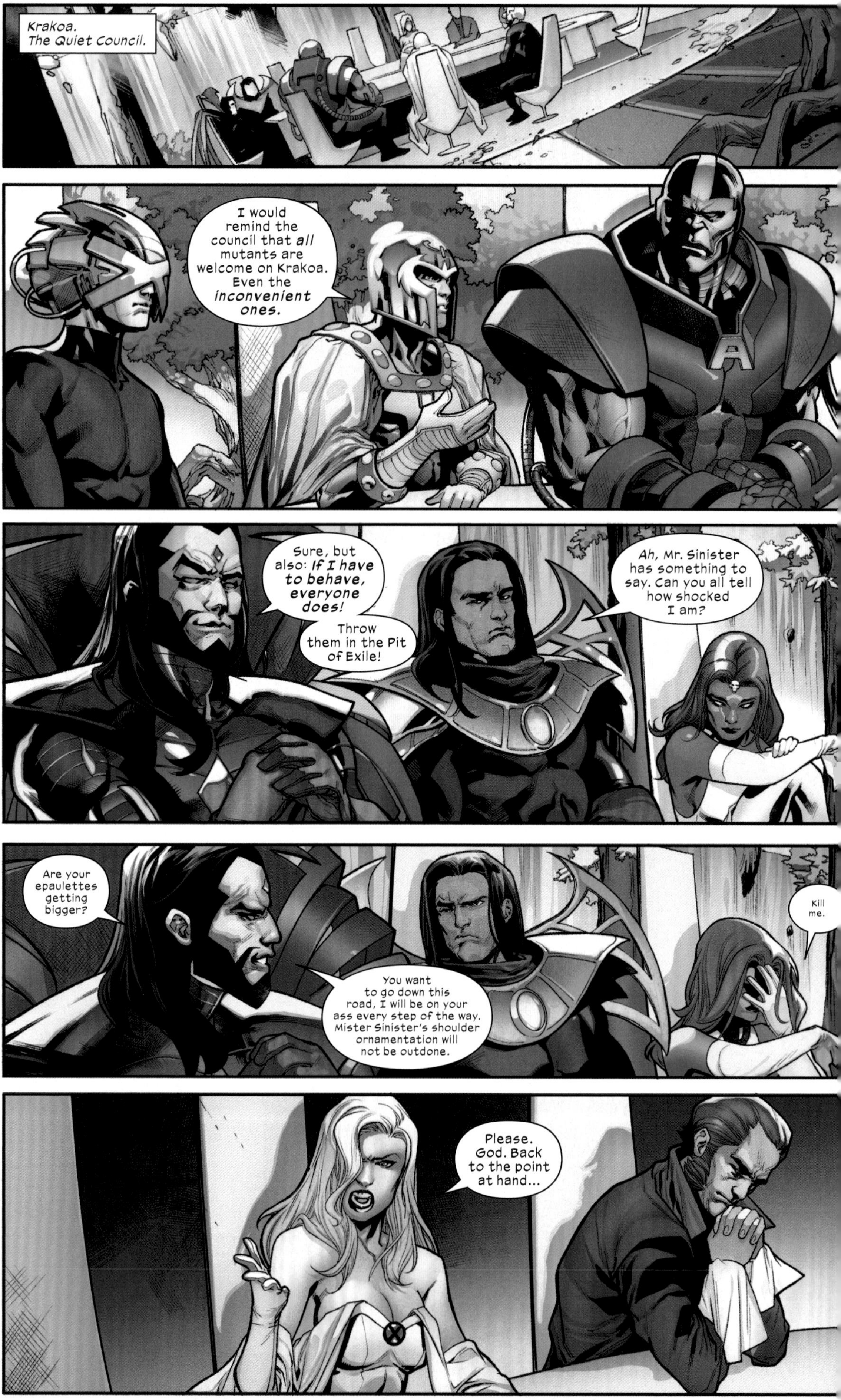
Krakoa. The Quiet Council.
I would remind the council that *all* mutants are welcome on Krakoa. Even the *inconvenient ones.*
Sure, but also: ***If I have to behave, everyone does!***
Throw them in the Pit of Exile!
Ah, Mr. Sinister has something to say. Can you all tell how shocked I am?
Are your epaulettes getting bigger?
You want to go down this road, I will be on your ass every step of the way. Mister Sinister's shoulder ornamentation will not be outdone.
Kill me.
Please. God. Back to the point at hand...

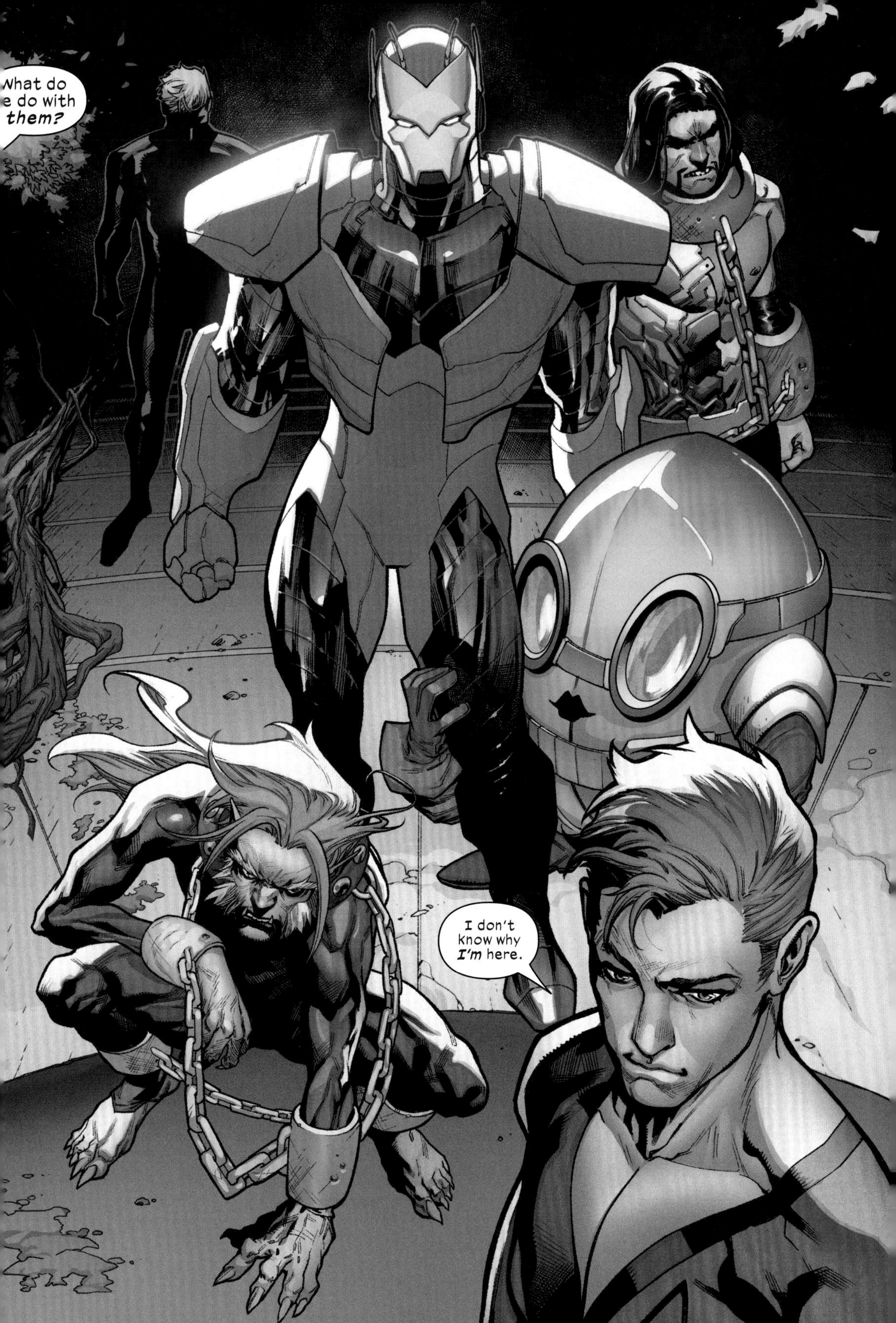
What do
e do with
them?
I don't
know why
I'm here.

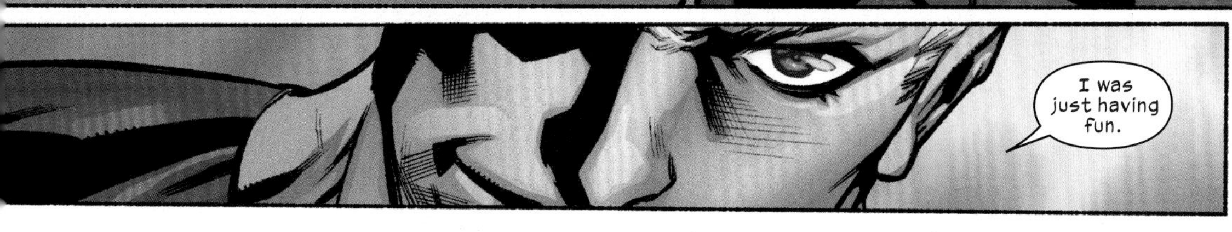
I was
just having
fun.

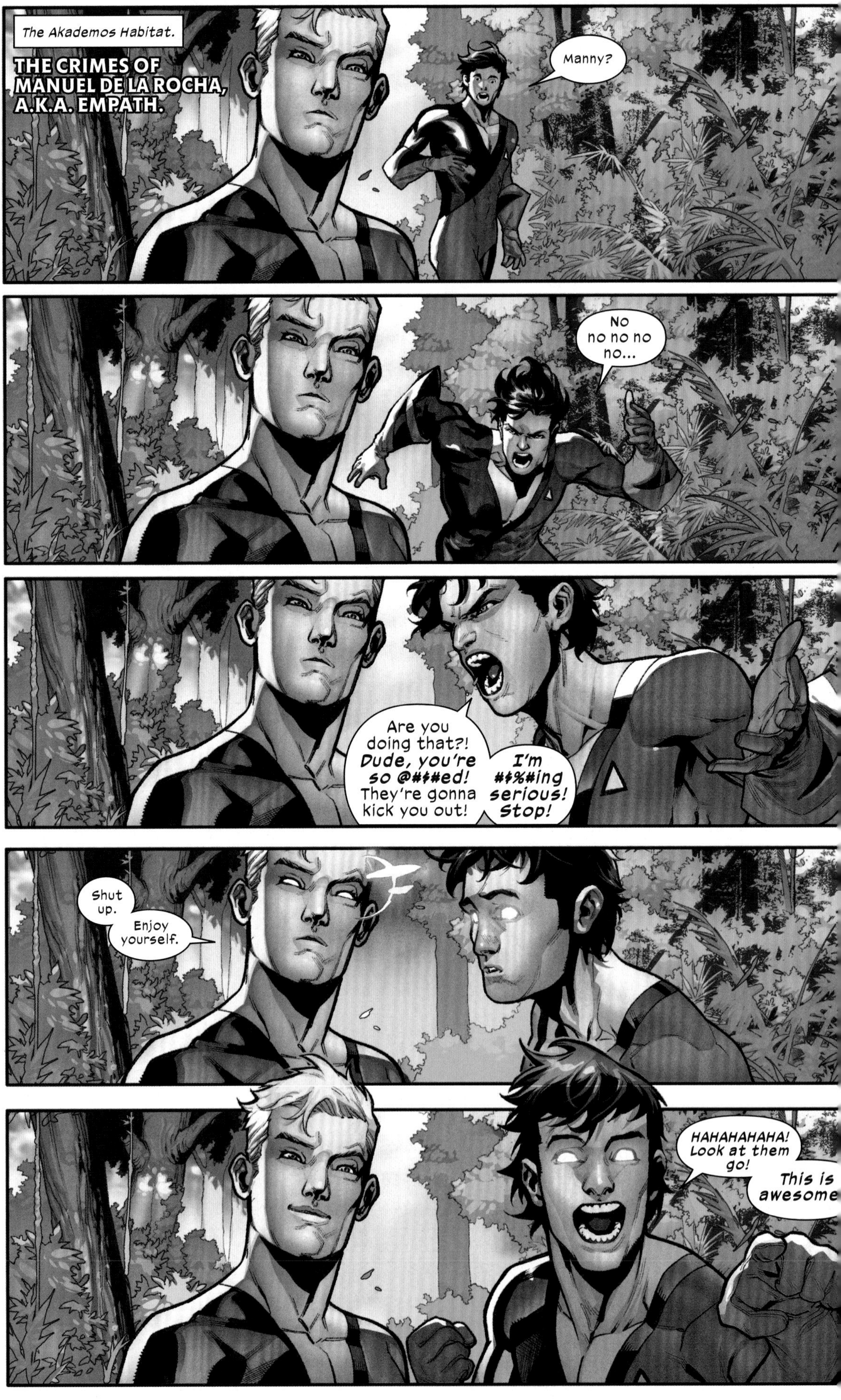
The Akademos Habitat.
THE CRIMES OF MANUEL DE LA ROCHA, A.K.A. EMPATH.
Manny?
No no no no no...
Are you doing that?! Dude, you're so @#$#ed! They're gonna kick you out!
I'm #$%#ing serious! Stop!
Shut up.
Enjoy yourself.
HAHAHAHAHA! Look at them go!
This is awesome

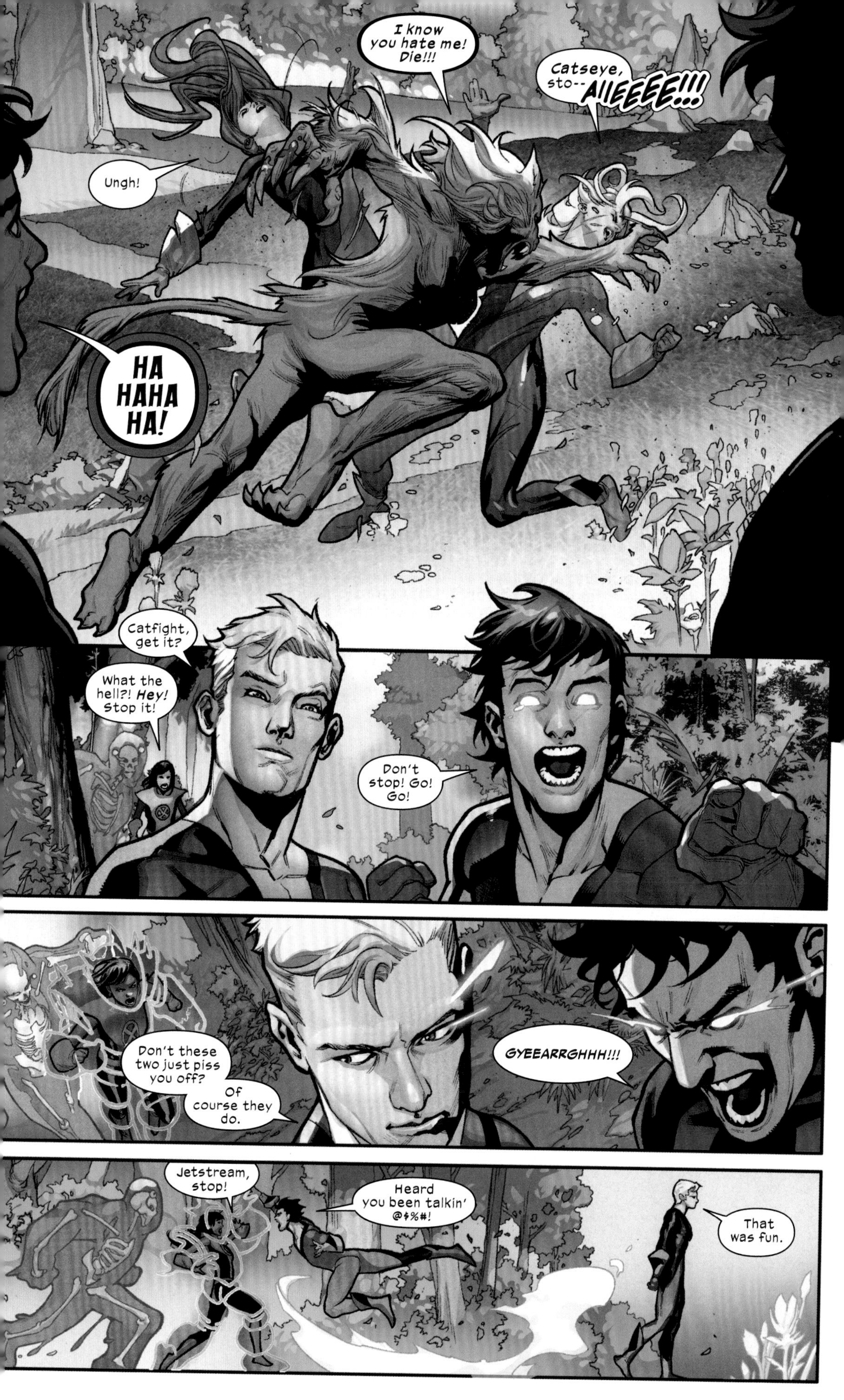
I know you hate me! Die!!!
Catseye, sto--AIIEEEE!!!
Ungh!
HA HAHA HA!
Catfight, get it?
What the hell?! Hey! Stop it!
Don't stop! Go! Go!
Don't these two just piss you off?
Of course they do.
GYEEARRGHHH!!!
Jetstream, stop!
Heard you been talkin' @$%#!
That was fun.

THE EMPATH PROBLEM

Notes on Manuel de la Rocha

I've finally analyzed the temporal psi-slices Emma harvested from Manuel de la Rocha's brain. The results were disturbing as expected, but for an alarming reason. They revealed a cold, sadistic mind ravaged not by psychosis or genetic defect, but bad data.

To explain: The brains of our species, like those of our *homo sapiens* cousins, come hardwired for environmental feedback. We touch a flame, we get hurt, we never touch the flame again.

So too do we look to our peers for emotional feedback. We hurt a friend, their tears shame us, we strive to bring back a smile. And so we learn to bargain, apologize, embrace and connect.

Not so Empath. Upon the activation of his X-gene (at an atypically young age), Manuel gained the power to control the emotions of others. He had only to flex his mind and all social feedback became positive. No matter how hurtful his actions, he only experienced love and adoration in return. His insults would inspire affection. His violence, adulation. His sadism, devotion. No action was so heinous as to alienate him from his peers, as they were under his thrall. Environmental cause and effect, the emotional data the mind relies on to form its reality, disappeared.

Manuel de la Rocha is a warped, profoundly unpleasant young man. A danger to every mutant on Krakoa. But the uncomfortable truth of his case is this: A violent sociopath was not gifted the X-gene, the X-gene created a violent sociopath.

Knowing this, what do we do with the other mutants whose gifts, in their expression, are intrinsically antisocial?

How do we rehabilitate them without fundamentally rejecting their mutant identity?

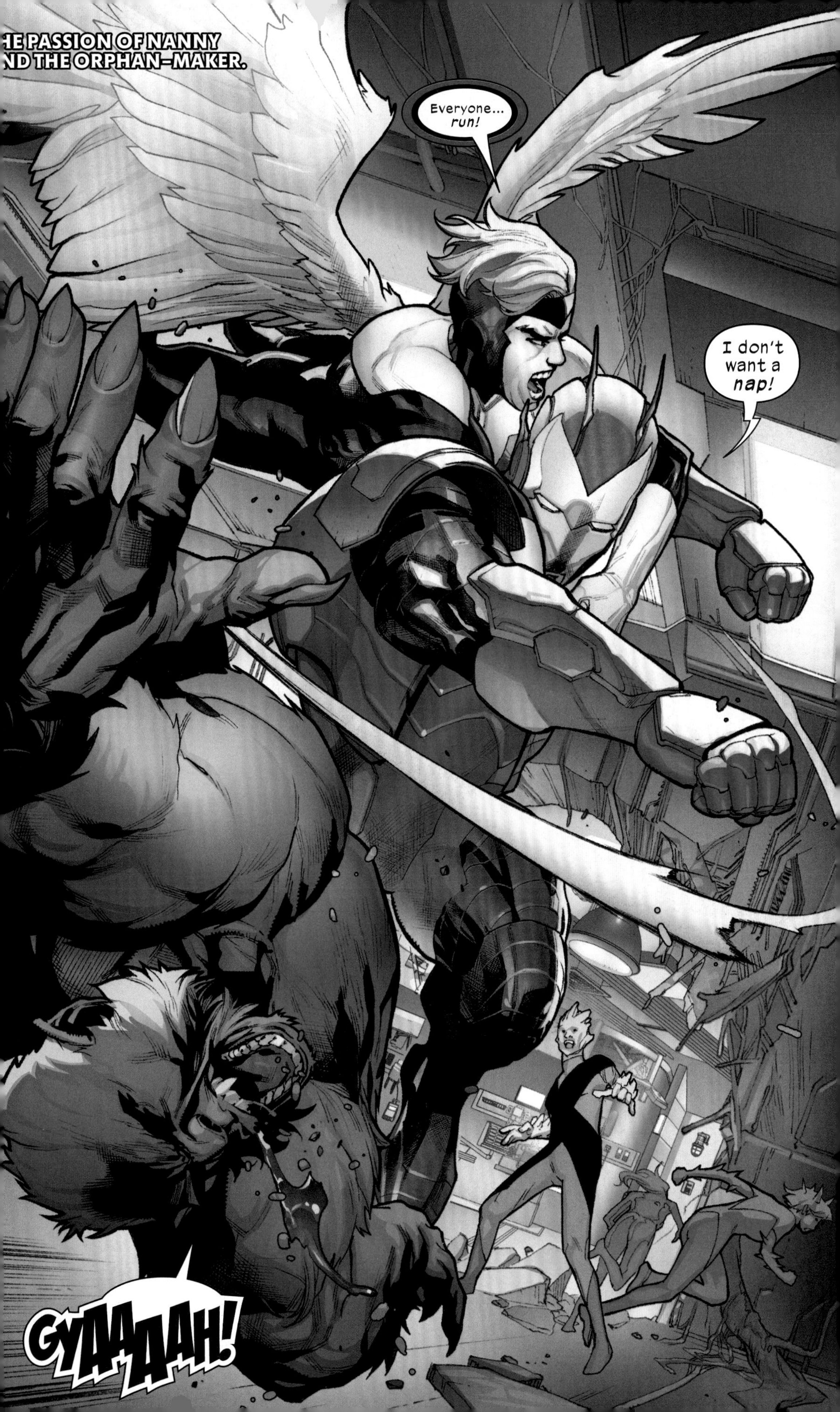
HE PASSION OF NANNY
ND THE ORPHAN-MAKER.
Everyone... *run!*
I don't want a *nap!*
GYAAAAAH!

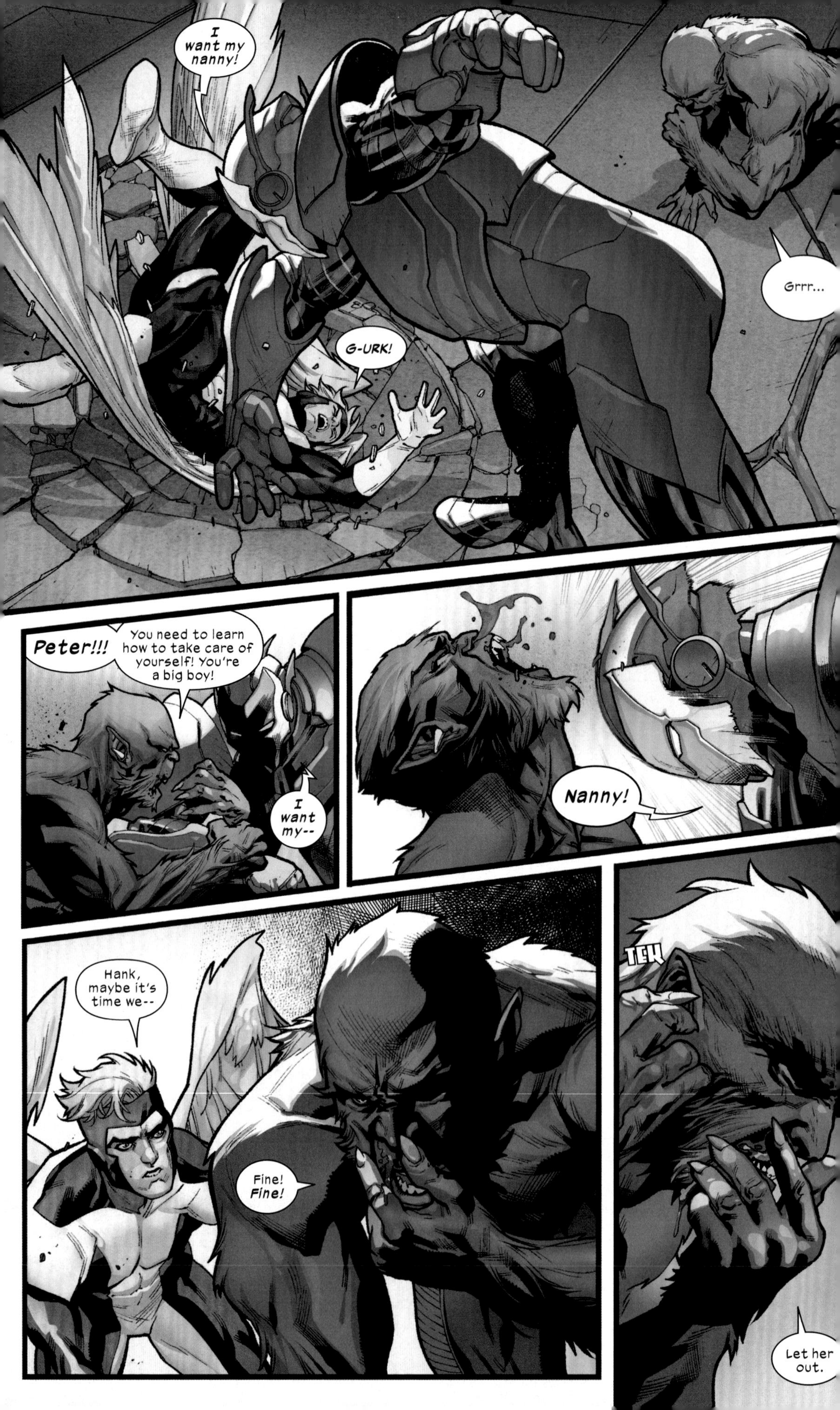
I want my nanny!
Grrr...
G-URK!
Peter!!!
You need to learn how to take care of yourself! You're a big boy!
I want my--
Nanny!
Hank, maybe it's time we--
Fine! Fine!
TEK
Let her out.

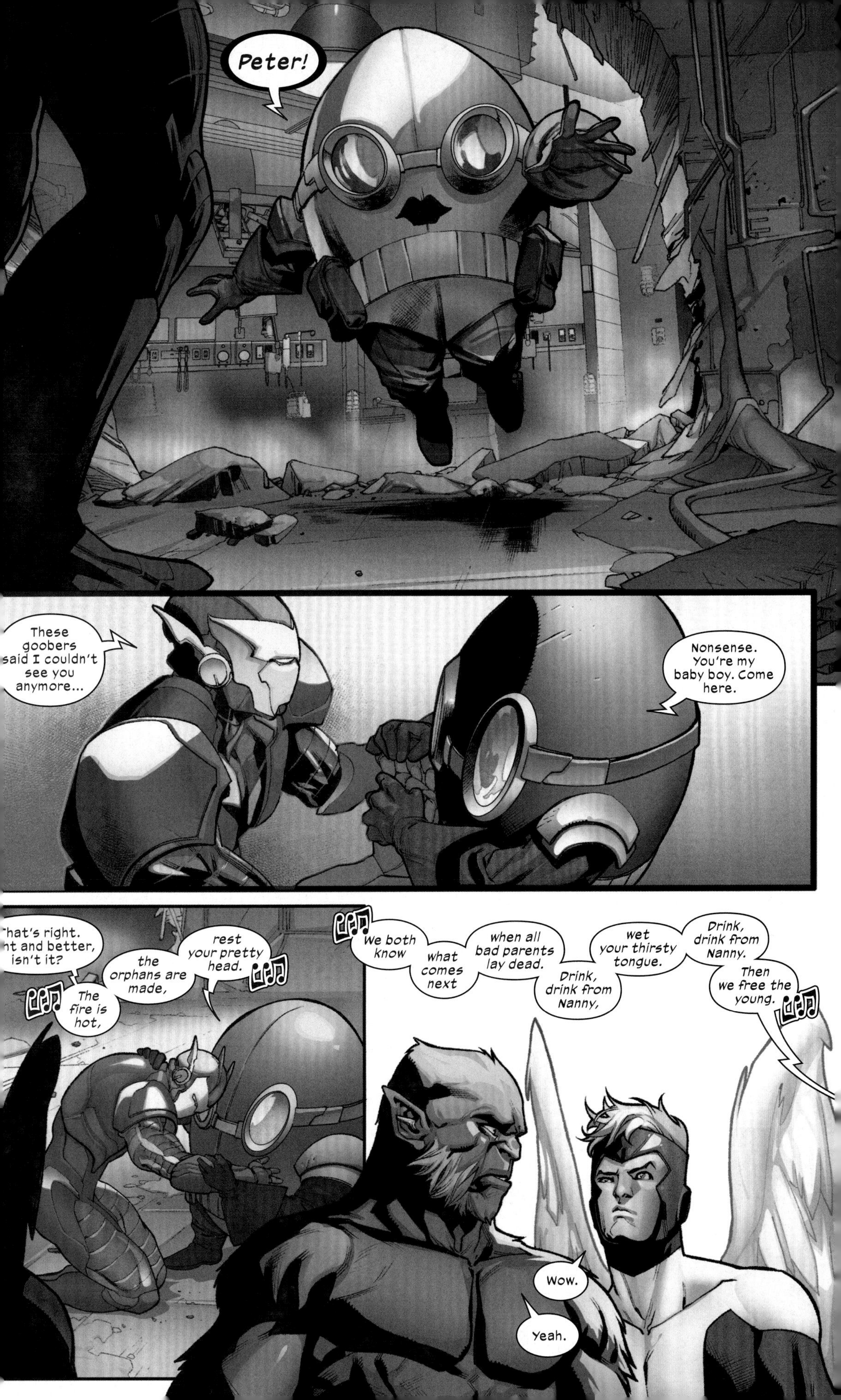
Peter!
These goobers said I couldn't see you anymore...
Nonsense. You're my baby boy. Come here.
hat's right.
nt and better, isn't it?
The fire is hot,
the orphans are made,
rest your pretty head.
We both know
what comes next
when all bad parents lay dead.
Drink, drink from Nanny,
wet your thirsty tongue.
Drink, drink from Nanny.
Then we free the young.
Wow.
Yeah.

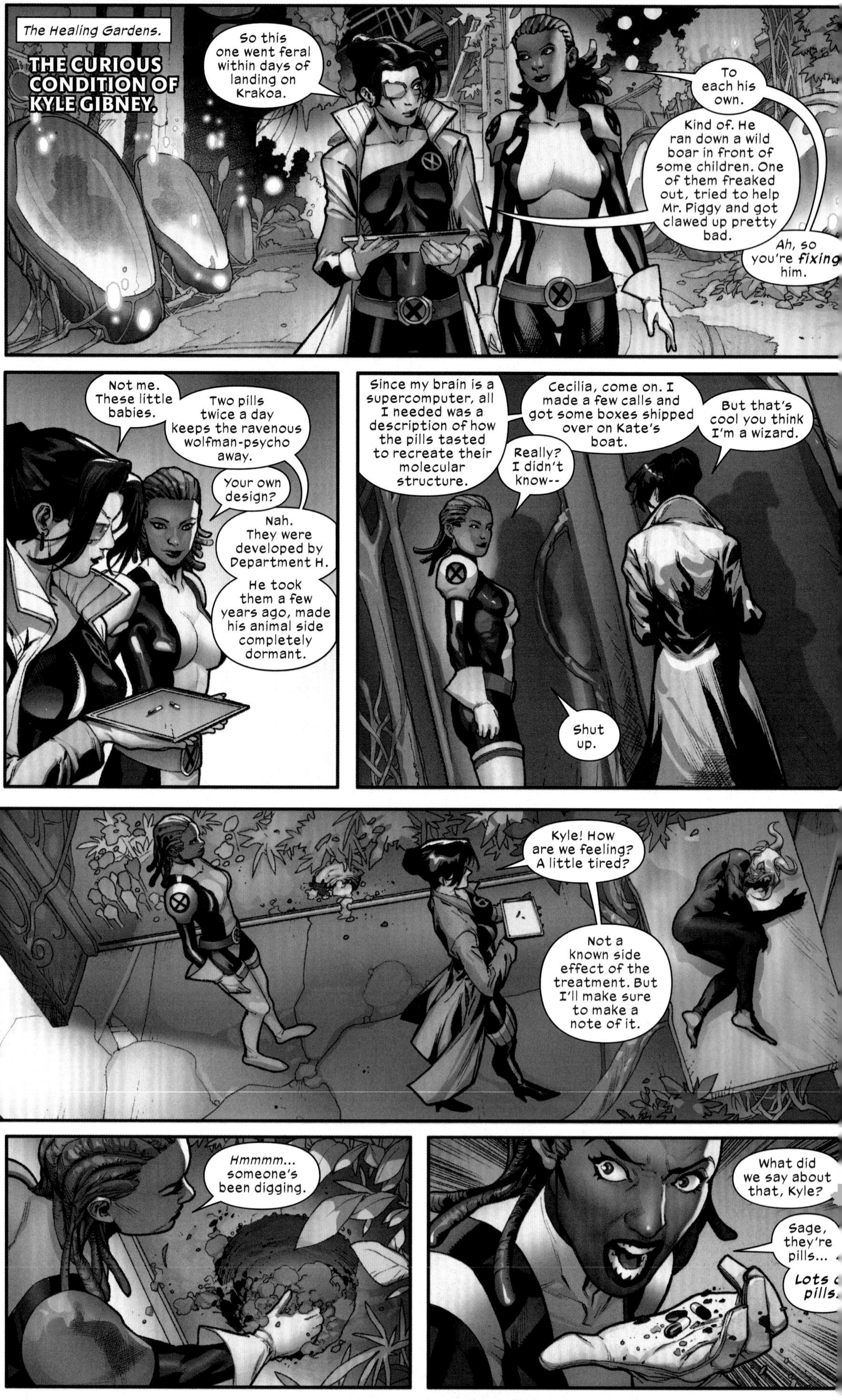

The Healing Gardens.
THE CURIOUS CONDITION OF KYLE GIBNEY.
So this one went feral within days of landing on Krakoa.
To each his own.
Kind of. He ran down a wild boar in front of some children. One of them freaked out, tried to help Mr. Piggy and got clawed up pretty bad.
Ah, so you're fixing him.
Not me. These little babies.
Two pills twice a day keeps the ravenous wolfman-psycho away.
Your own design?
Nah. They were developed by Department H.
He took them a few years ago, made his animal side completely dormant.
Since my brain is a supercomputer, all I needed was a description of how the pills tasted to recreate their molecular structure.
Cecilia, come on. I made a few calls and got some boxes shipped over on Kate's boat.
Really? I didn't know--
But that's cool you think I'm a wizard.
Shut up.
Kyle! How are we feeling? A little tired?
Not a known side effect of the treatment. But I'll make sure to make a note of it.
Hmmmm... someone's been digging.
What did we say about that, Kyle?
Sage, they're pills...

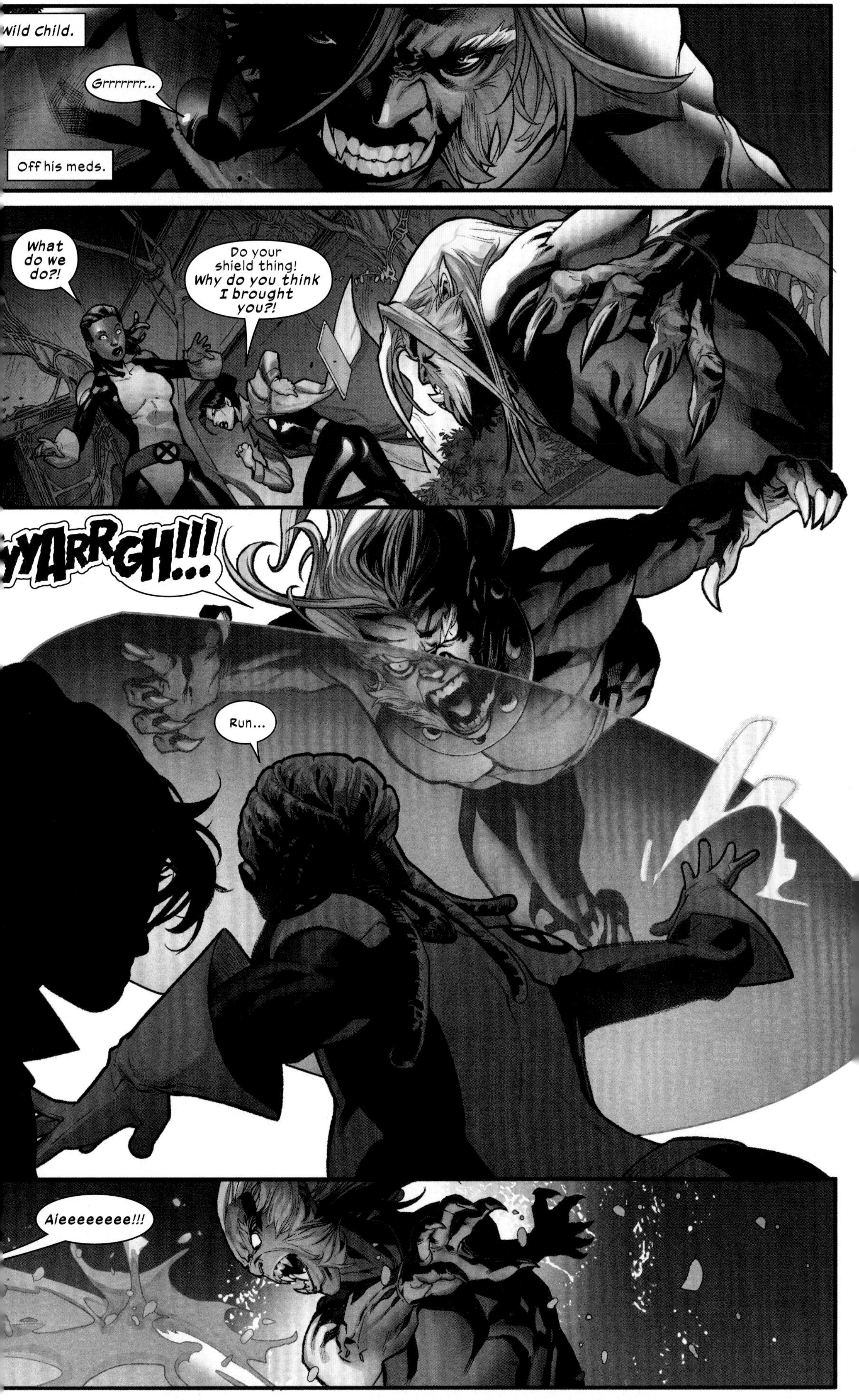
Wild Child.
Grrrrrrr...
Off his meds.
What do we do?!
Do your shield thing! Why do you think I brought you?!
YYARRRGH!!!
Run...
Aieeeeeeee!!!

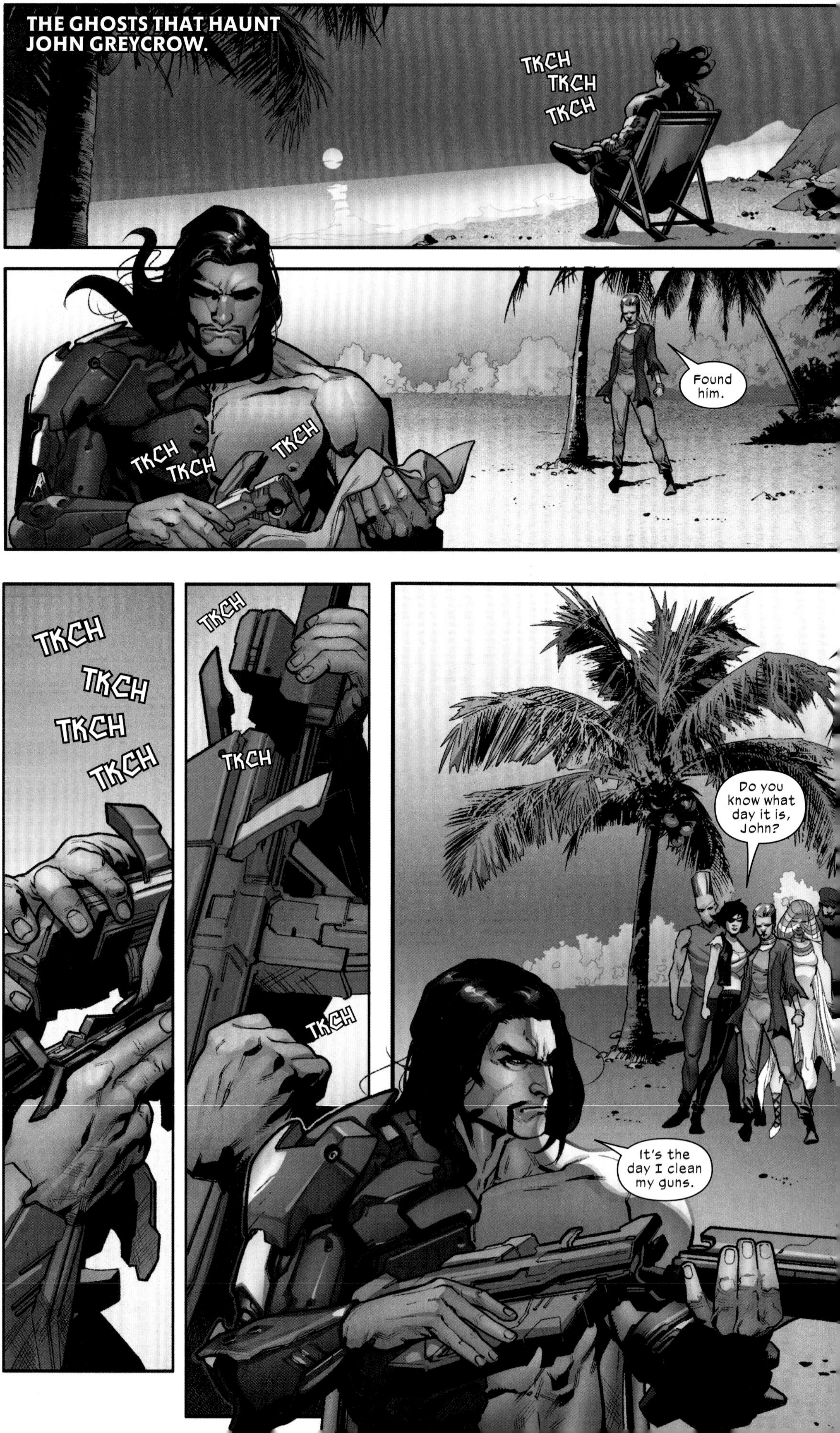
THE GHOSTS THAT HAUNT JOHN GREYCROW.
TKCH
TKCH
TKCH
TKCH
TKCH
TKCH
Found him.
TKCH
TKCH
TKCH
TKCH
TKCH
TKCH
TKCH
Do you know what day it is, John?
It's the day I clean my guns.

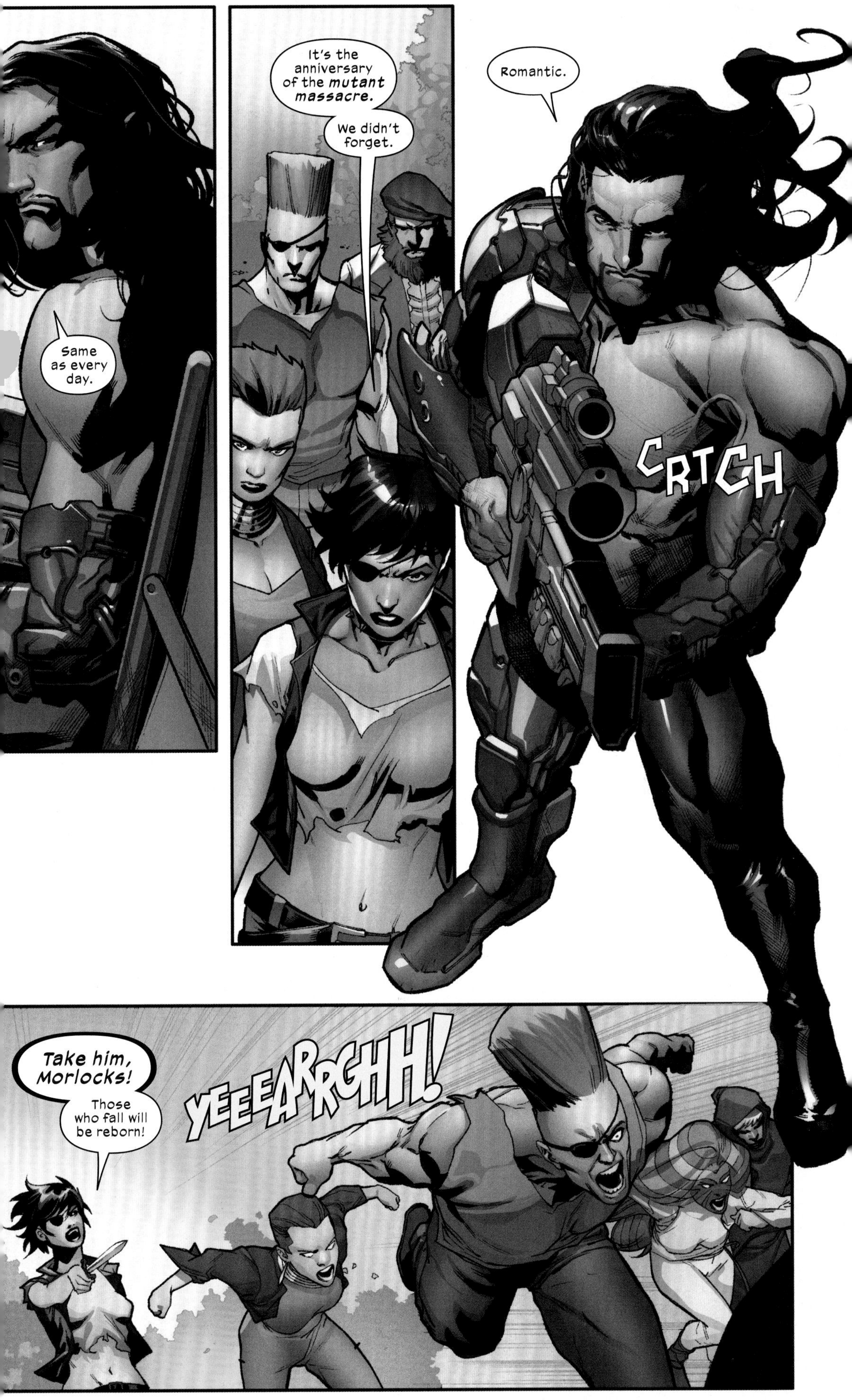
Same as every day.
It's the anniversary of the *mutant massacre.*
We didn't forget.
Romantic.
CRTCH
Take him, Morlocks!
Those who fall will be reborn!
YEEEARRGHH!

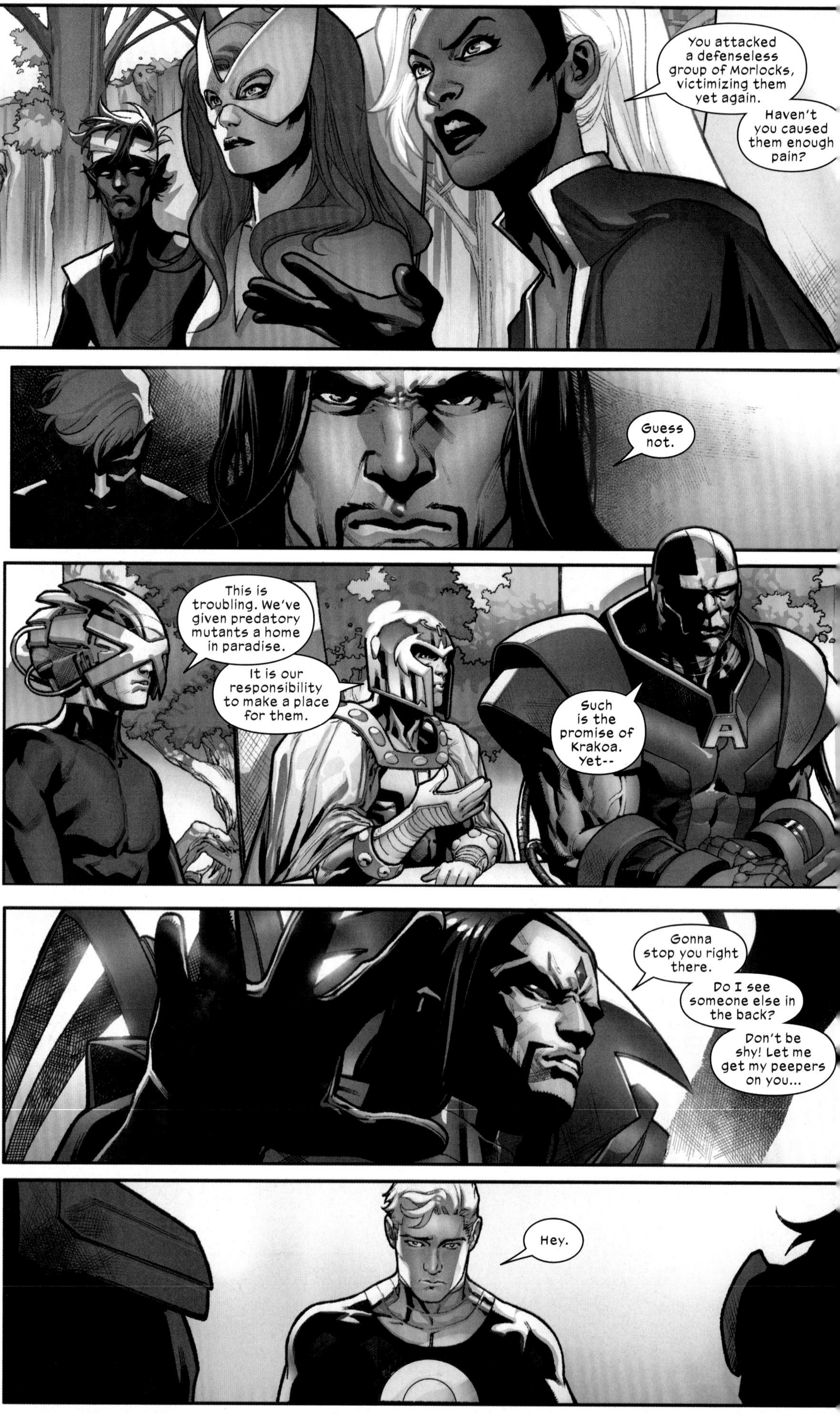
You attacked a defenseless group of Morlocks, victimizing them yet again.
Haven't you caused them enough pain?
Guess not.
This is troubling. We've given predatory mutants a home in paradise.
It is our responsibility to make a place for them.
Such is the promise of Krakoa. Yet--
Gonna stop you right there.
Do I see someone else in the back?
Don't be shy! Let me get my peepers on you...
Hey.

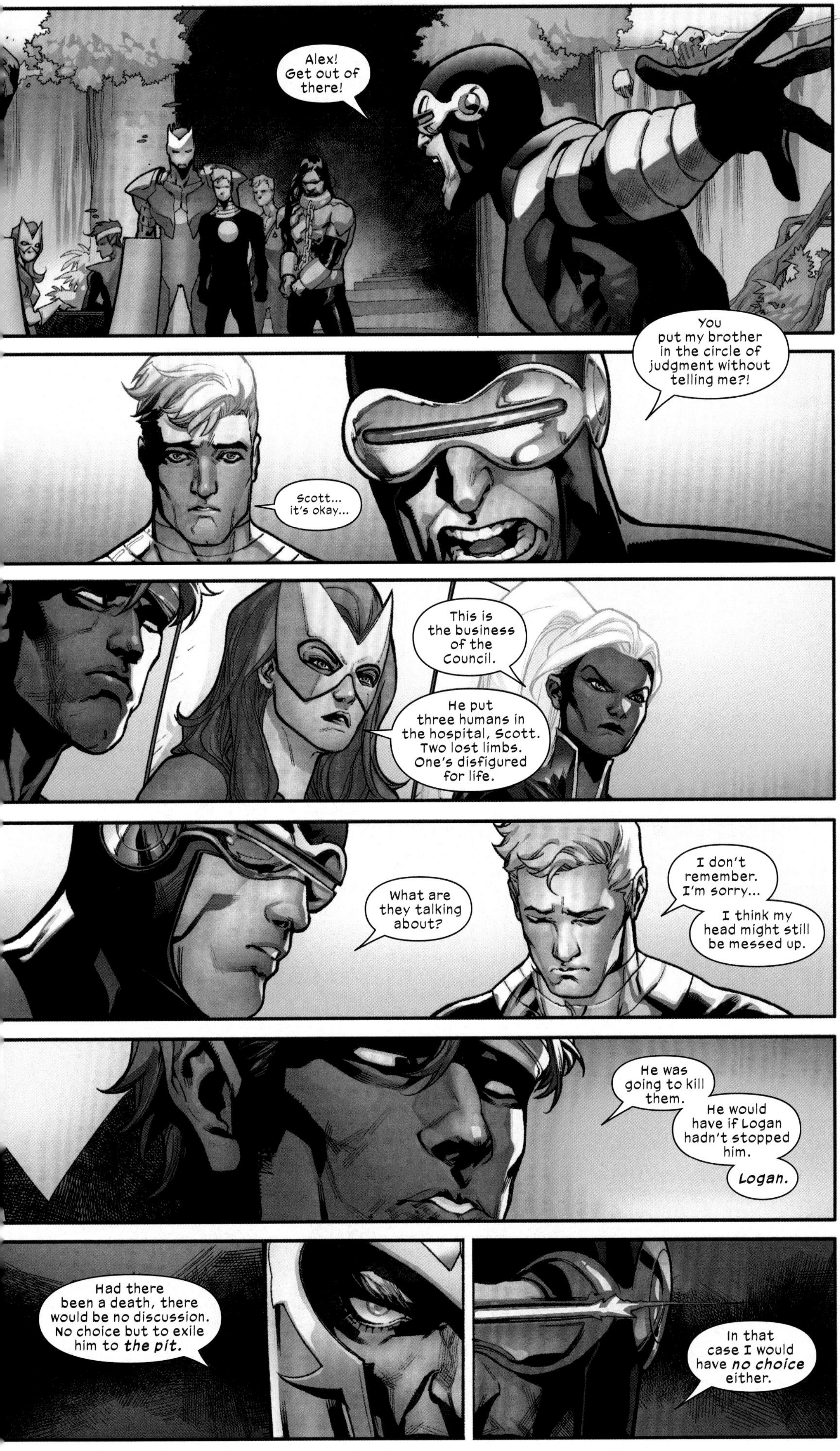

Alex! Get out of there!
You put my brother in the circle of judgment without telling me?!
Scott... it's okay...
This is the business of the Council.
He put three humans in the hospital, Scott. Two lost limbs. One's disfigured for life.
What are they talking about?
I don't remember. I'm sorry...
I think my head might still be messed up.
He was going to kill them.
He would have if Logan hadn't stopped him.
Logan.
Had there been a death, there would be no discussion. No choice but to exile him to the pit.
In that case I would have no choice either.

Everyone relax! Unclench please! Eyes over here! I've had an idea!

Yaaaaay!!!

Oh, clean up those poopy pants, Scotty. I'm here to save the day!

Come on, you're so much prettier when you smile!

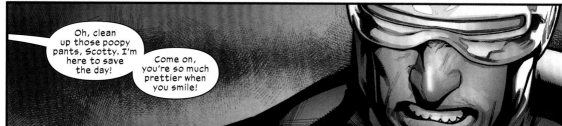

These aren't predators! Th are square pe straining heroic against roun holes.

That was a metaphor.

@#$% you.

What will we, the Quiet Council of Krakoa, do with our outcasts? Our unwanted?

Medication? Incarceration?

These are human solutions. They are sweaty and they are dumb and they are gee dee boring.

I know everyone on this council looks up to me, but I have a confession: I too know the cerebral itch of madness.

And I know madness can be put to good use. Even these crazy @#$%& right here.

Cover your ea Peter.

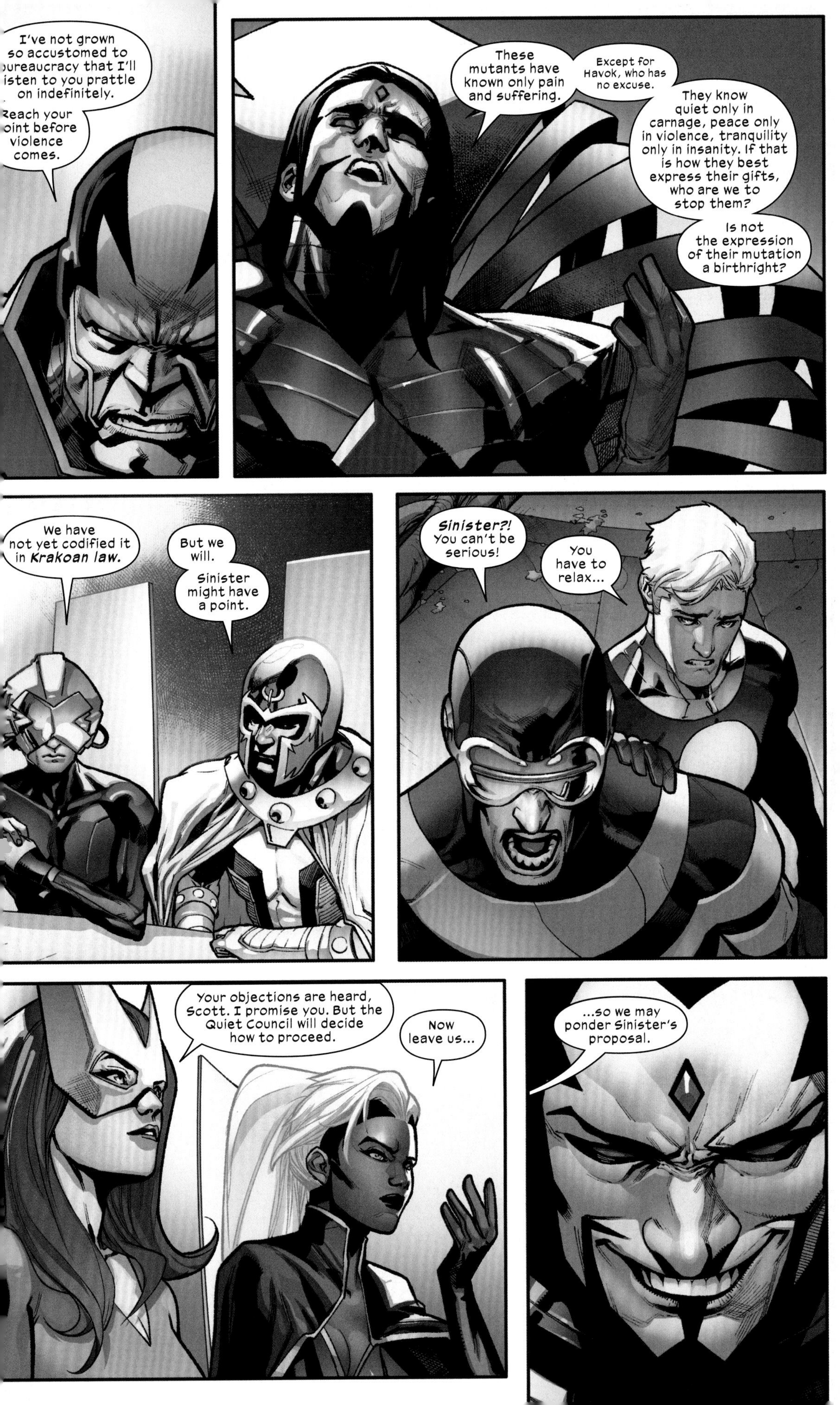
I've not grown so accustomed to bureaucracy that I'll listen to you prattle on indefinitely.
Reach your point before violence comes.
These mutants have known only pain and suffering.
Except for Havok, who has no excuse.
They know quiet only in carnage, peace only in violence, tranquility only in insanity. If that is how they best express their gifts, who are we to stop them?
Is not the expression of their mutation a birthright?
We have not yet codified it in *Krakoan law.*
But we will.
Sinister might have a point.
Sinister?! You can't be serious!
You have to relax...
Your objections are heard, Scott. I promise you. But the Quiet Council will decide how to proceed.
Now leave us...
...so we may ponder Sinister's proposal.

Scott Summers requested I look over the minutes of the recent Quiet Council meeting. Upon review I can see why. On paper the developments are indeed alarming, and I understand why Scott is ringing every alarm he can find.

But having slept on it, I do see the faintest shimmers of wisdom in giving Mr. Sinister a team of troubled mutants. Could it hurt them to have a mentor who understands what it's like to be unwell? God knows they've received enough finger wagging and sideways glances to cure them a thousand times over if that was going to do the trick.

I sniffed around and heard rumblings you'd like to see them in the field as soon as next month. After much thought I can throw my weight behind you as long as any missions follow these criteria:

CHANCE OF HUMAN CASUALTIES IS NIL

Placing these mutants in situations where their intrinsic overenthusiasm may lead to dead humans, and therefore banishment to the Pit of Exile, is unacceptable. I will not stand by while our most at-risk mutants are re-traumatized by that barbaric punishment.

VIOLENT OVERREACTION IS THE IDEAL

These are bulls and the world is a china shop. We don't let them out of their pen unless the goal is lots of broken china.

THERE IS THERAPEUTIC VALUE IN THE CARNAGE

The missions should allow these problem mutants to express themselves in ways frowned upon by polite society. In this freedom perhaps they will find healing.

If you can promise me these considerations, we're in business. And I'll just have to find myself another friend who has a house on the moon.

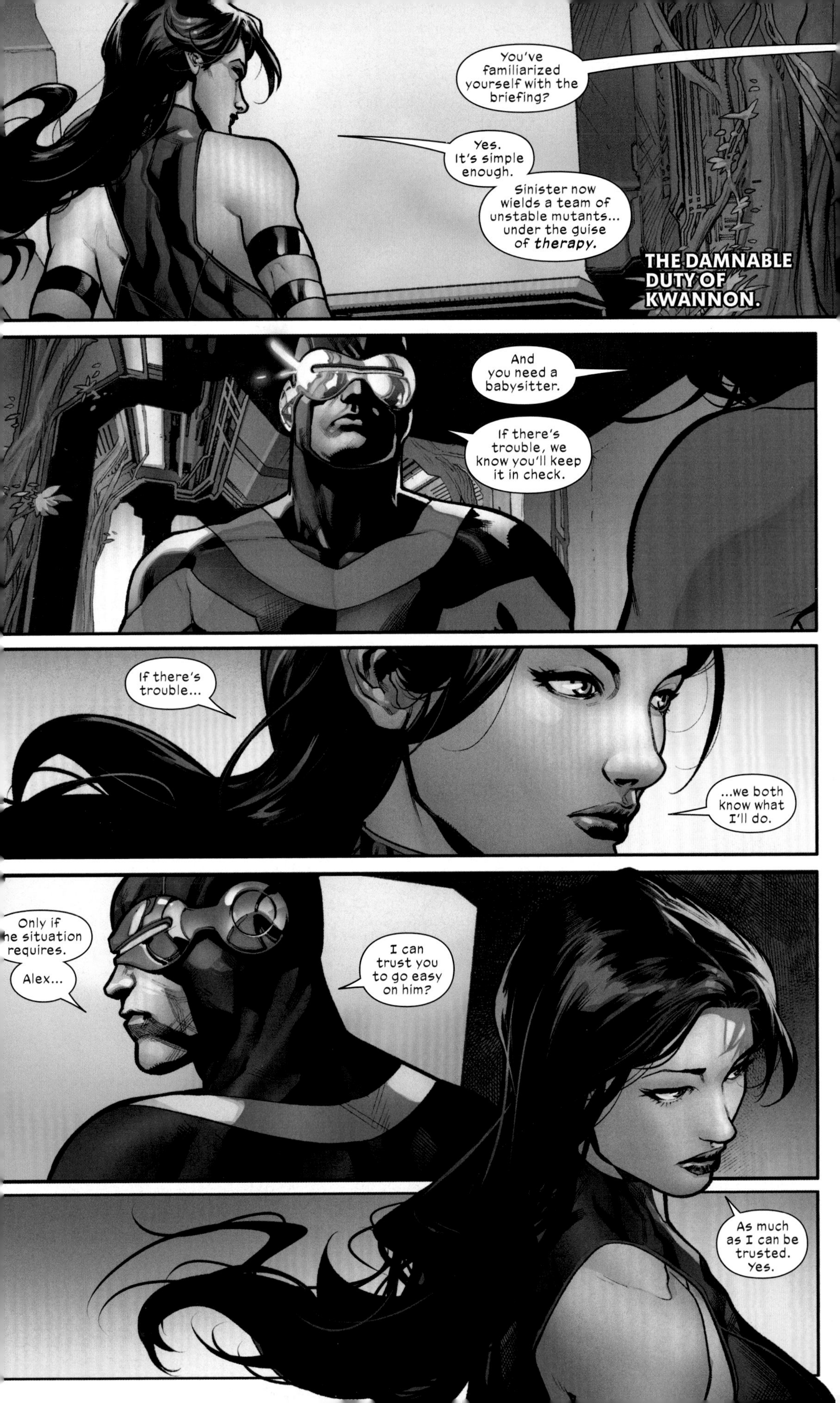
You've familiarized yourself with the briefing?
Yes. It's simple enough.
Sinister now wields a team of unstable mutants... under the guise of *therapy.*
THE DAMNABLE DUTY OF KWANNON.
And you need a babysitter.
If there's trouble, we know you'll keep it in check.
If there's trouble...
...we both know what I'll do.
Only if he situation requires.
Alex...
I can trust you to go easy on him?
As much as I can be trusted. Yes.

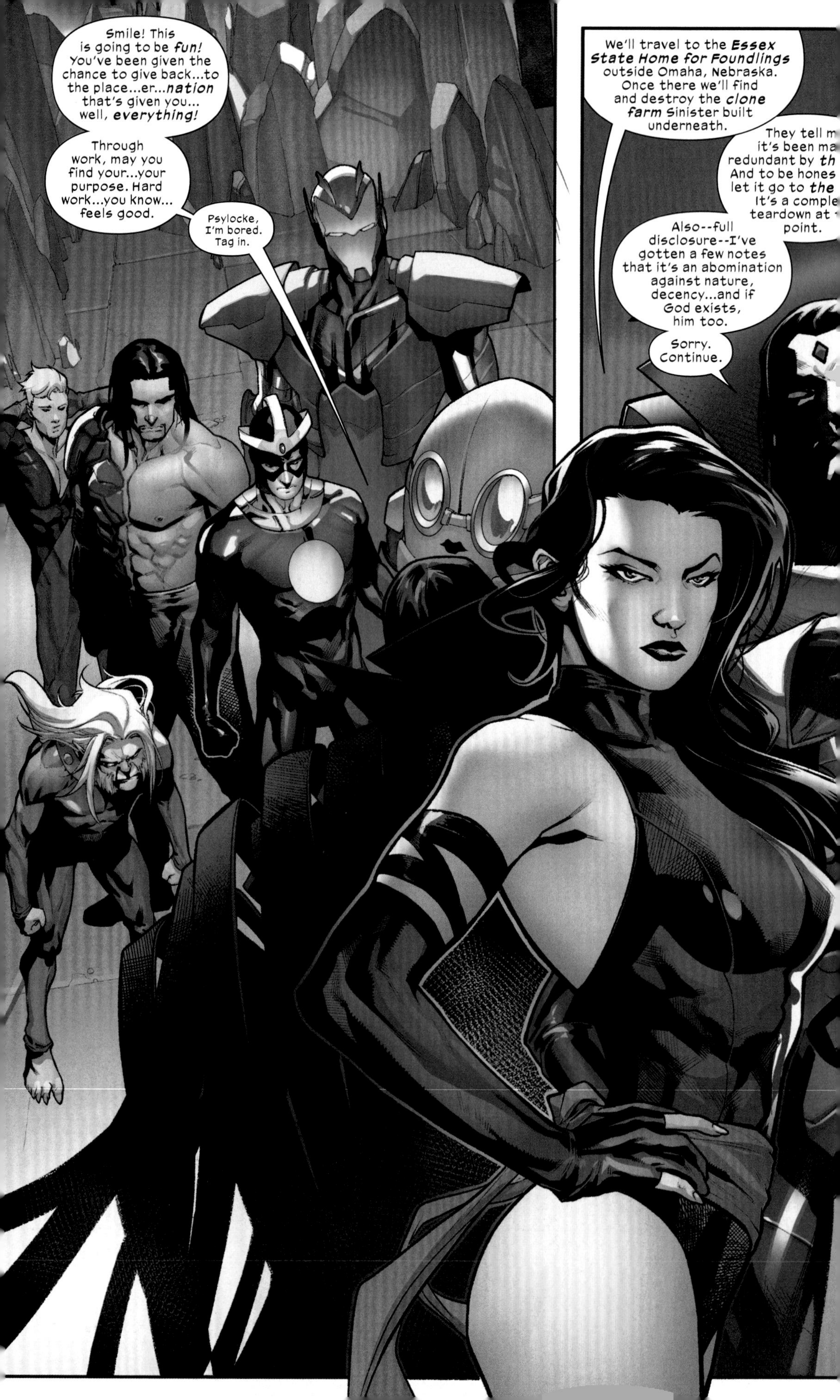

Smile! This is going to be *fun!* You've been given the chance to give back...to the place...er...*nation* that's given you... well, *everything!*
Through work, may you find your...your purpose. Hard work...you know... feels good.
Psylocke, I'm bored. Tag in.
We'll travel to the *Essex State Home for Foundlings* outside Omaha, Nebraska. Once there we'll find and destroy the *clone farm* Sinister built underneath.
They tell m it's been ma redundant by *th* And to be hones let it go to *the* It's a comple teardown at point.
Also--full disclosure--I've gotten a few notes that it's an abomination against nature, decency...and if God exists, him too.
Sorry. Continue.

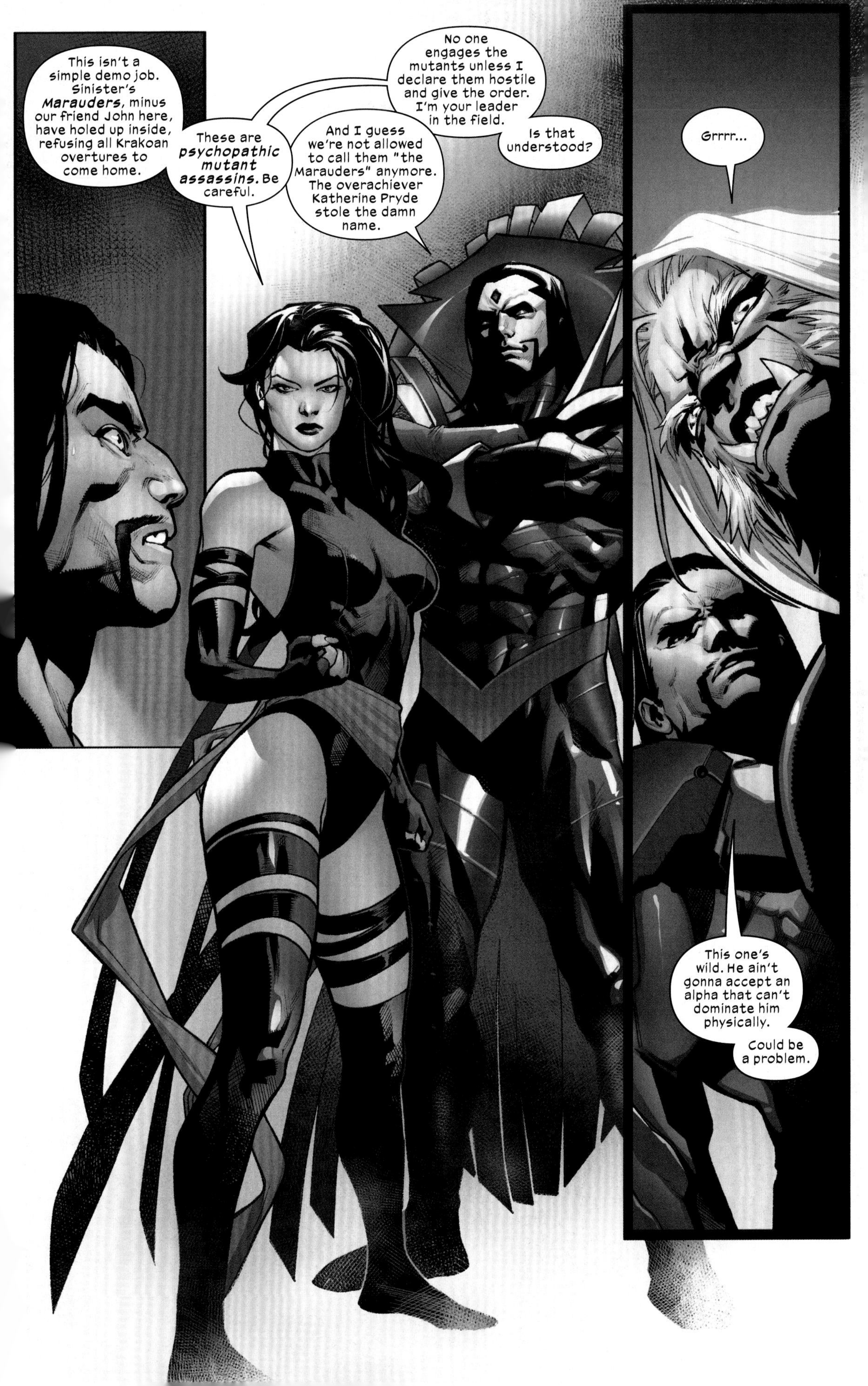

This isn't a simple demo job. Sinister's *Marauders*, minus our friend John here, have holed up inside, refusing all Krakoan overtures to come home.
These are *psychopathic mutant assassins.* Be careful.
And I guess we're not allowed to call them "the Marauders" anymore. The overachiever Katherine Pryde stole the damn name.
No one engages the mutants unless I declare them hostile and give the order. I'm your leader in the field.
Is that understood?
Grrrr...
This one's wild. He ain't gonna accept an alpha that can't dominate him physically.
Could be a problem.

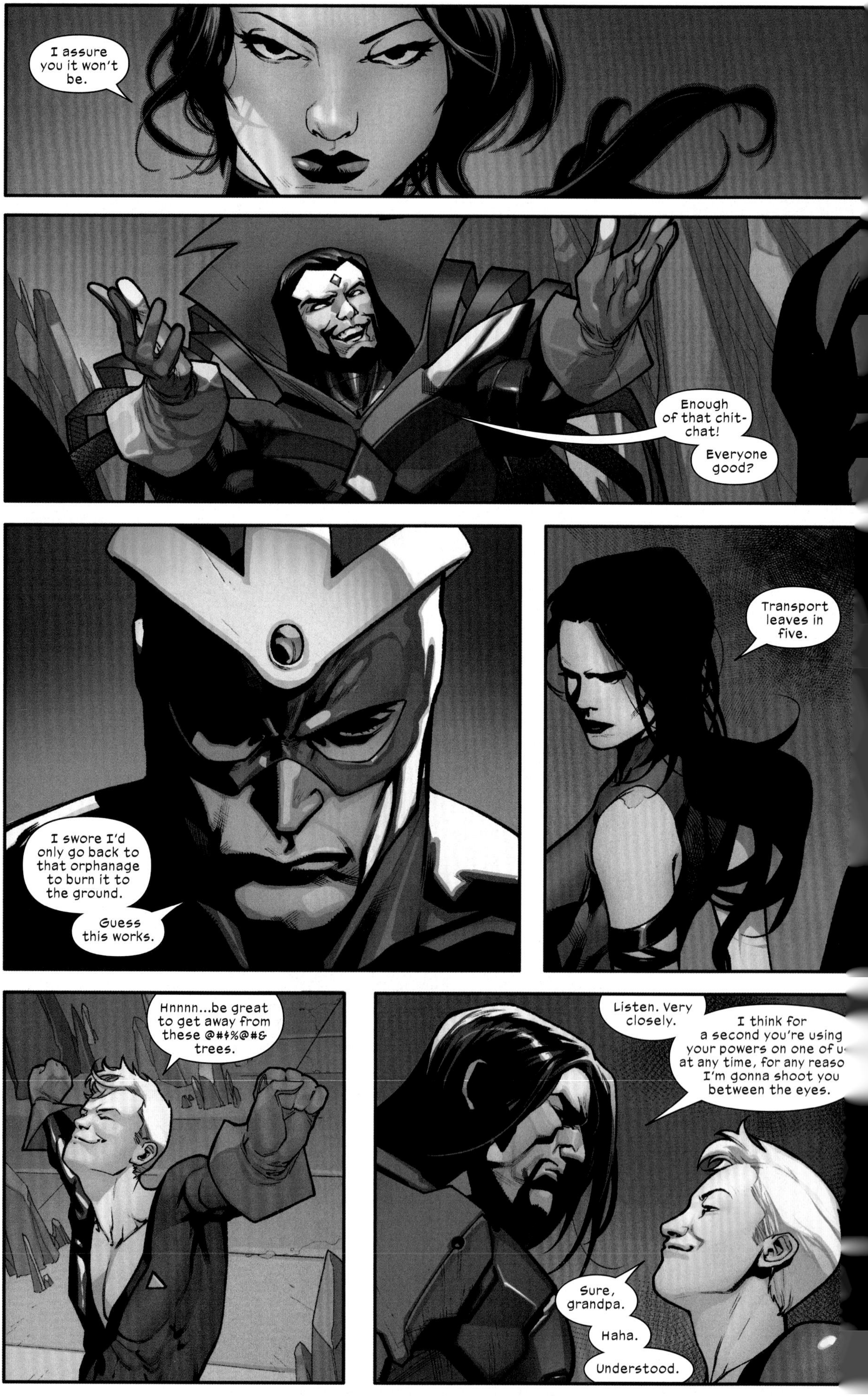

I assure you it won't be.
Enough of that chit-chat!
Everyone good?
I swore I'd only go back to that orphanage to burn it to the ground.
Guess this works.
Transport leaves in five.
Hnnnn...be great to get away from these @#$%@#& trees.
Listen. Very closely.
I think for a second you're using your powers on one of u at any time, for any reaso I'm gonna shoot you between the eyes.
Sure, grandpa.
Haha.
Understood.

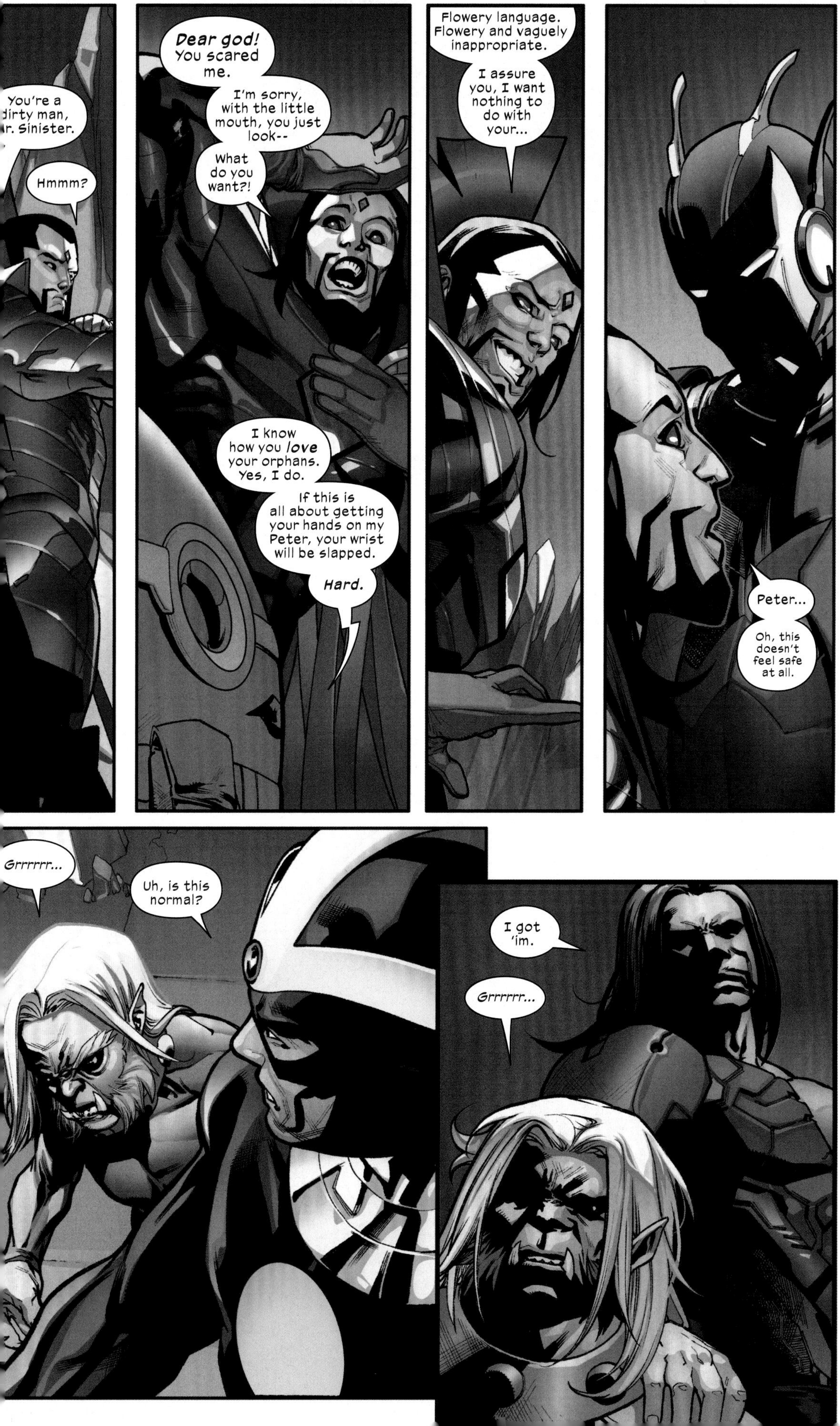

You're a dirty man, r. Sinister.
Hmmm?
Dear god! You scared me.
I'm sorry, with the little mouth, you just look--
What do you want?!
I know how you *love* your orphans. Yes, I do.
If this is all about getting your hands on my Peter, your wrist will be slapped.
Hard.
Flowery language. Flowery and vaguely inappropriate.
I assure you, I want nothing to do with your...
Peter...
Oh, this doesn't feel safe at all.
Grrrrrr...
Uh, is this normal?
I got 'im.
Grrrrrr...

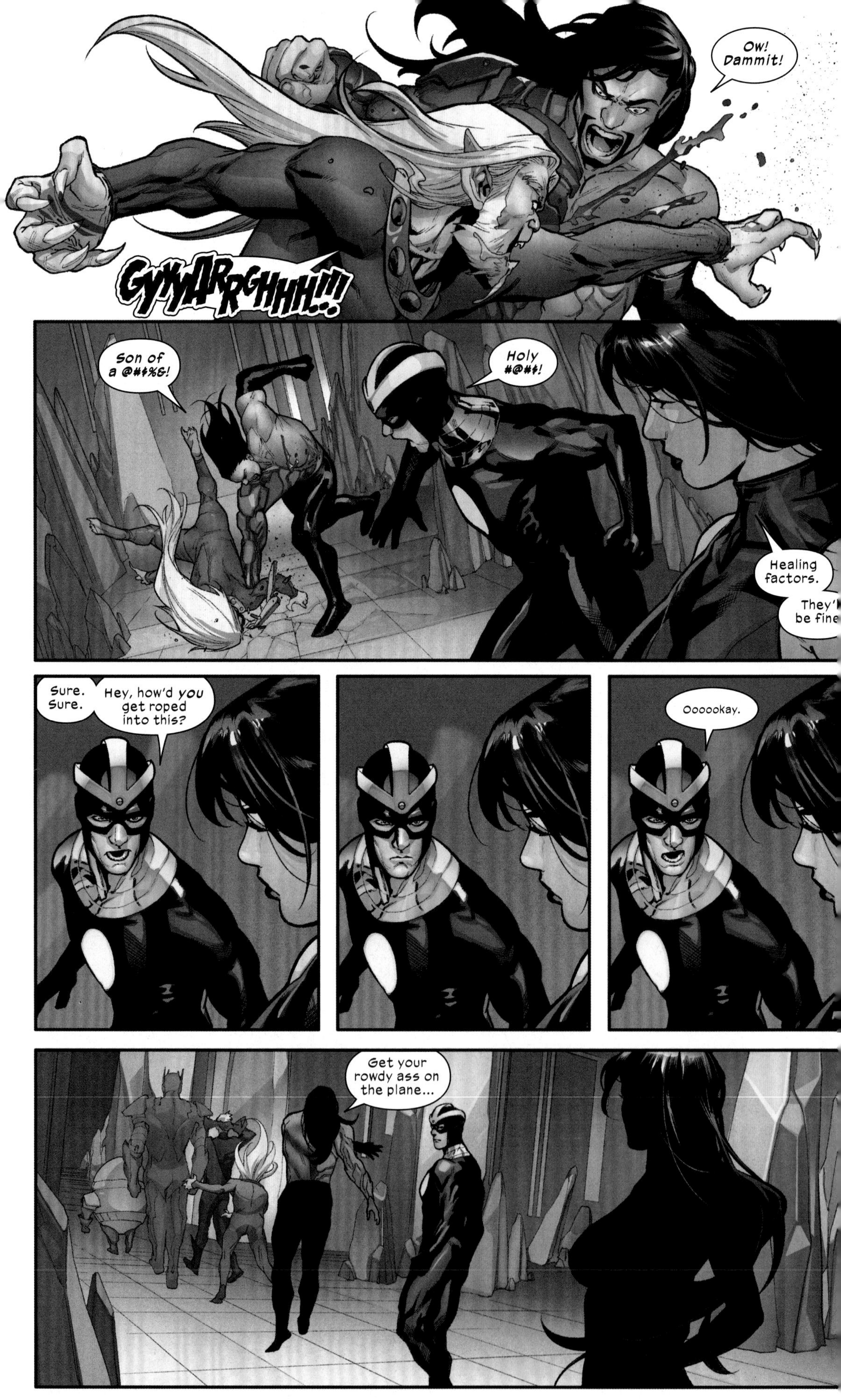
Ow! Dammit!
GYYYARRRGHHH!!!
Son of a @#$%&!
Holy #@#$!
Healing factors.
They'l be fine
Sure. Sure.
Hey, how'd you get roped into this?
Oooookay.
Get your rowdy ass on the plane...

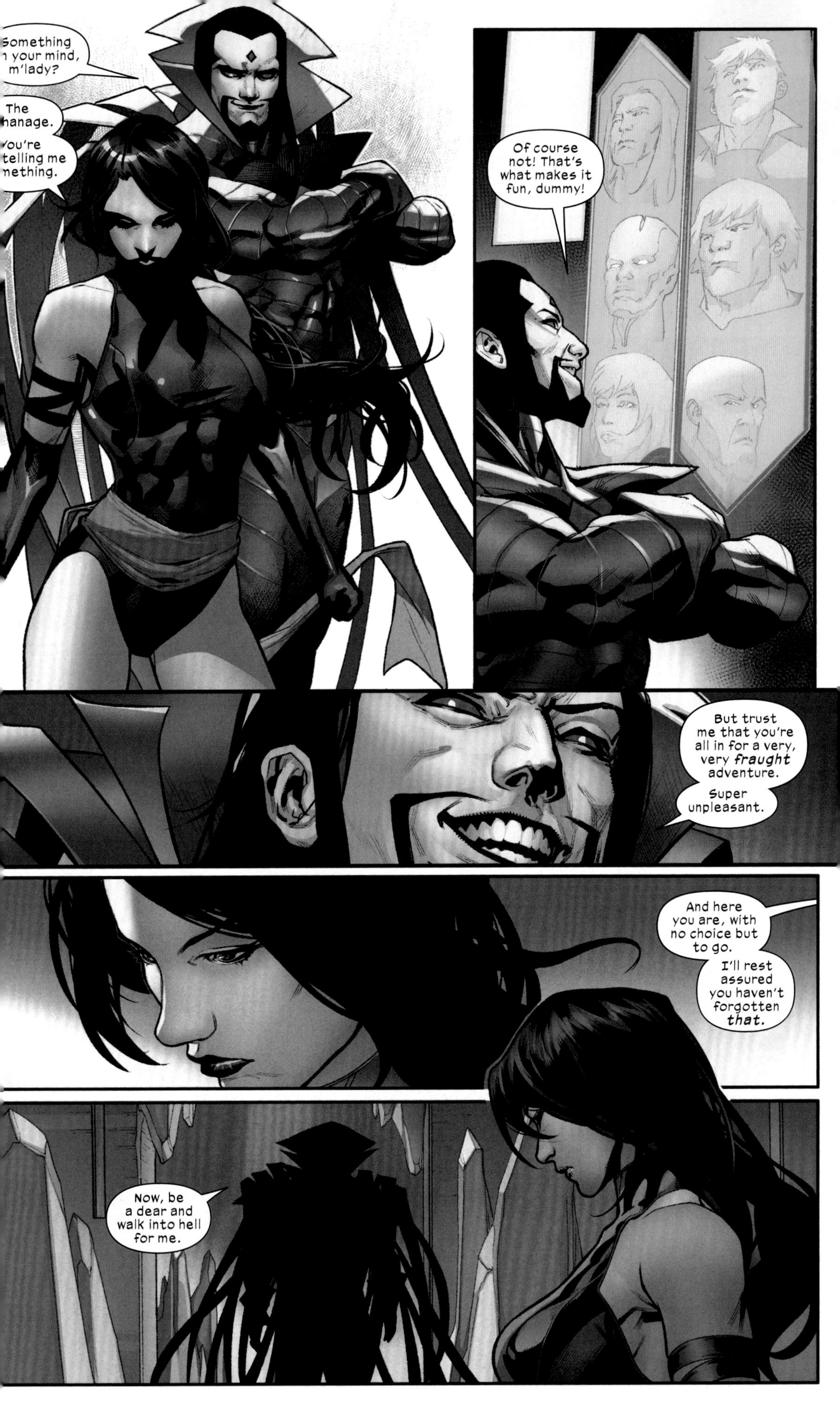

Something
n your mind, m'lady?
The
nanage.
ou're telling me
nething.
Of course not! That's what makes it fun, dummy!
But trust me that you're all in for a very, very *fraught* adventure.
Super unpleasant.
And here you are, with no choice but to go.
I'll rest assured you haven't forgotten *that.*
Now, be a dear and walk into hell for me.

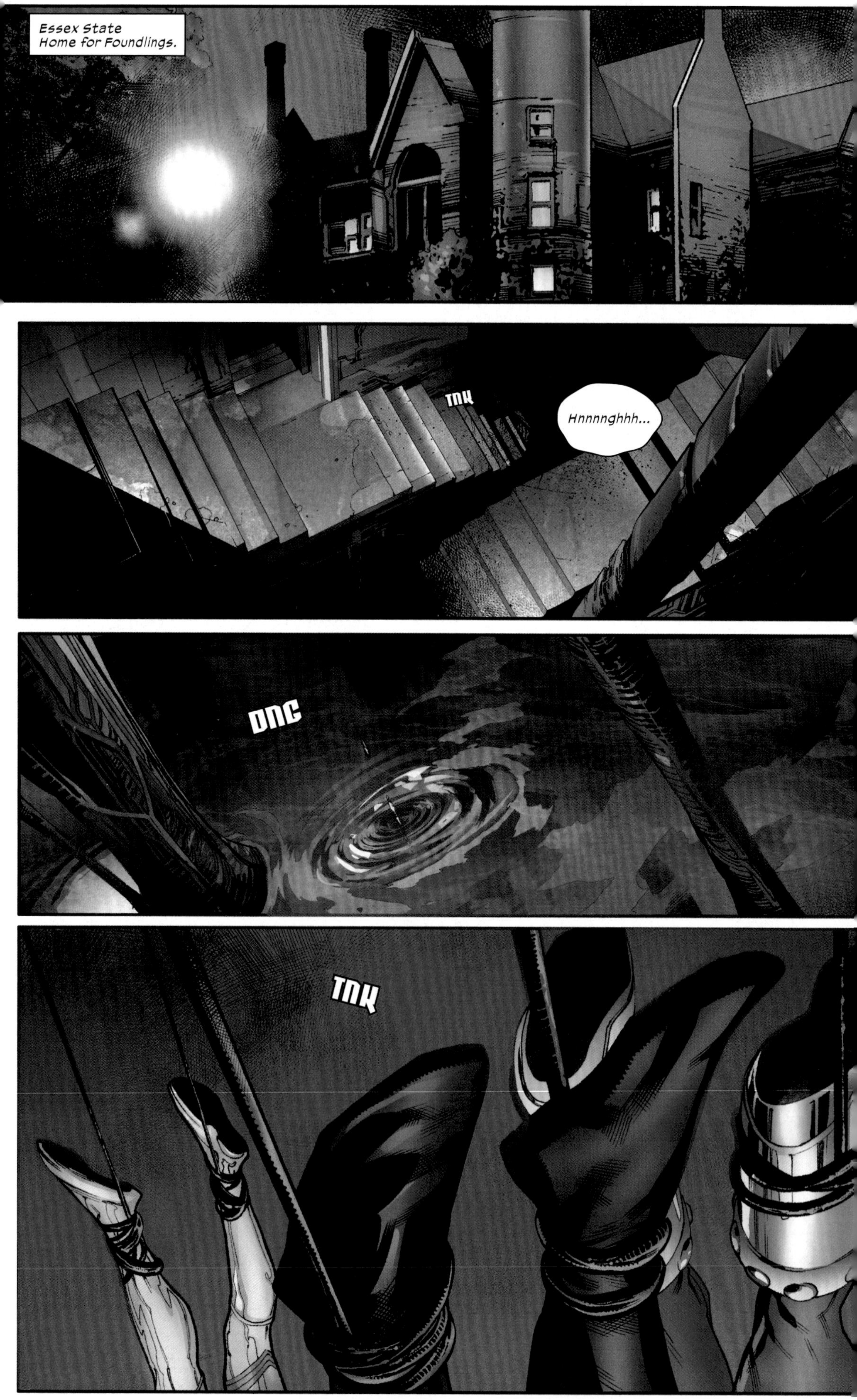

Essex State
Home for Foundlings.
TNK
Hnnnnghhh...
DNC
TNK

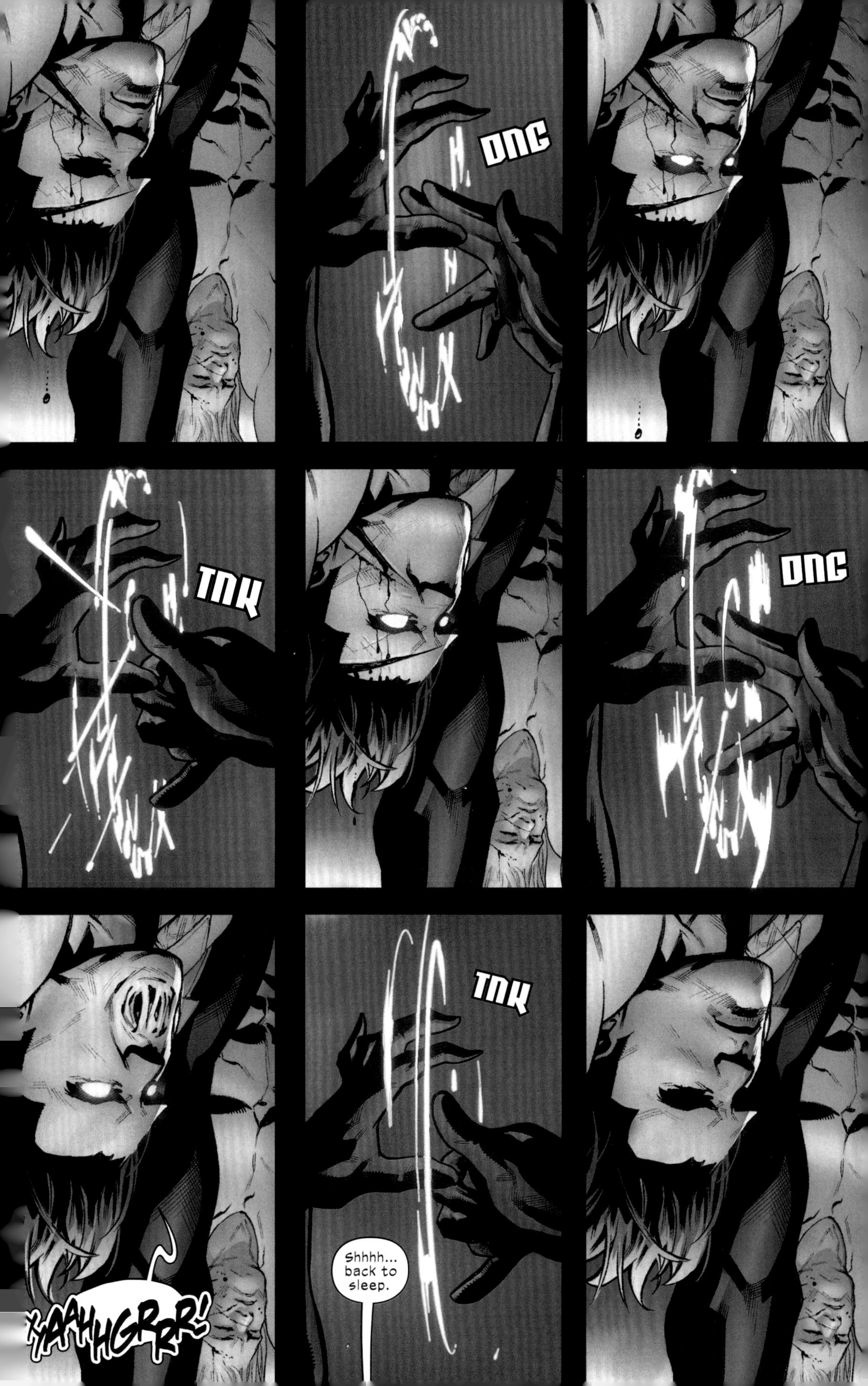
DNG
TNK
DNG
YAAHHGRRR!
TNK
Shhhh... back to sleep.

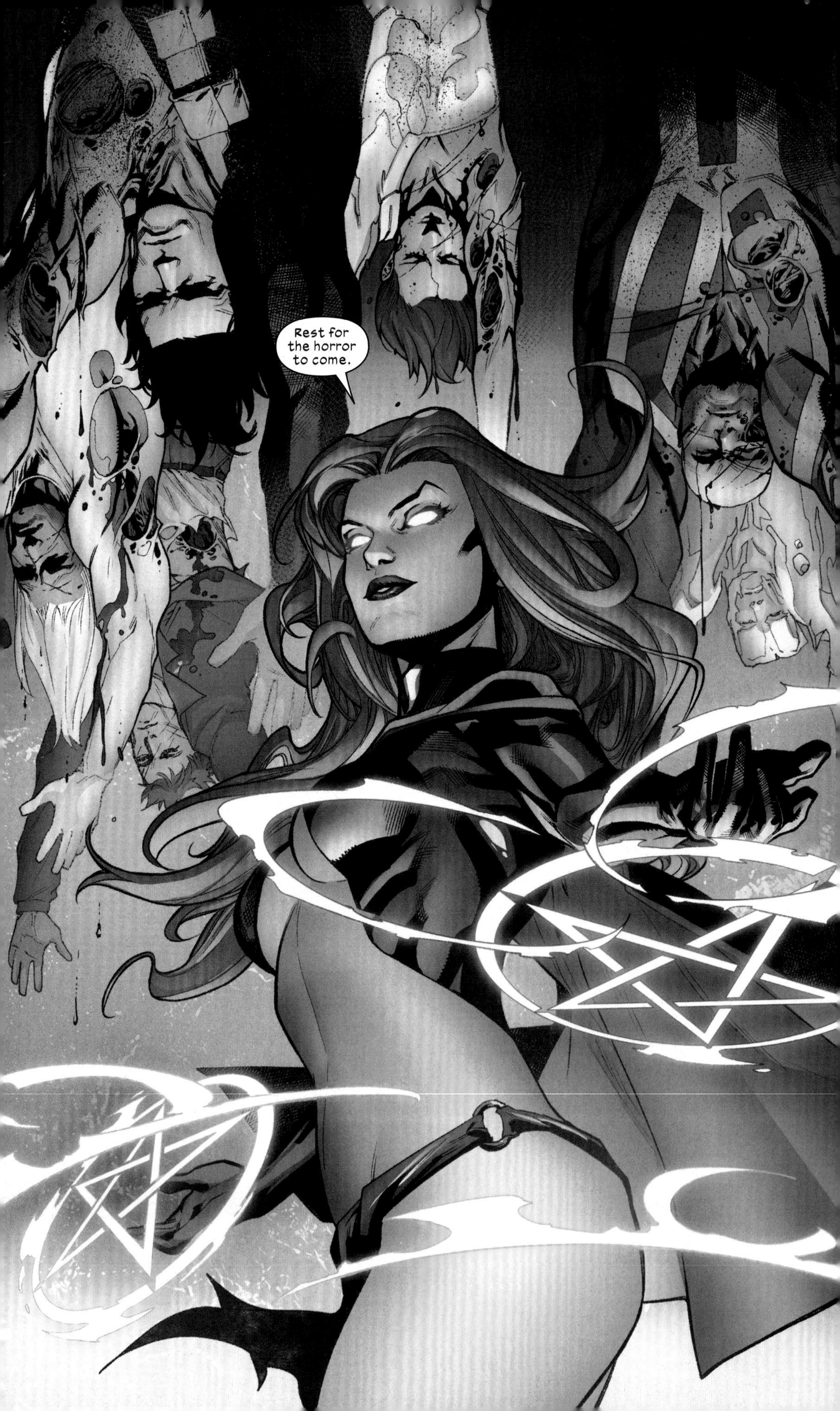
Rest for the horror to come.

[bad__]
[news_]

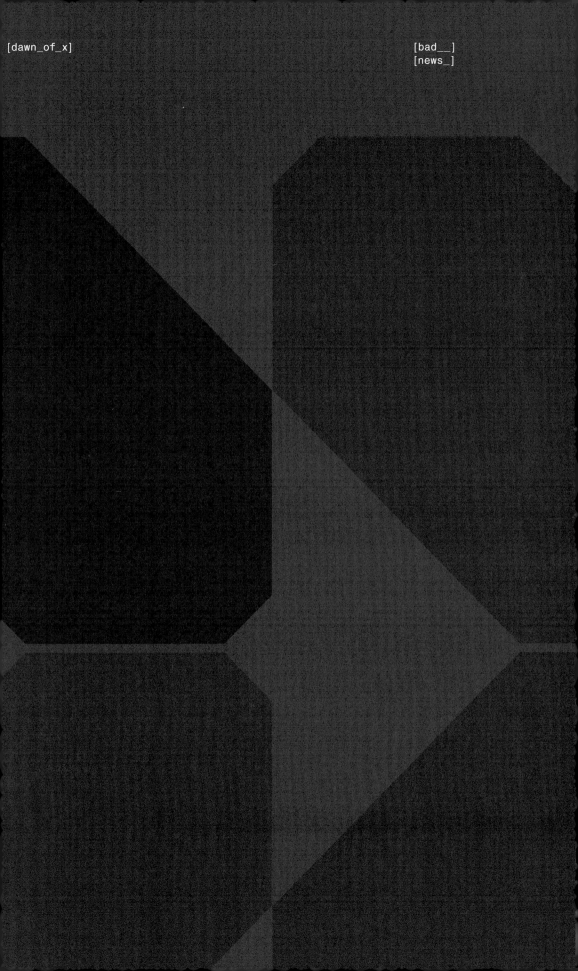

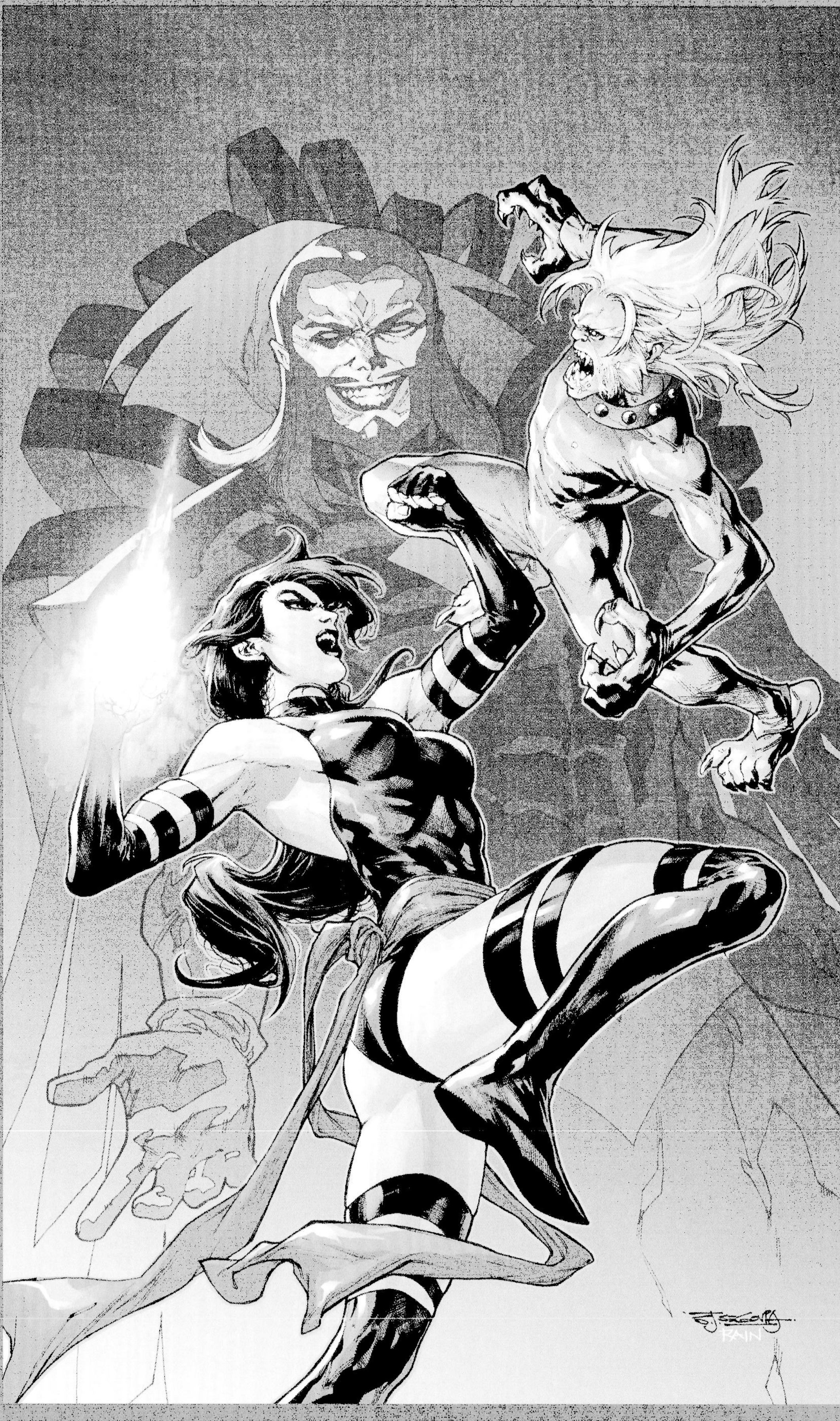
RAIN

Blood Work

⌐[hell_[0.2]
[ions_[0.2]

Those whose violence you do not understand have often seen horrors you cannot imagine.

-NIGHTCRAWLER

⌐[hell_[0.X]
[ions_[0.X]

[hell_[0.2].....]
[ions_[0.2].....]

[Hellions_alpha.]

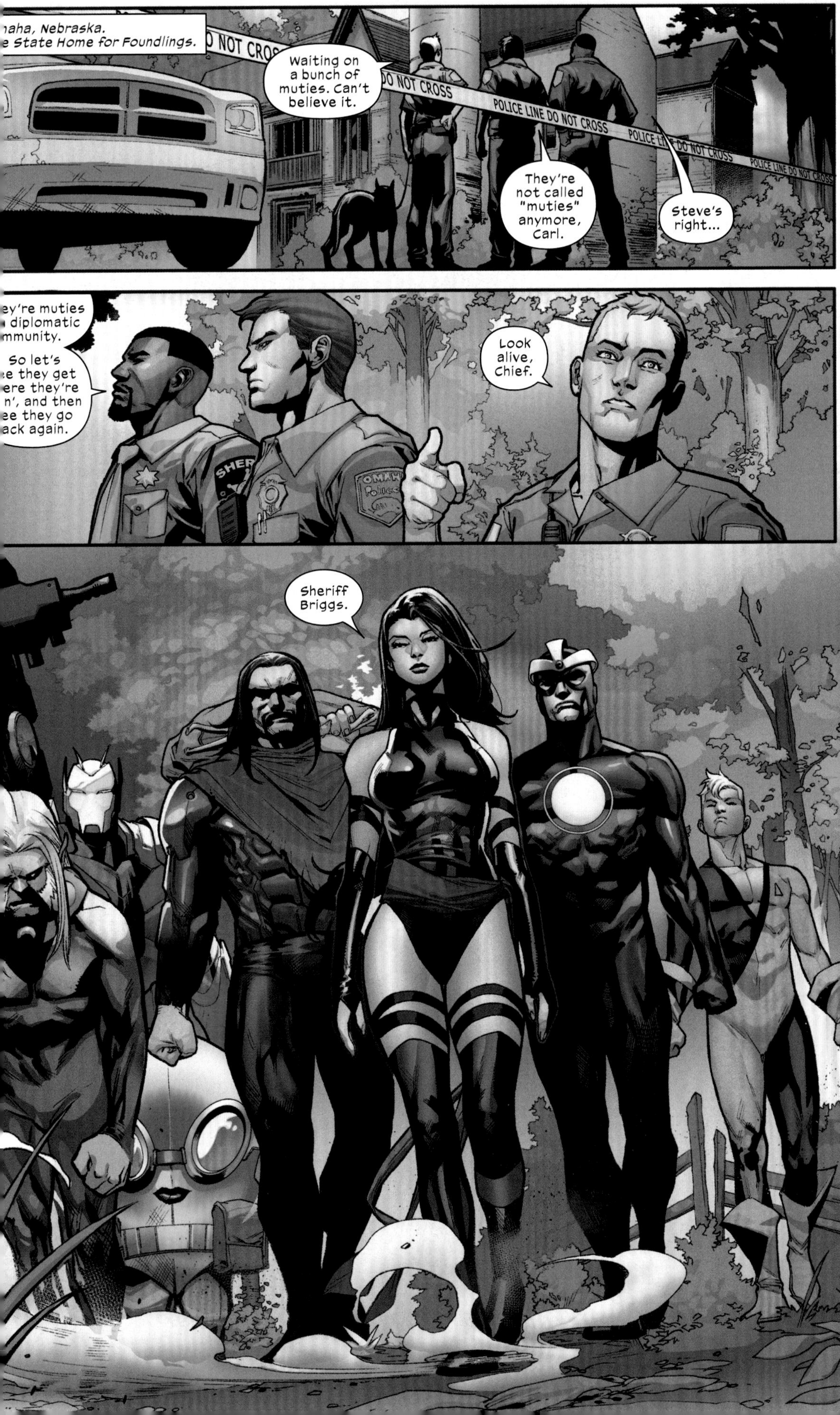

naha, Nebraska.
e State Home for Foundlings.
O NOT CROSS
Waiting on a bunch of muties. Can't believe it.
DO NOT CROSS
POLICE LINE DO NOT CROSS
POLICE LINE DO NOT CROSS
POLICE LINE DO NOT CROSS
They're not called "muties" anymore, Carl.
Steve's right...
ey're muties diplomatic mmunity.
So let's e they get ere they're n', and then ee they go ack again.
Look alive, Chief.
Sheriff Briggs.

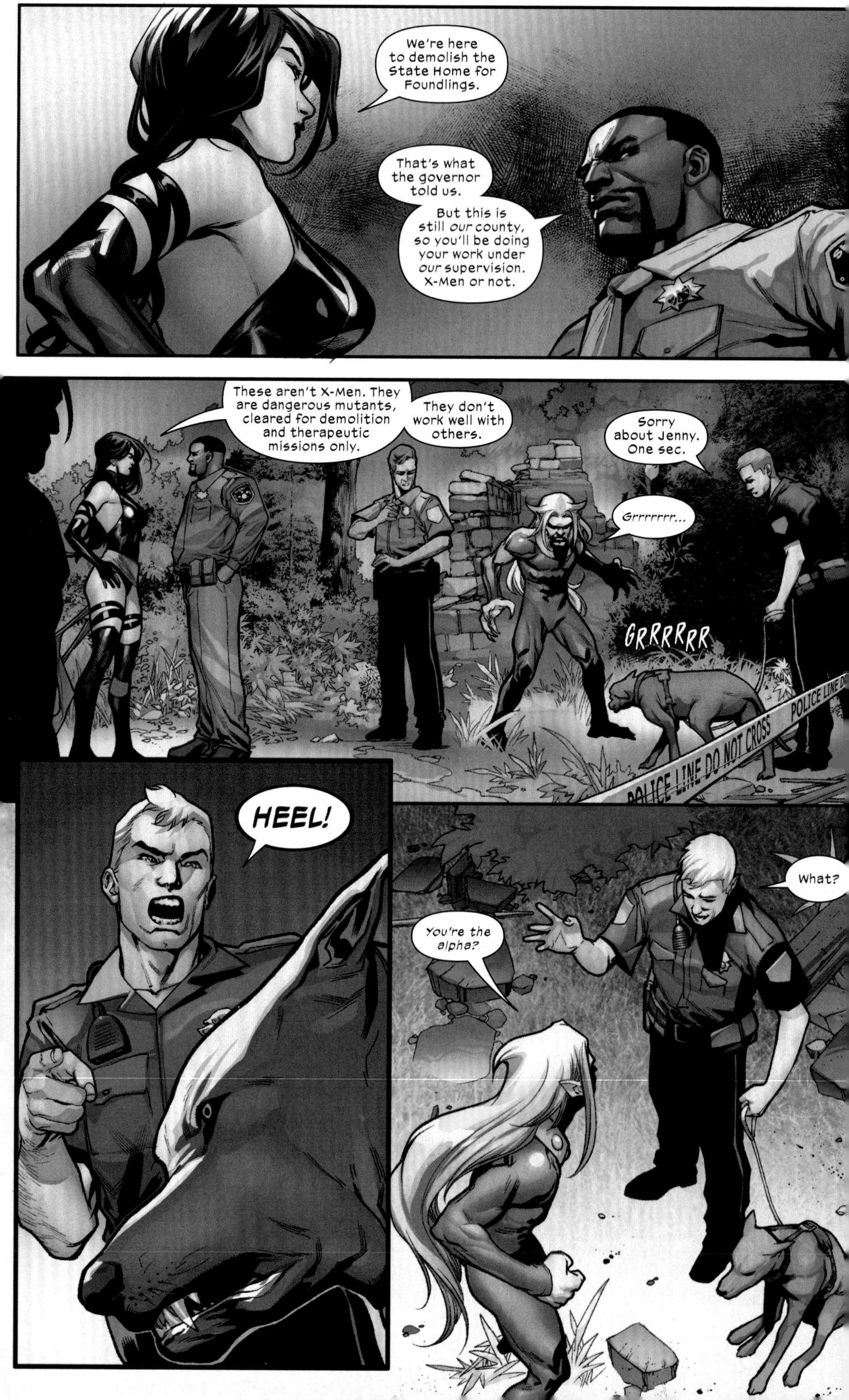

We're here to demolish the State Home for Foundlings.
That's what the governor told us.
But this is still *our* county, so you'll be doing your work under *our* supervision. X-Men or not.
These aren't X-Men. They are dangerous mutants, cleared for demolition and therapeutic missions only.
They don't work well with others.
Sorry about Jenny. One sec.
Grrrrrrr...
GRRRRRR
POLICE LINE DO NOT CROSS
HEEL!
What?
You're the alpha?

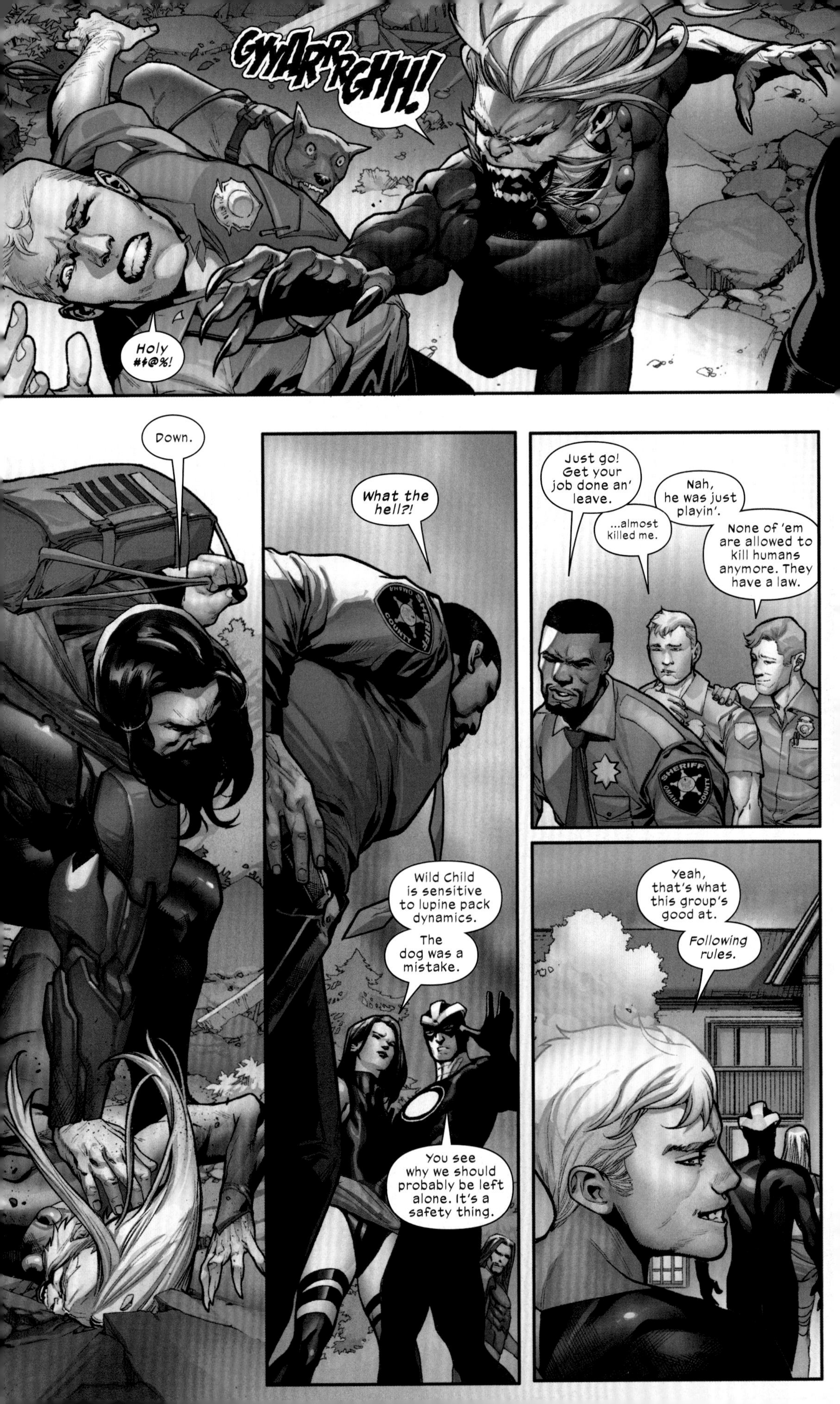
GWARRRCHH!
Holy #$@%!
Down.
What the hell?!
Wild Child is sensitive to lupine pack dynamics.
The dog was a mistake.
You see why we should probably be left alone. It's a safety thing.
Just go! Get your job done an' leave.
...almost killed me.
Nah, he was just playin'.
None of 'em are allowed to kill humans anymore. They have a law.
Yeah, that's what this group's good at.
Following rules.

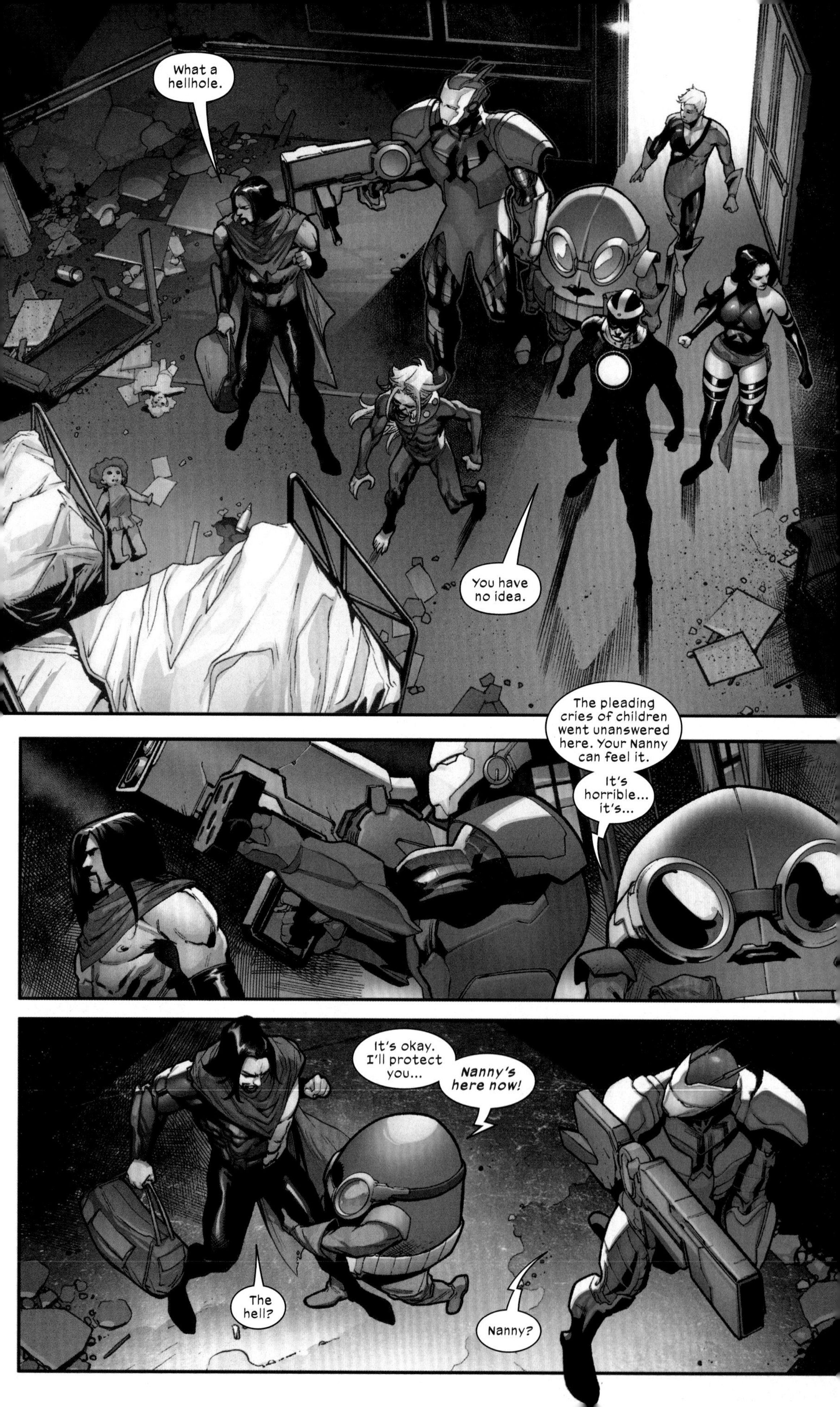
What a hellhole.
You have no idea.
The pleading cries of children went unanswered here. Your Nanny can feel it.
It's horrible... it's...
It's okay. I'll protect you...
Nanny's here now!
The hell?
Nanny?

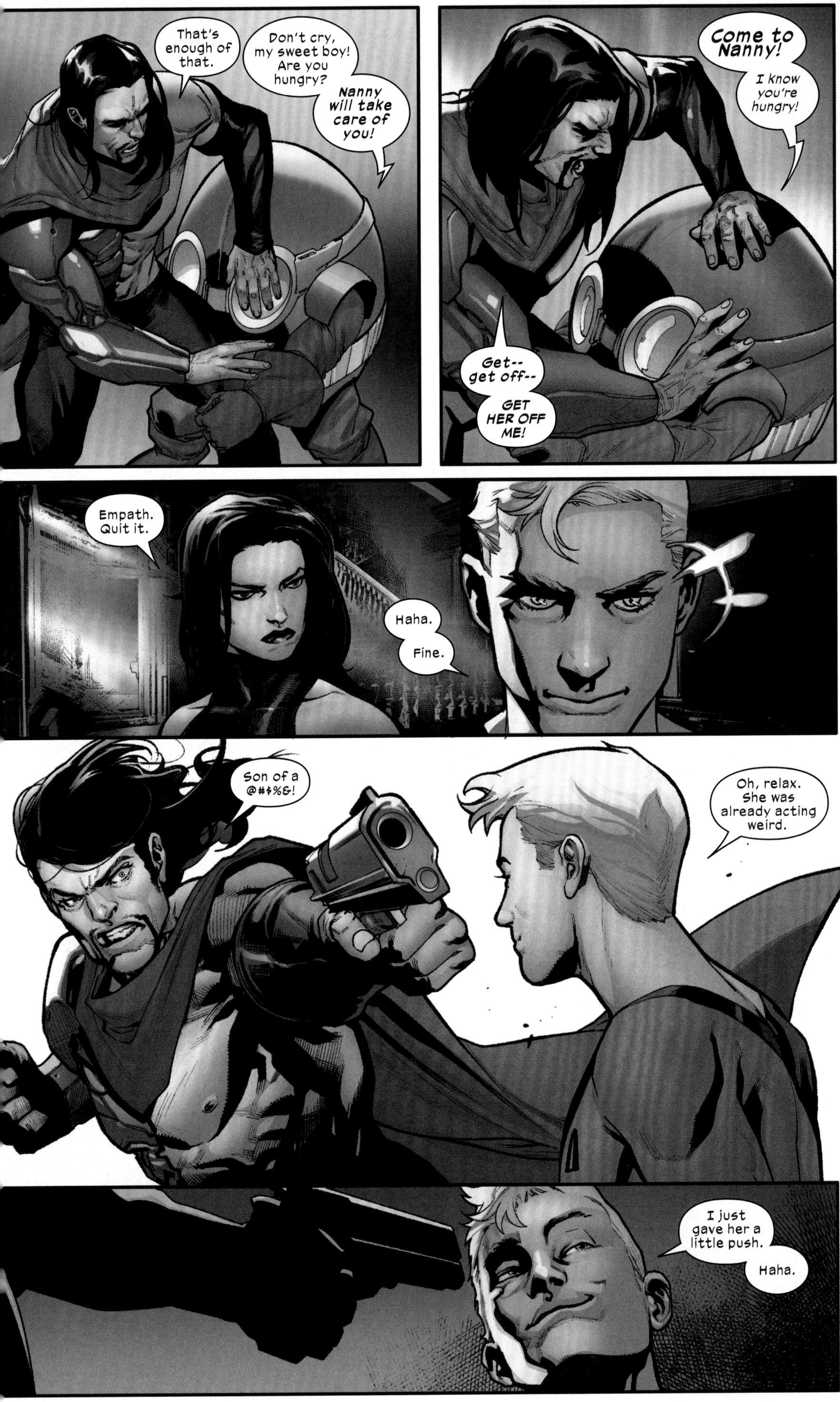
That's enough of that.
Don't cry, my sweet boy! Are you hungry?
Nanny will take care of you!
Come to Nanny!
I know you're hungry!
Get-- get off--
GET HER OFF ME!
Empath. Quit it.
Haha.
Fine.
Son of a @#$%&!
Oh, relax. She was already acting weird.
I just gave her a little push.
Haha.

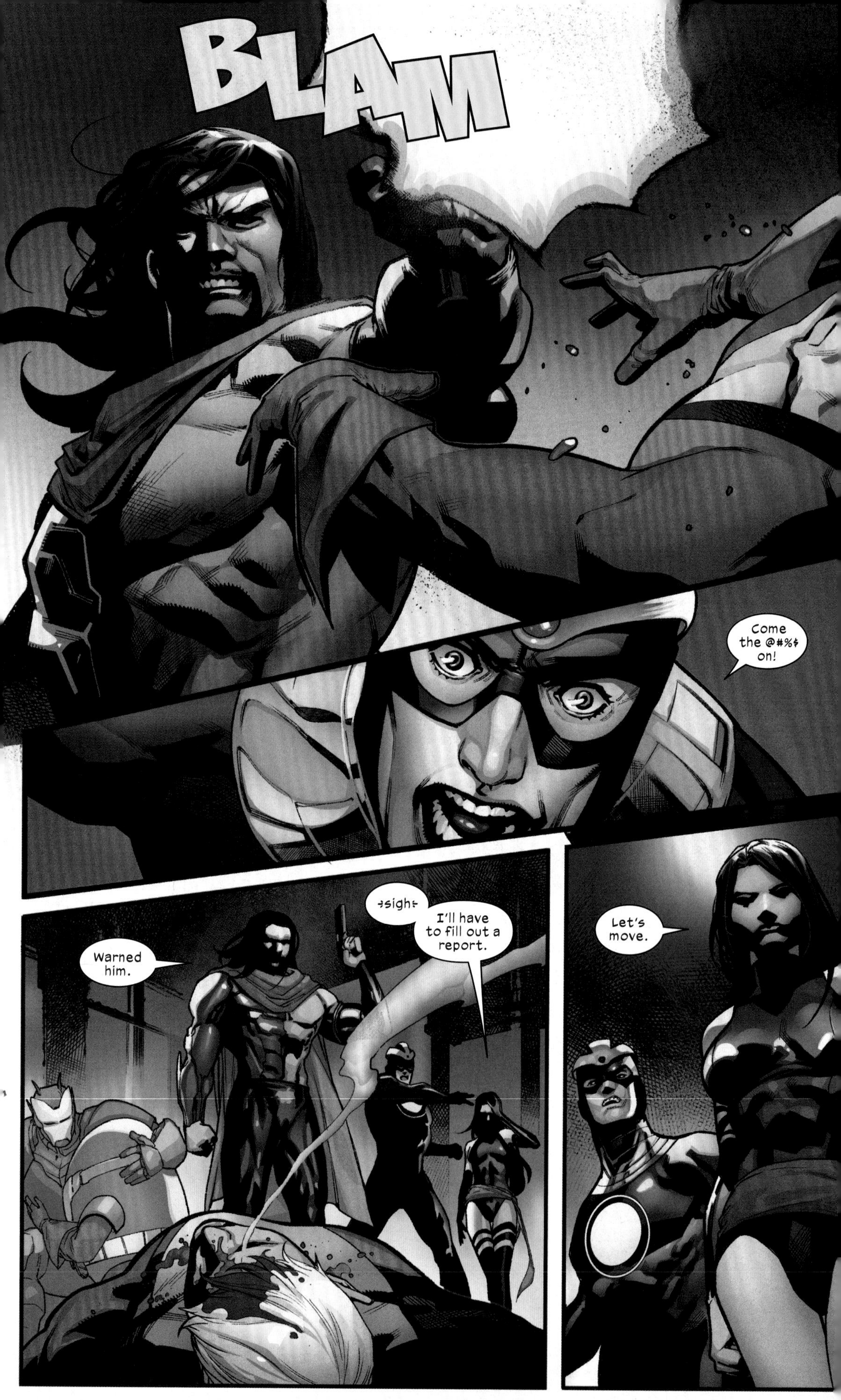
BLAM
Come the @#%$ on!
Warned him.
-sigh-
I'll have to fill out a report.
Let's move.

Hey, I'm starting to think--

--what with the public execution back there--

--that maybe I'm not a great fit for this team.

The Quiet Council disagrees.

I think they'd disagree with what happened back there too.

Perhaps. But they know the damage you all carry.

And that vanquishing demons is messy work.

I don't have demons. Look at me...I'm in the orphanage Scott and I were sent to as kids. Where Mr. Sinister had us separated.

And I'm fine.

I'm telepathic, Alex. Your mind screams at me.

Just like the rest of them.

None of us are fine.

Hmm?

Hee hee hee

Look alive!

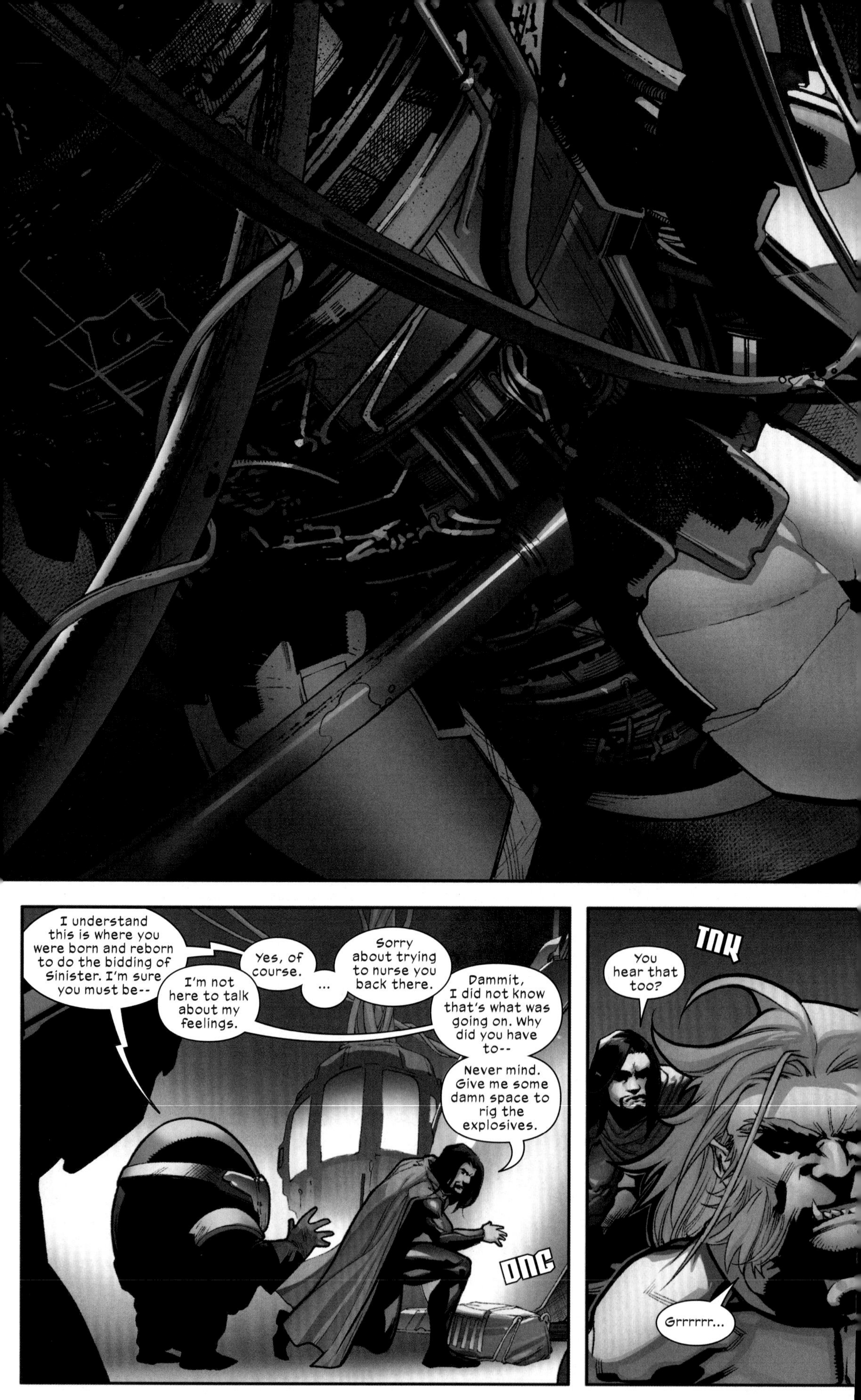
I understand this is where you were born and reborn to do the bidding of Sinister. I'm sure you must be--
I'm not here to talk about my feelings.
Yes, of course.
...
Sorry about trying to nurse you back there.
Dammit, I did not know that's what was going on. Why did you have to--
Never mind. Give me some damn space to rig the explosives.
DNC
TNK
You hear that too?
Grrrrrr...

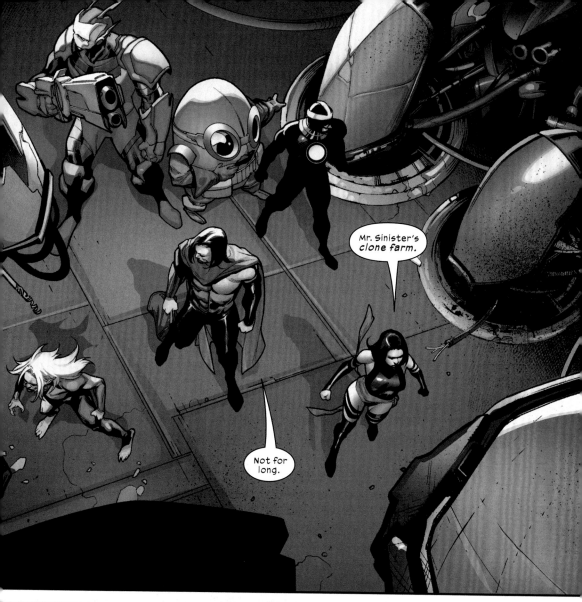

Mr. Sinister's *clone farm.*

Not for long.

JNC

garf!

Something's wrong.

Wha...

TNK

Th-that wasn't there.

What?

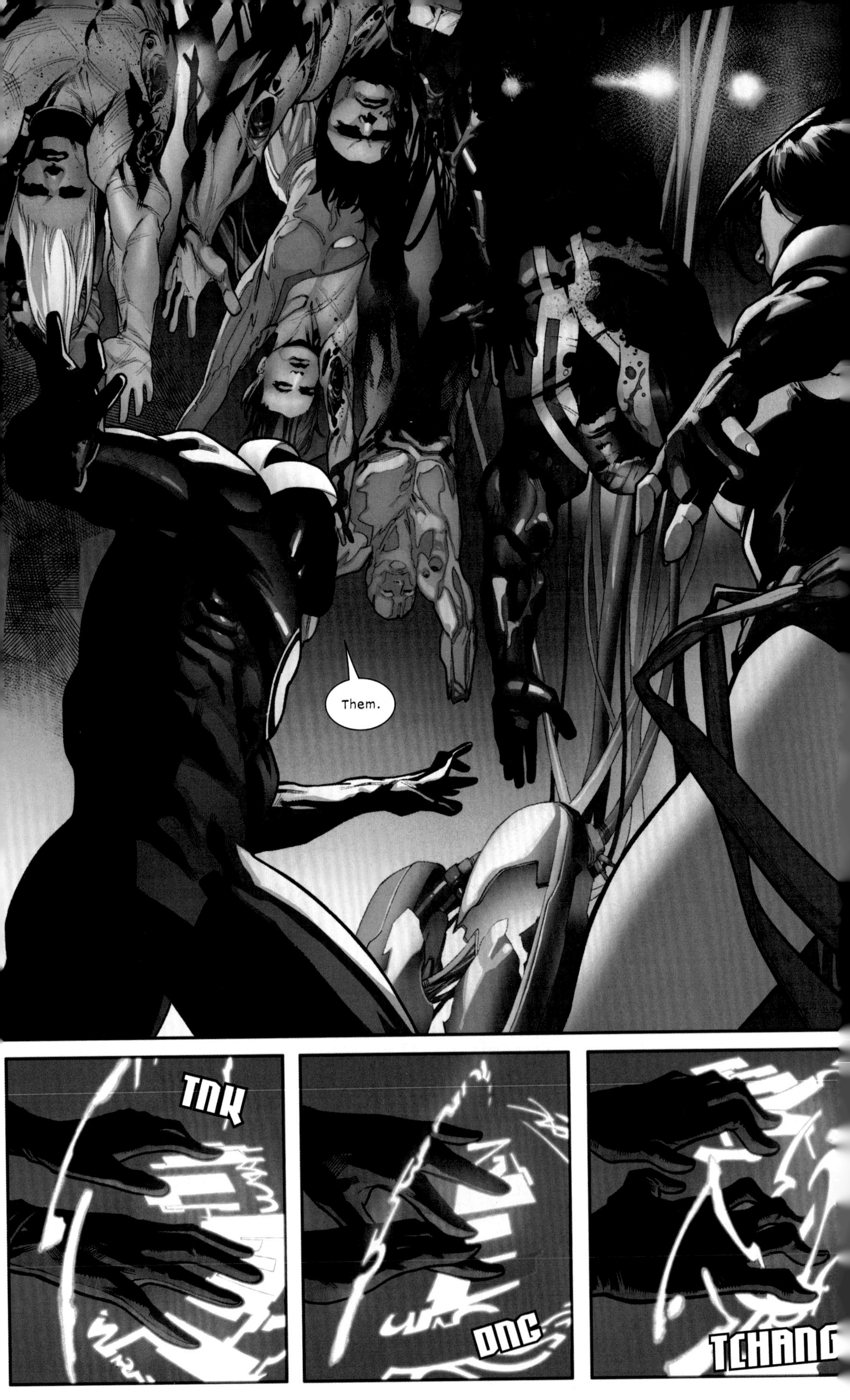
Them.
TNK
DNG
TCHANG

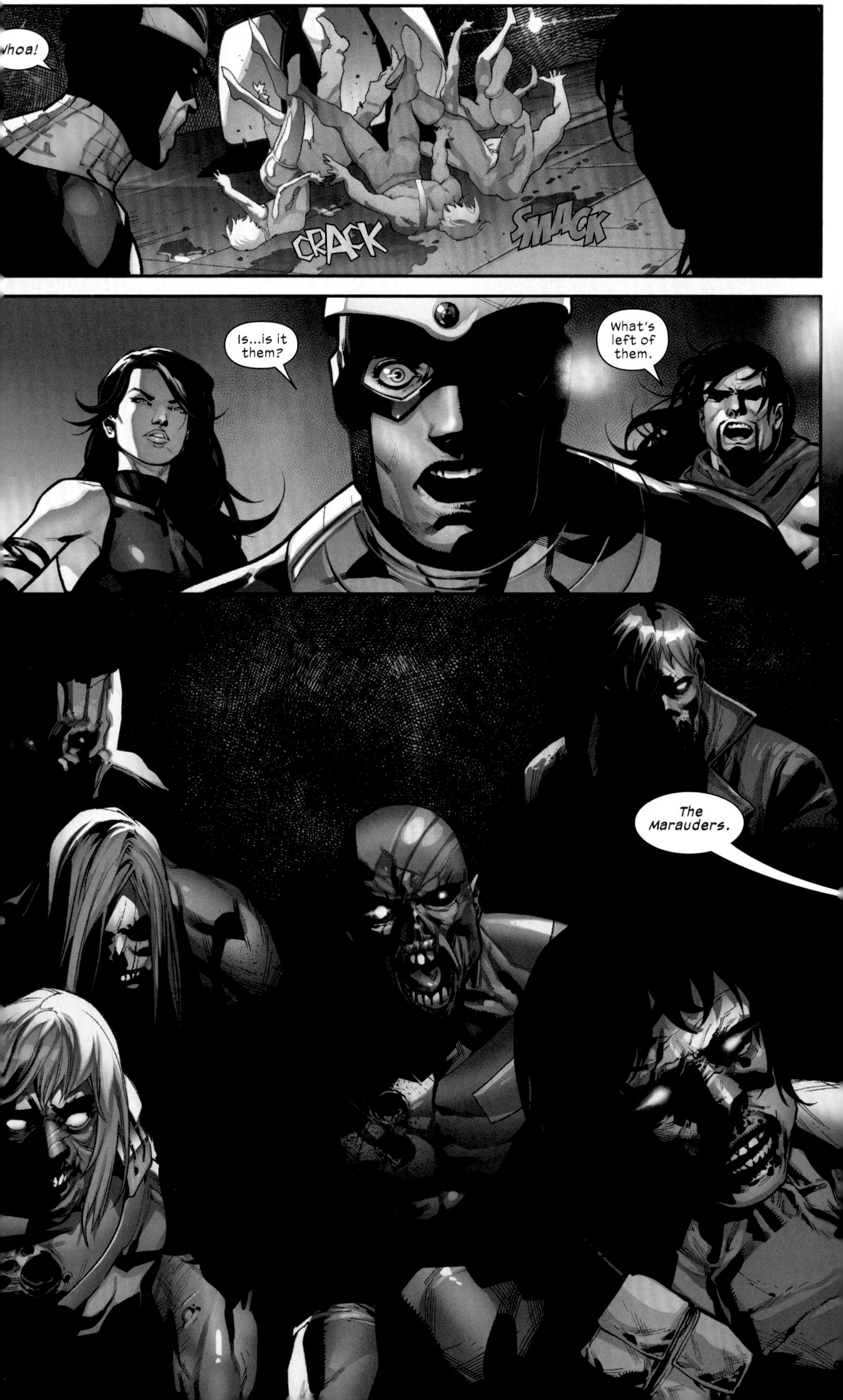

hoa!
CRACK
SMACK
Is...is it them?
What's left of them.
The Marauders.

THE CONUNDRUM OF
MR. SINISTER'S (LEGACY) MARAUDERS

John Greycrow paid me a visit asking after his former teammates again. I can only call his demeanor "stoic desperation," which would have been amusing if not for the high caliber weapon he assembled and disassembled compulsively as we talked. I'm truly saddened that whatever trauma he's endured compels him to hide his completely natural concern for his comrades. I'll order a temporal psi-topsy from Emma to get to the bottom of that, but to the subject at hand:

Bringing the legacy Marauders to Krakoa is not as simple as it seems. At least not as simple as Mr. Greycrow appears (despite his best efforts) to hope. Mr. Sinister was resurrecting clones of his mutant assassins back when Krakoa was just a murderous island we didn't know how to explain to our friends. To call his resurrection protocols lax does not adequately sum up how antithetical his procedures were to current Krakoan best practices. All that is to say the current iteration of the Marauders are clones of clones of clones, most likely suffering from generation loss and genetic corruption (some, no doubt, intentional.) Are these current Marauders the most natural versions of themselves? If not, don't they deserve to be?

I won't try to force a decision (not a priority, I understand,) but for now we should apply some political pressure towards Sinister dismantling his clone farm. Once we know we're dealing with the last of the line, we can assess the Marauders' genetic integrity and discern if the whole lot of them aren't better left for The Five to sort out.

I don't want to sound like Kurt, but I'd be excited to see what could be made of these mutants if they were resurrected with a little love.

—

ARCLIGHT: Manual techtonic disruption.

RIPTIDE: Hyper rotation. Uber-keratin pentaquill excretion.

HARPOON: Bio-energetic, bio-luminous projectiles.

BLOCKBUSTER: Strong guy.

PRISM: Energy absorption/refraction. Biotransparency.

SCRAMBLER: Electro/Bioelectrosystemic disruption.

—

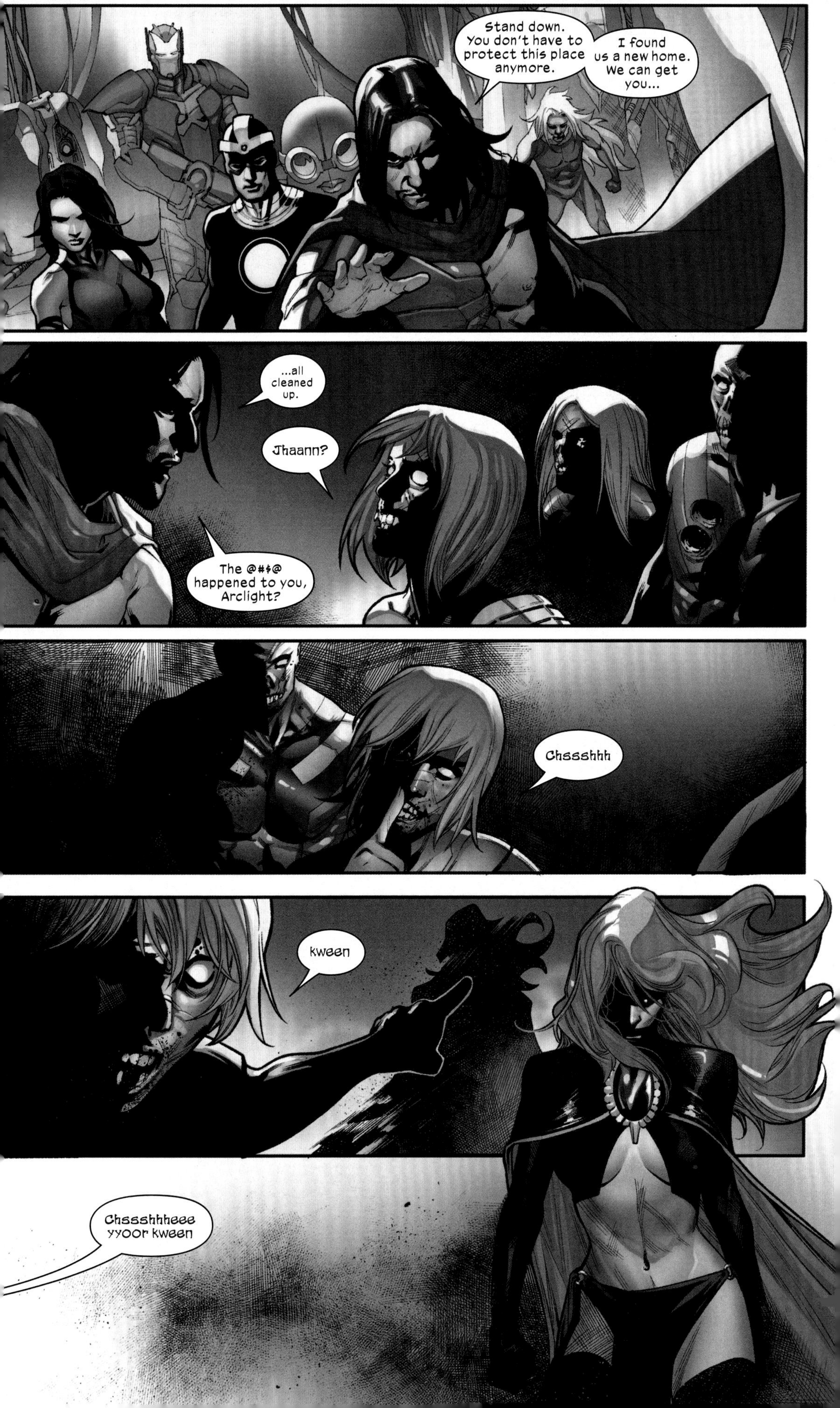

Stand down. You don't have to protect this place anymore.
I found us a new home. We can get you...
...all cleaned up.
Jhaann?
The @#$@ happened to you, Arclight?
Chssshhh
kween
Chssshhheee yyoor kween

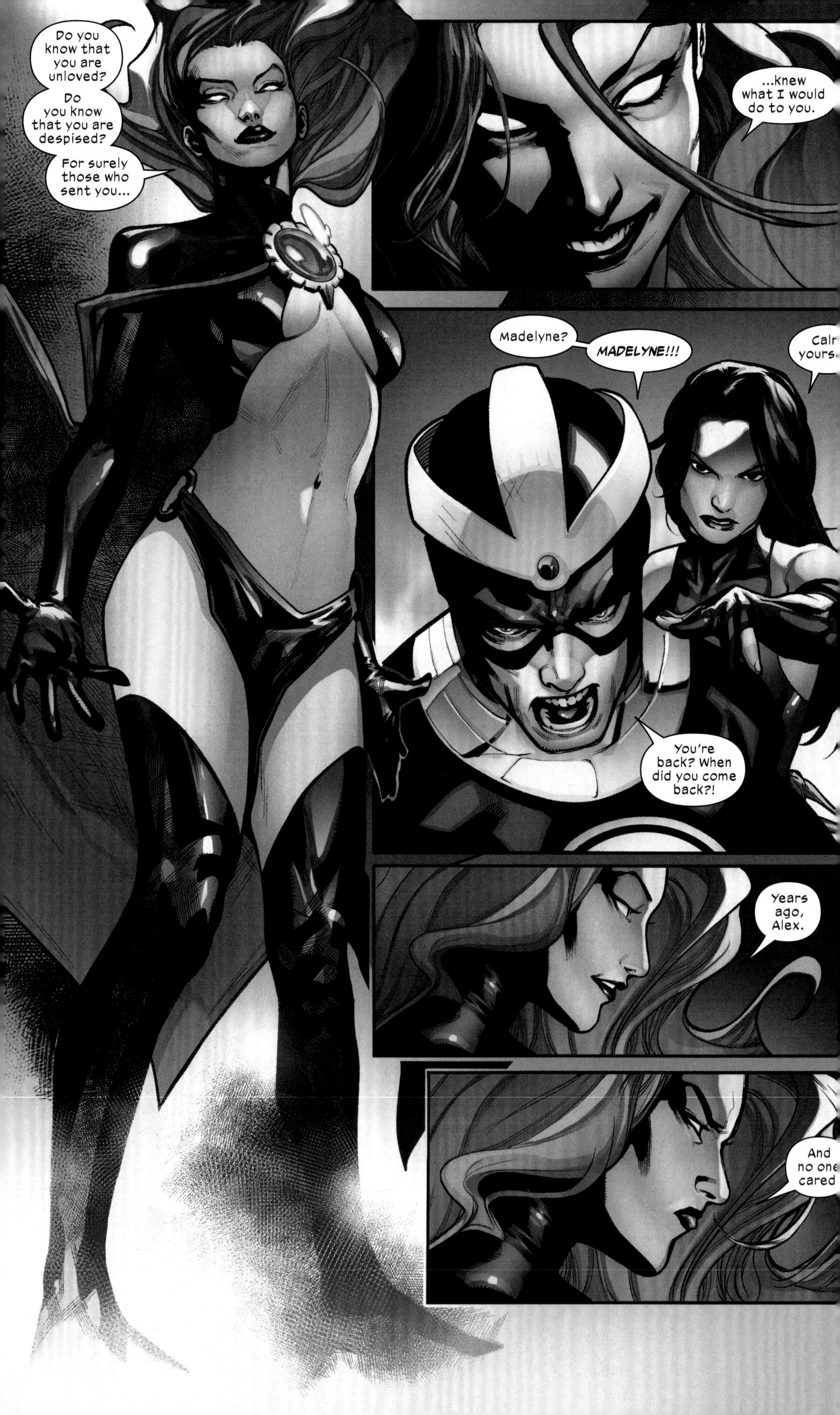
Do you know that you are unloved?
Do you know that you are despised?
For surely those who sent you...
...knew what I would do to you.
Madelyne?
MADELYNE!!!
Calr yours
You're back? When did you come back?!
Years ago, Alex.
And no one cared

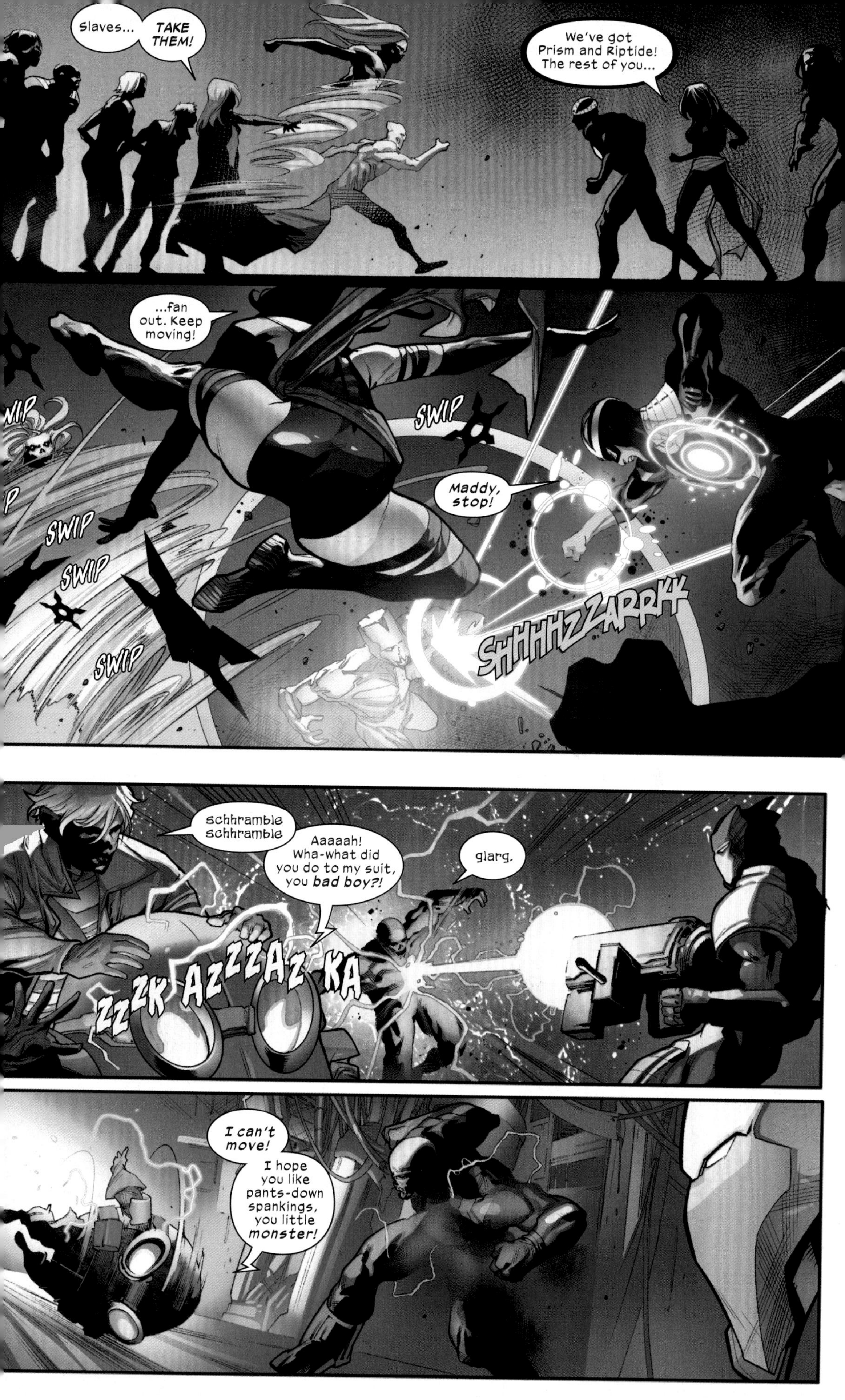
Slaves... TAKE THEM!
We've got Prism and Riptide! The rest of you...
...fan out. Keep moving!
SWIP
SWIP
SWIP
SWIP
Maddy, stop!
SHHHHZZARRK
schhramble schhramble
Aaaaah! Wha-what did you do to my suit, you bad boy?!
glarg.
ZZZK AZZZAZ KA
I can't move!
I hope you like pants-down spankings, you little monster!

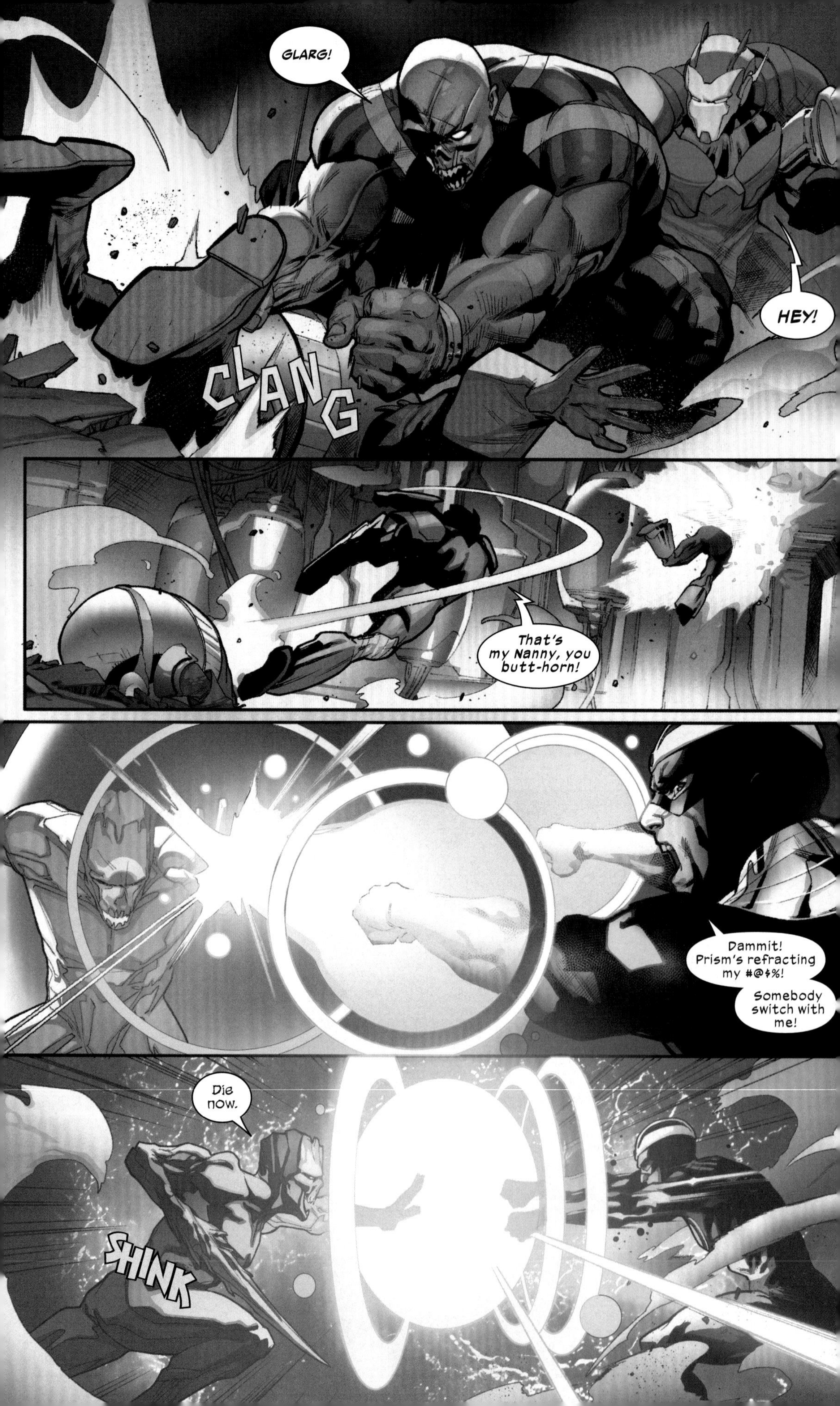
GLARG!
HEY!
CLANG
That's my Nanny, you butt-horn!
Dammit! Prism's refracting my #@$%!
Somebody switch with me!
Die now.
SHINK

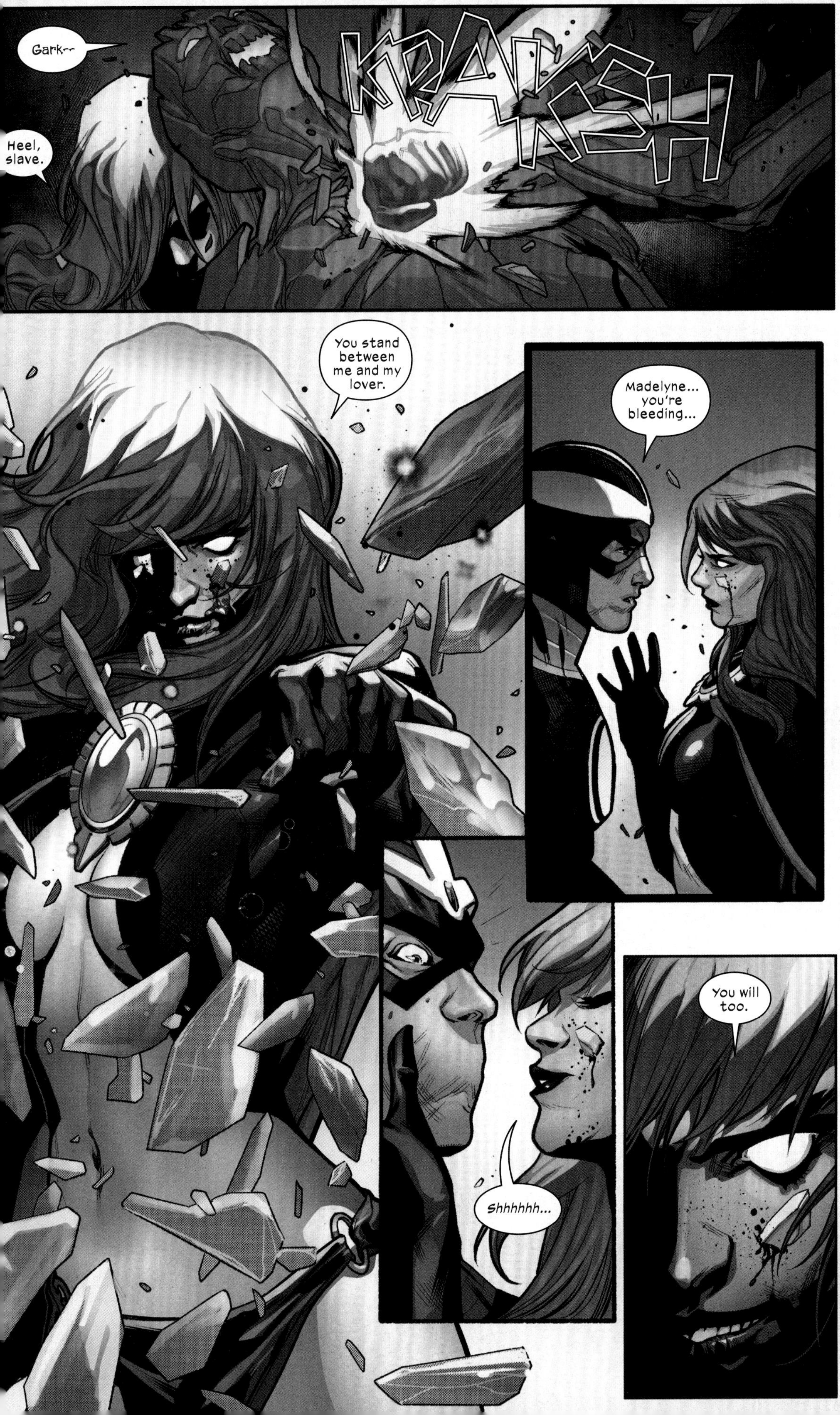
Gark--
KRAKKOOOSH
Heel, slave.
You stand between me and my lover.
Madelyne... you're bleeding...
Shhhhhh...
You will too.

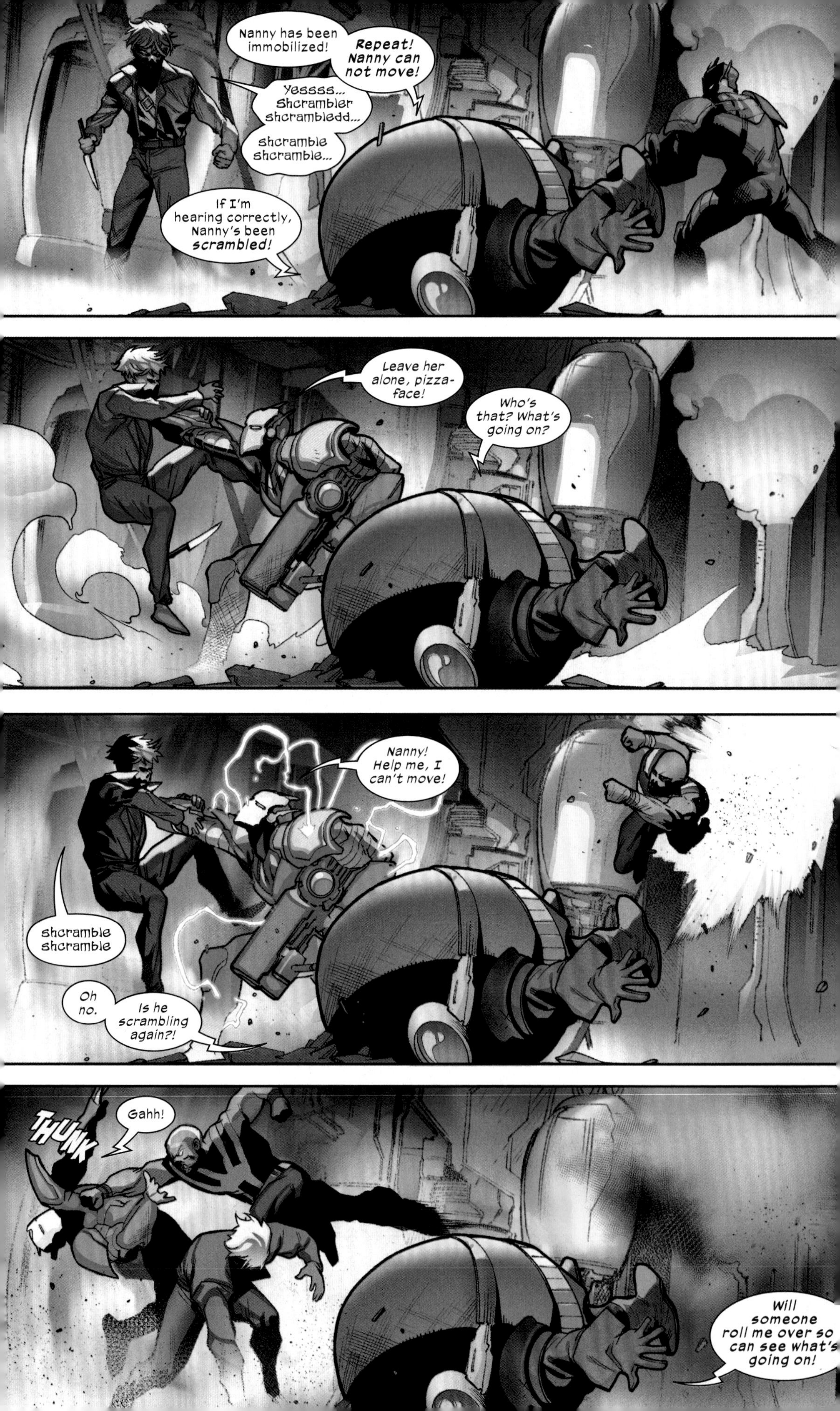
Nanny has been immobilized!
Repeat! Nanny can not move!
Yessss... Shcrambler shcrambledd...
shcramble shcramble...
If I'm hearing correctly, Nanny's been scrambled!
Leave her alone, pizza-face!
Who's that? What's going on?
Nanny! Help me, I can't move!
shcramble shcramble
Oh no.
Is he scrambling again?!
THUNK
Gahh!
Will someone roll me over so can see what's going on!

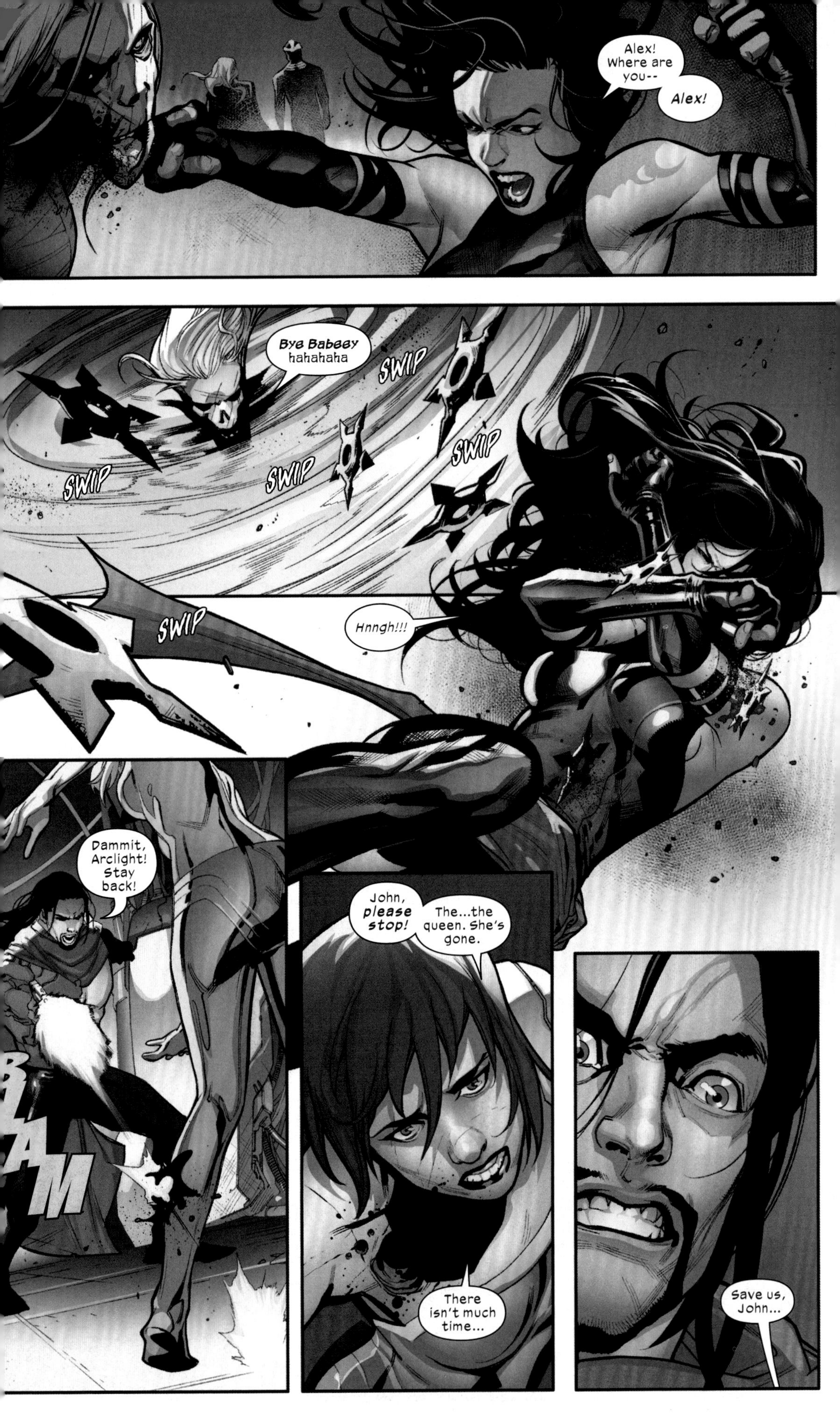

Alex! Where are you--
Alex!
Bye Babeey hahahaha
SWIP
SWIP
SWIP
SWIP
SWIP
Hnngh!!!
Dammit, Arclight! Stay back!
BLAM
John, please stop!
The...the queen. She's gone.
There isn't much time...
Save us, John...

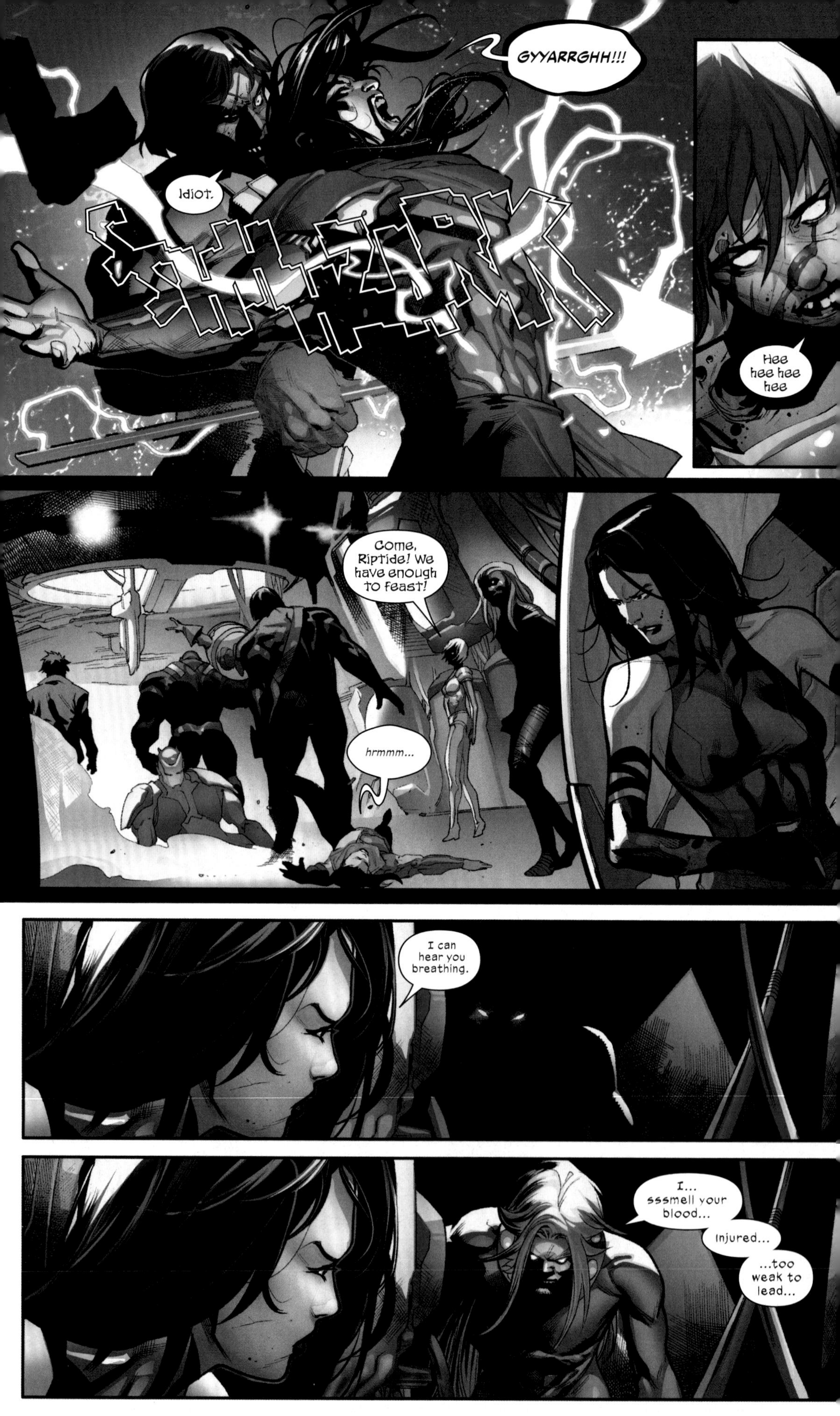
GYYARRGHH!!!
Idiot.
Hee hee hee hee
Come, Riptide! We have enough to feast!
hrmmm...
I can hear you breathing.
I... sssmell your blood...
Injured...
...too weak to lead...

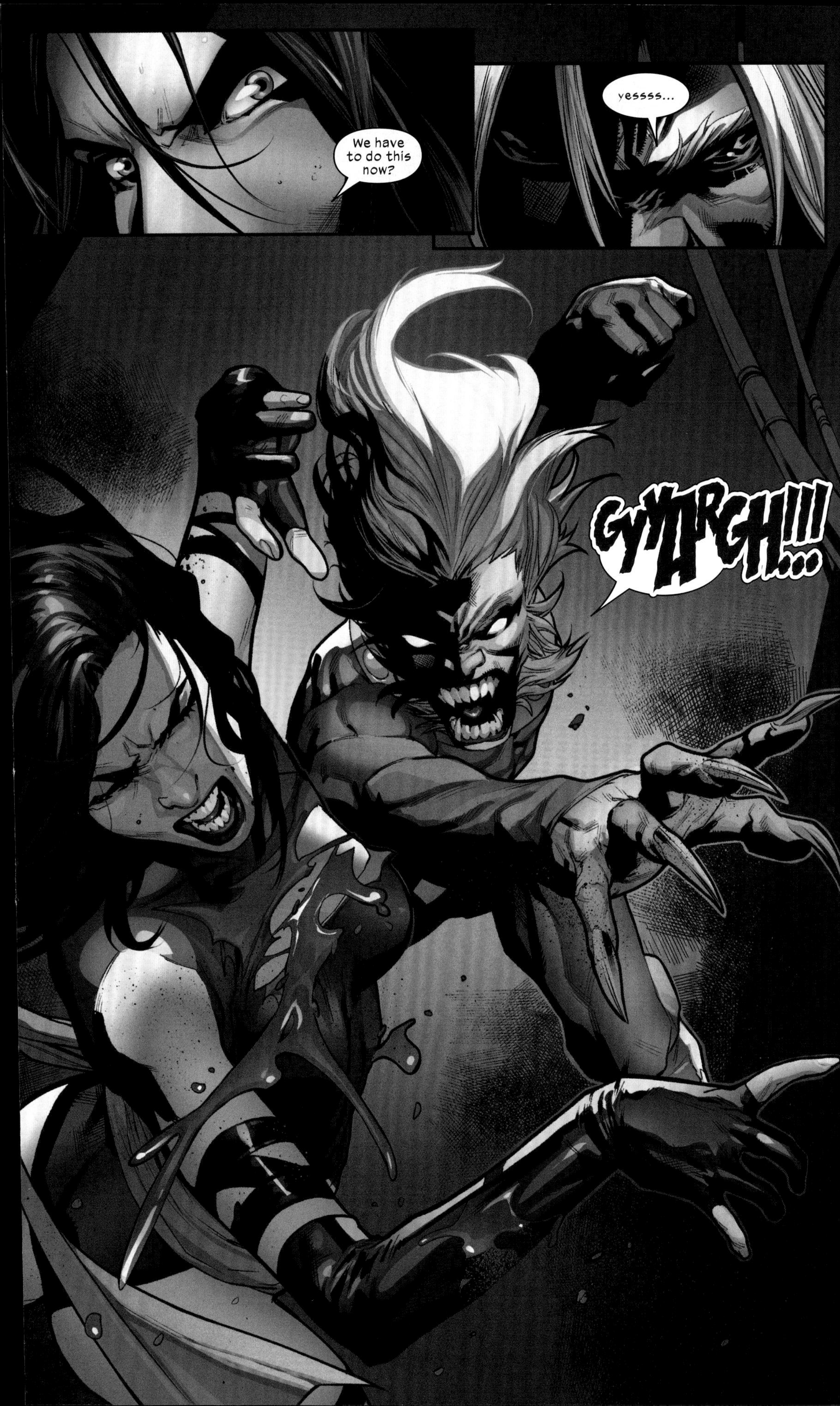
We have to do this now?
yessss...
GYYARGH!!!...

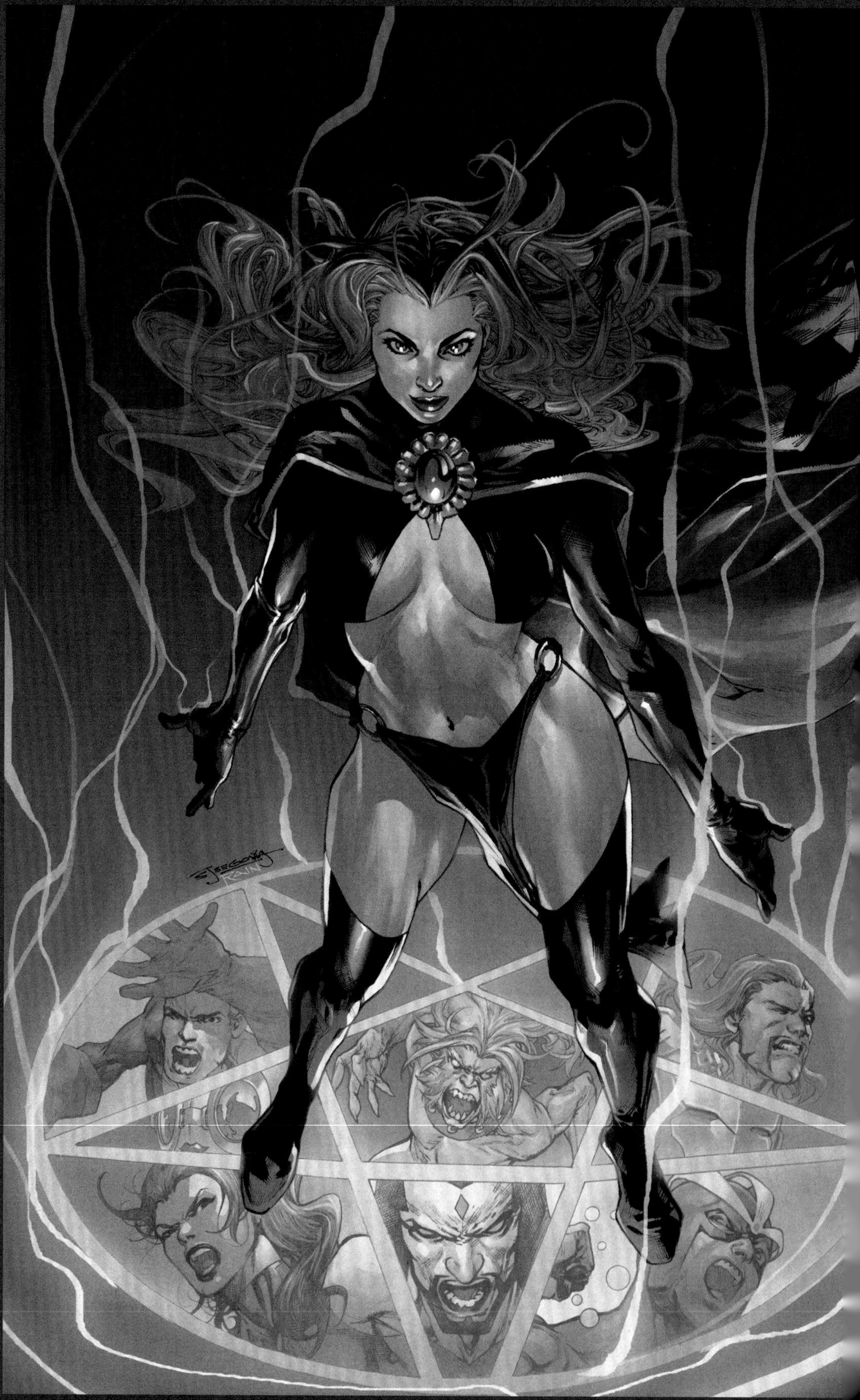

Nothing People

[hell_[0.3]
[ions_[0.3]

I do wonder which binds us more... Xavier's ideals or the trauma of being mutant. The dream or the pain.

-NIGHTCRAWLER

[hell_[0.X]
[ions_[0.X]

[hell_[0.3].....]
[ions_[0.3].....]

[Hellions_alpha.]

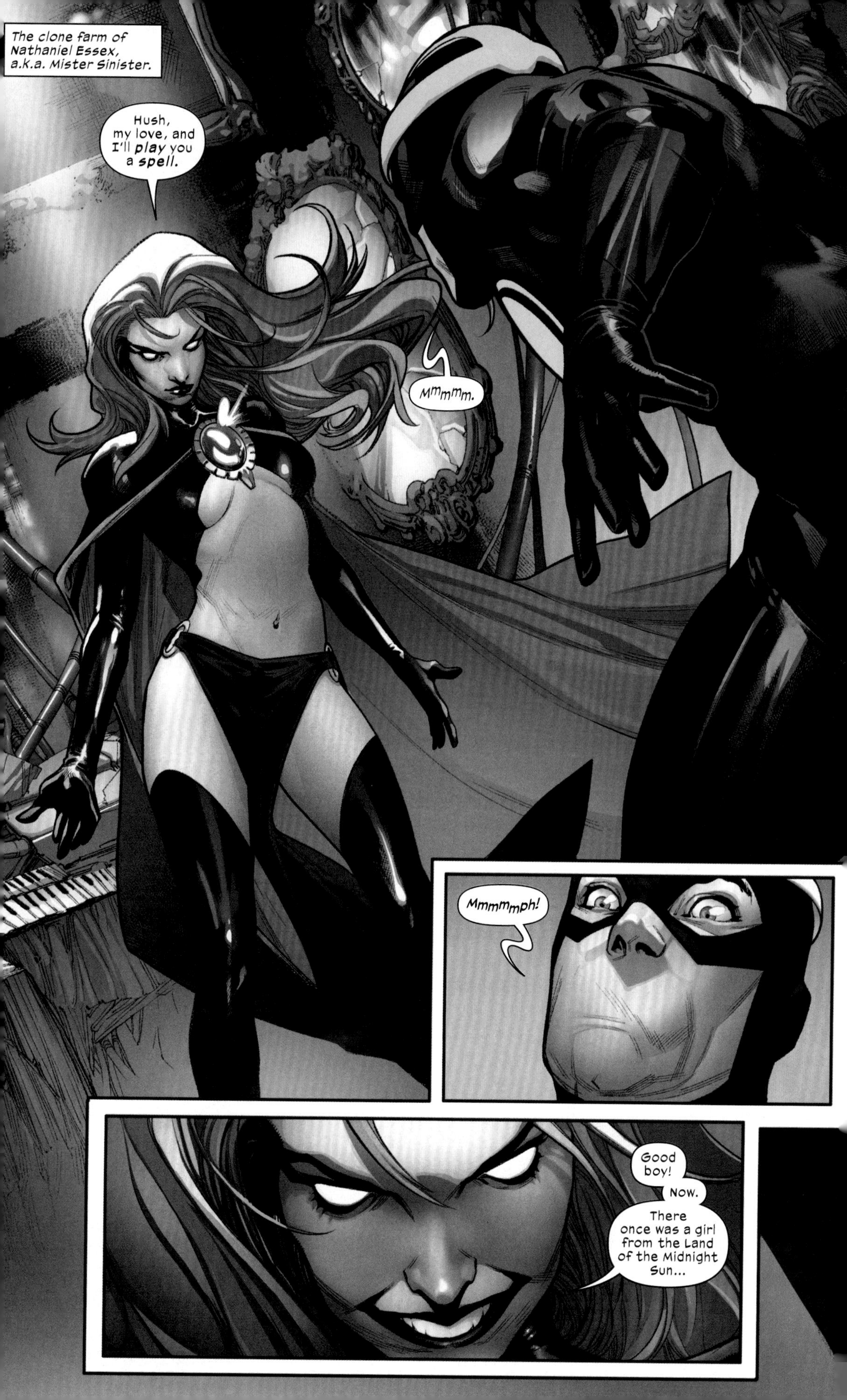
The clone farm of Nathaniel Essex, a.k.a. Mister Sinister.
Hush, my love, and I'll **play** you a **spell**.
Mmmmm.
Mmmmmph!
Good boy!
Now.
There once was a girl from the Land of the Midnight Sun...

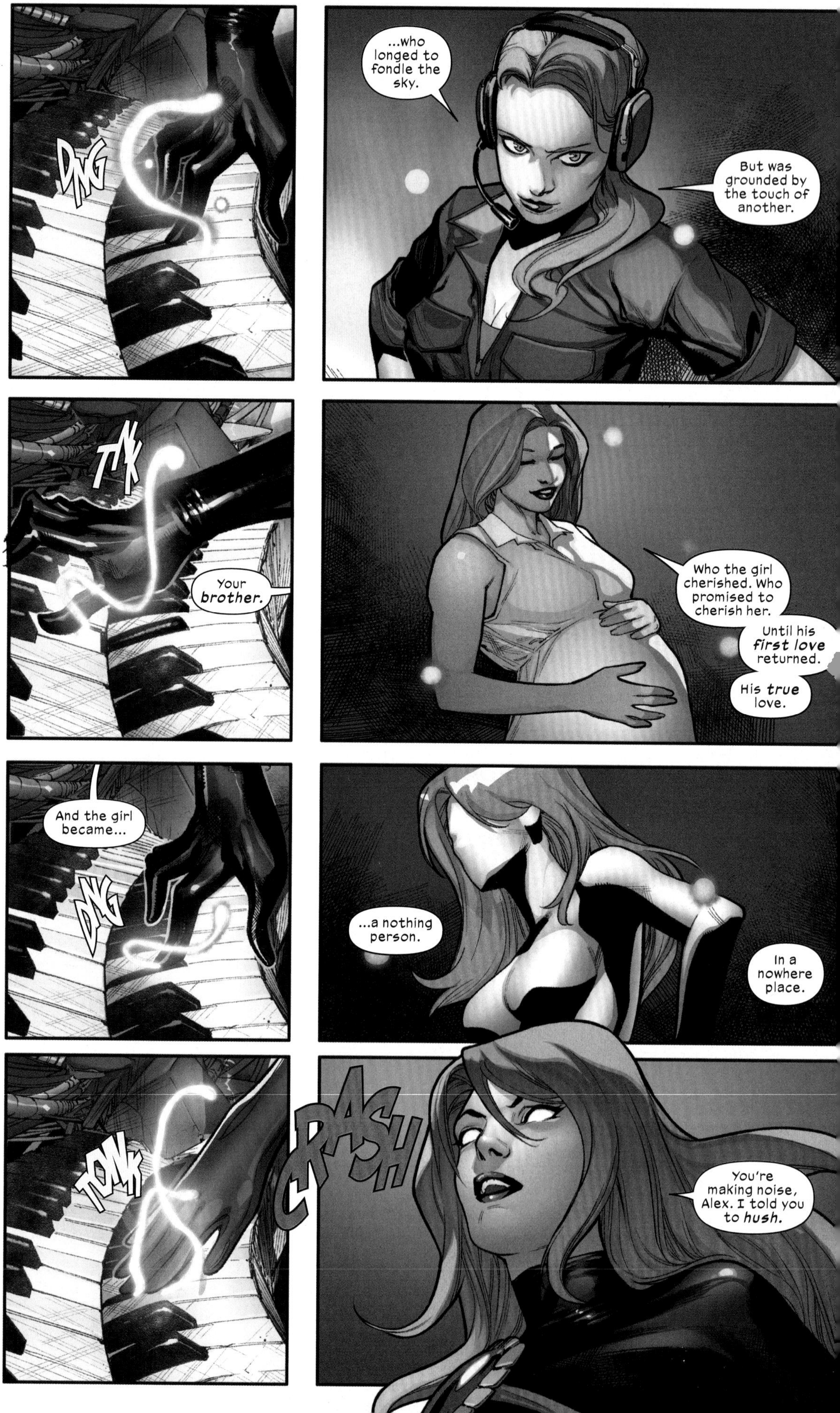
DNG
...who longed to fondle the sky.
But was grounded by the touch of another.
TINK
Your brother.
Who the girl cherished. Who promised to cherish her.
Until his first love returned.
His true love.
And the girl became...
DNG
...a nothing person.
In a nowhere place.
TONK
CRASH
You're making noise, Alex. I told you to hush.

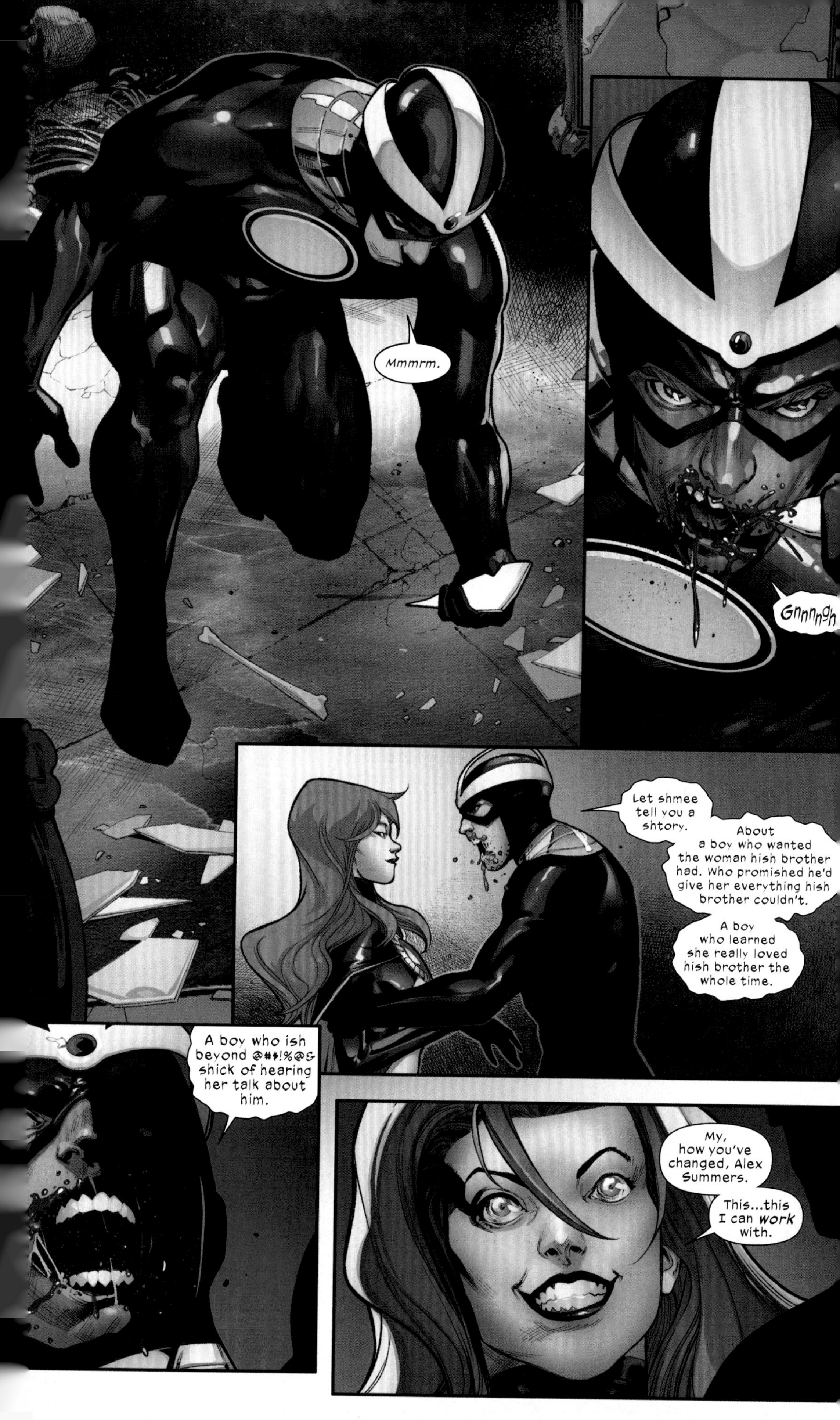
Mmmrm.
Gnnnngh
Let shmee tell you a shtory.
About a boy who wanted the woman hish brother had. Who promished he'd give her everything hish brother couldn't.
A boy who learned she really loved hish brother the whole time.
A boy who ish beyond @#$!%@& shick of hearing her talk about him.
My, how you've changed, Alex Summers.
This...this I can *work* with.

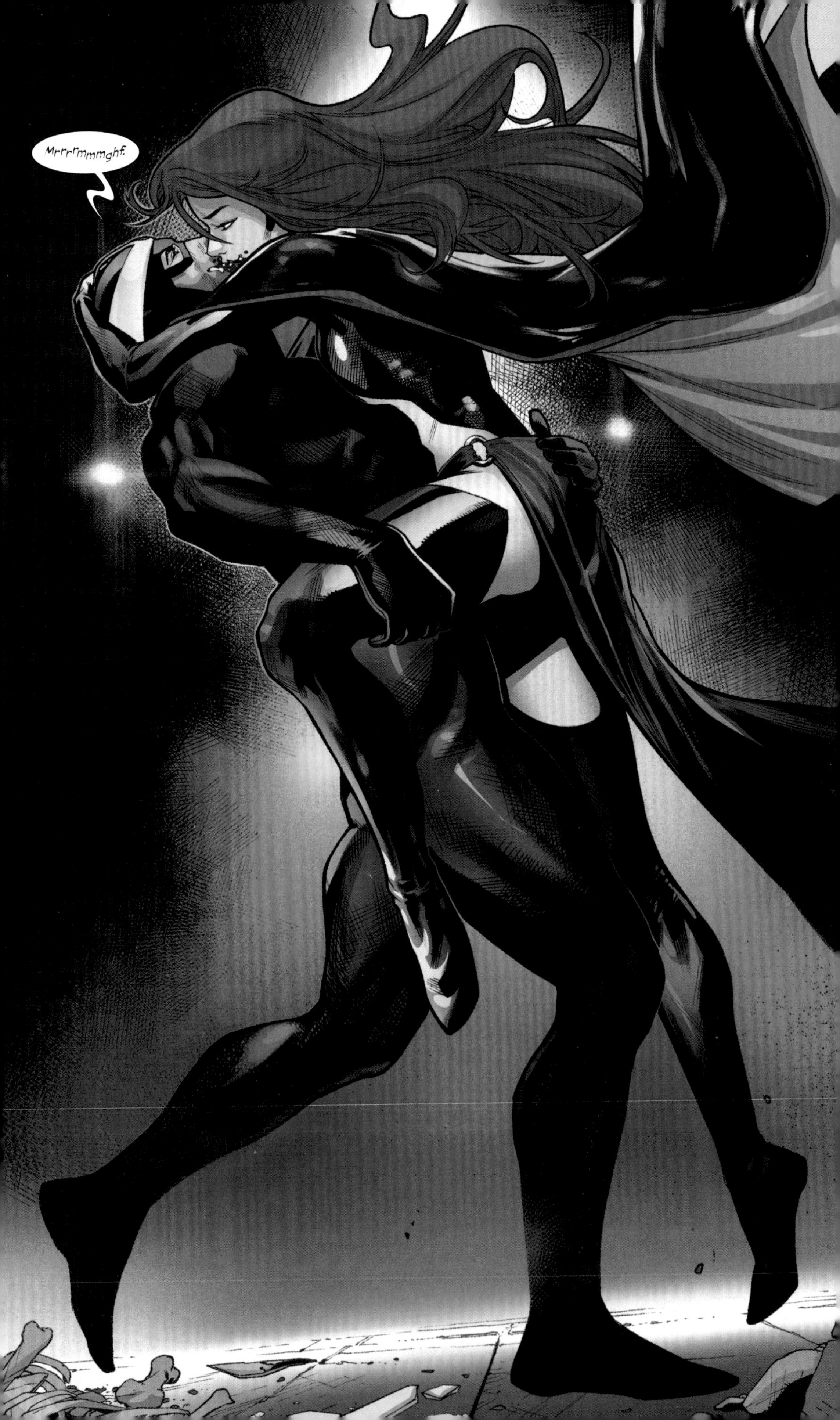
Mrrrrmmmghf.

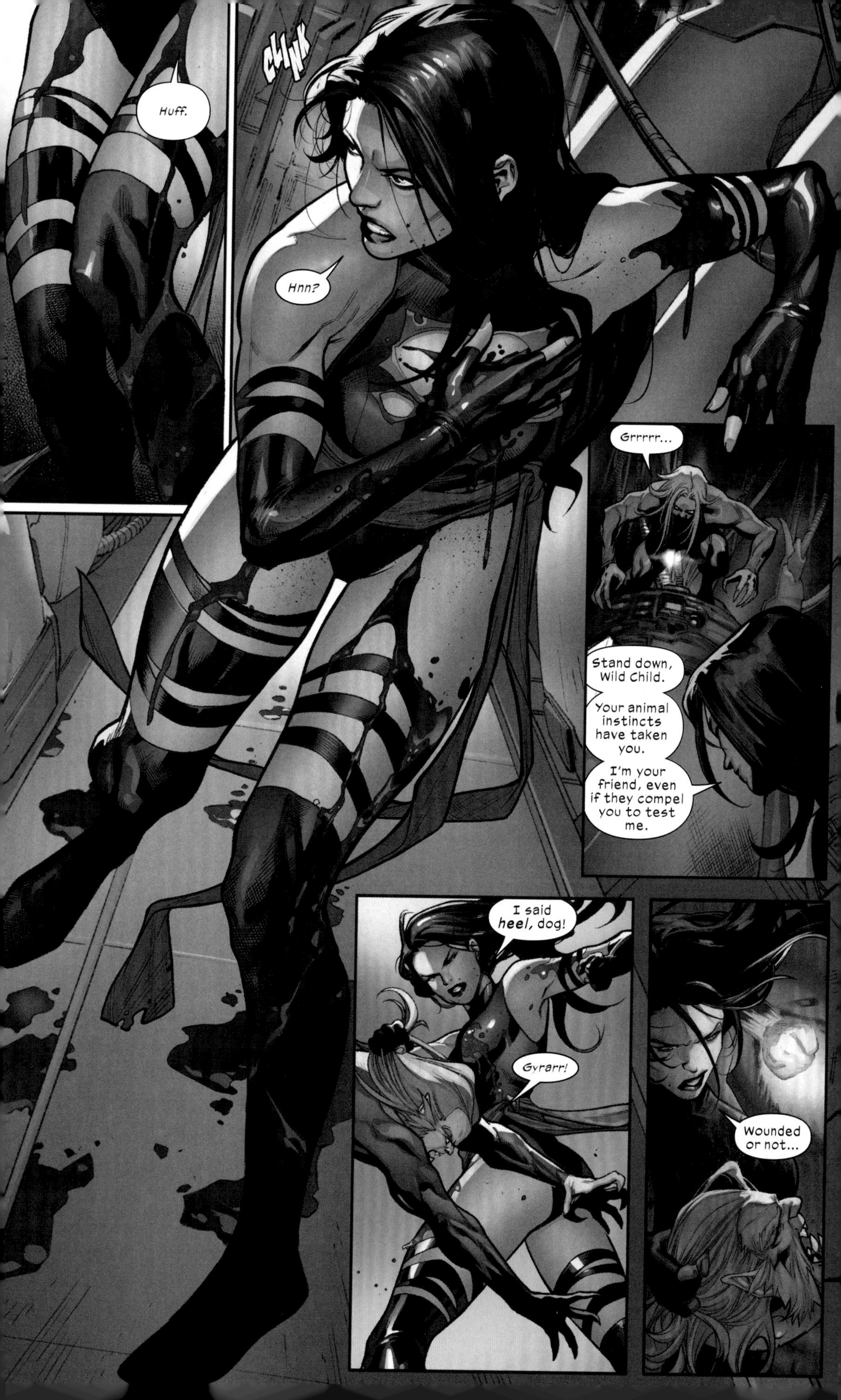

Huff.
CLINK
Hnn?
Grrrrr...
Stand down, Wild Child.
Your animal instincts have taken you.
I'm your friend, even if they compel you to test me.
I said heel, dog!
Gyrarr!
Wounded or not...

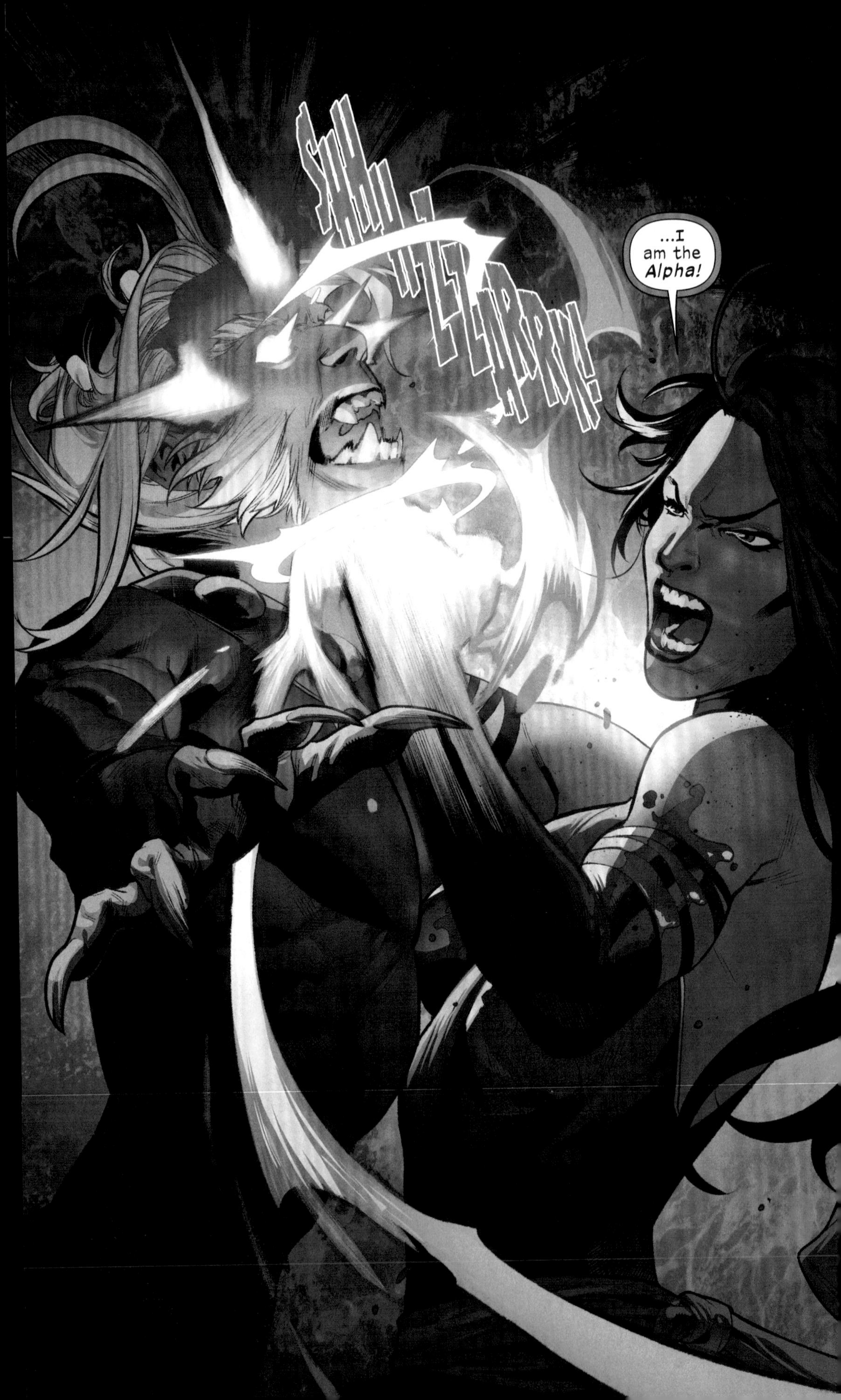
...I am the *Alpha!*

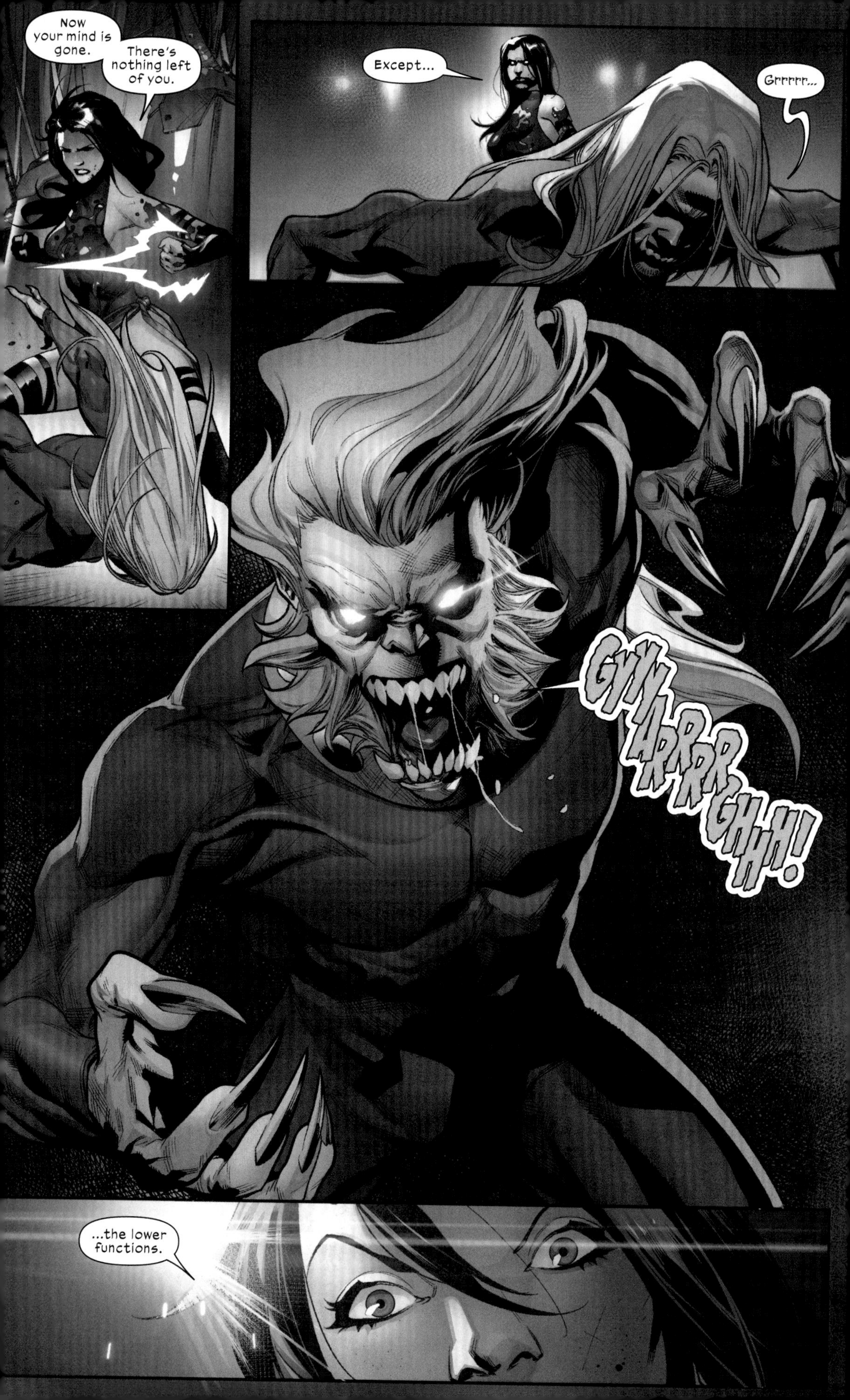
Now your mind is gone.
There's nothing left of you.
Except...
Grrrrr...
GYYARRRRGHHH!
...the lower functions.

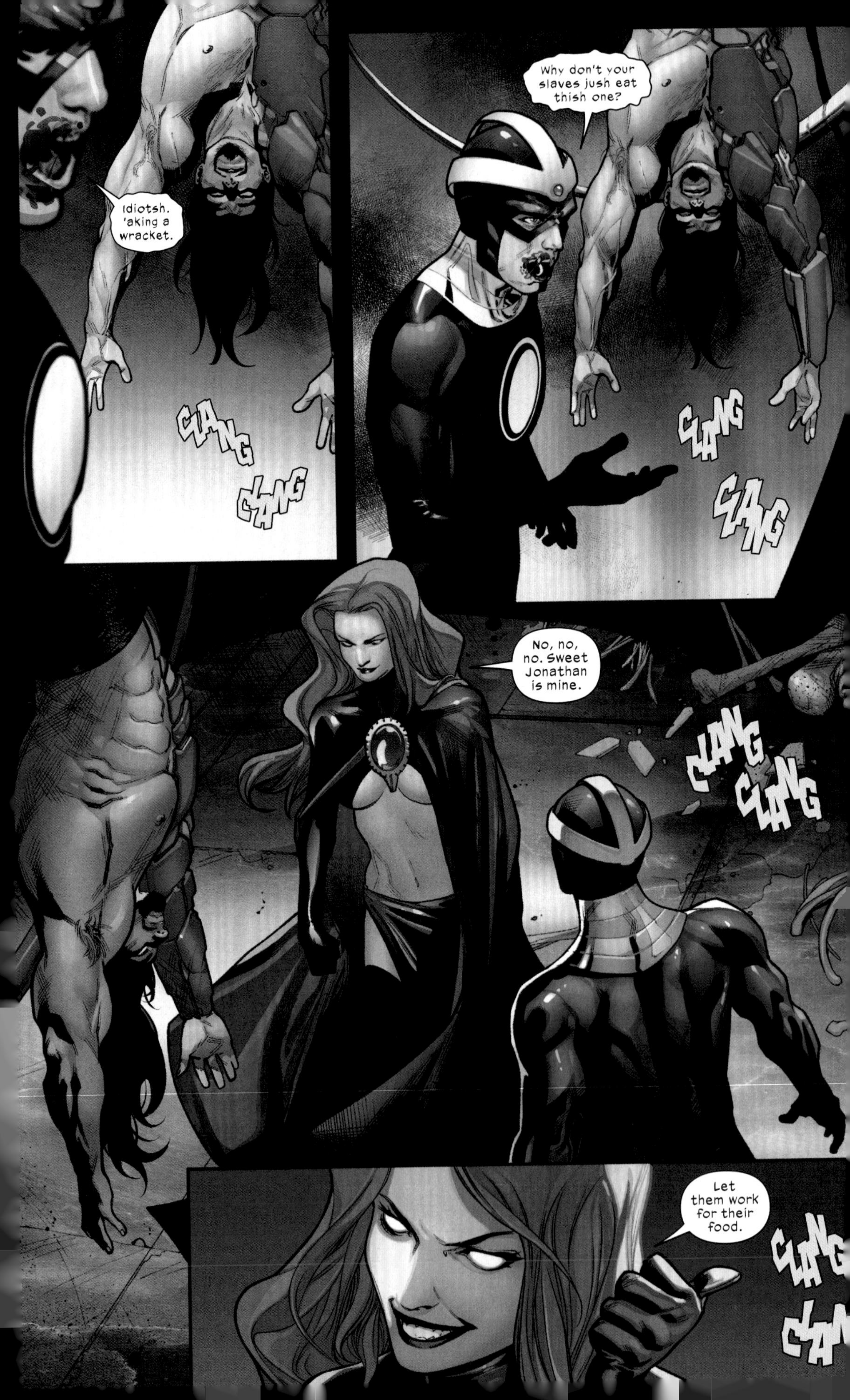
Idiotsh. 'aking a wracket.
CLANG
CLANG
Why don't your slaves jush eat thish one?
CLANG
CLANG
No, no, no. Sweet Jonathan is mine.
CLANG
CLANG
Let them work for their food.

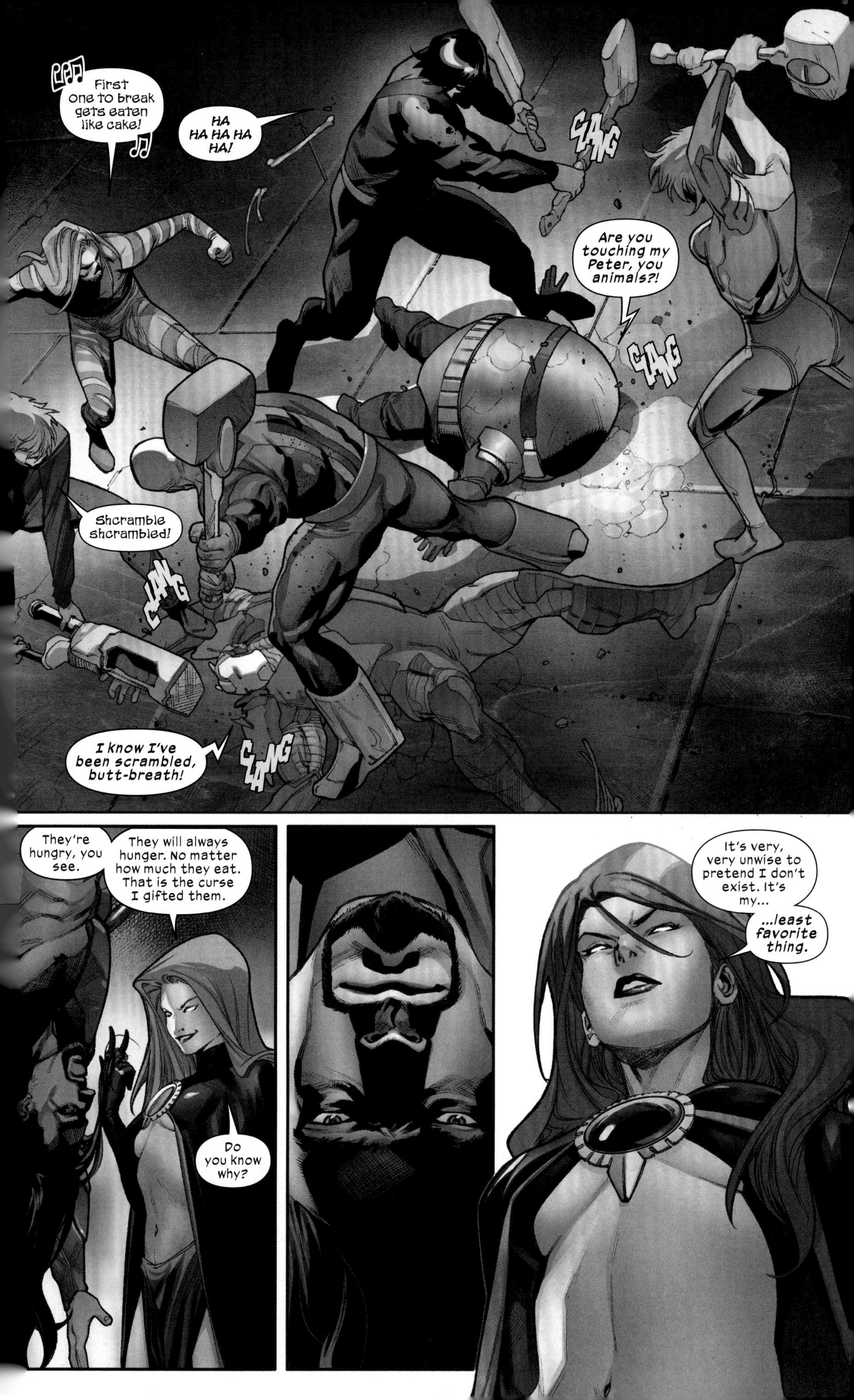
First one to break gets eaten like cake!
HA HA HA HA HA!
CLANG
Are you touching my Peter, you animals?!
CLANG
Shcramble shcrambled!
CLANG
I know I've been scrambled, butt-breath!
CLANG
They're hungry, you see.
They will always hunger. No matter how much they eat. That is the curse I gifted them.
Do you know why?
It's very, very unwise to pretend I don't exist. It's my...
...least favorite thing.

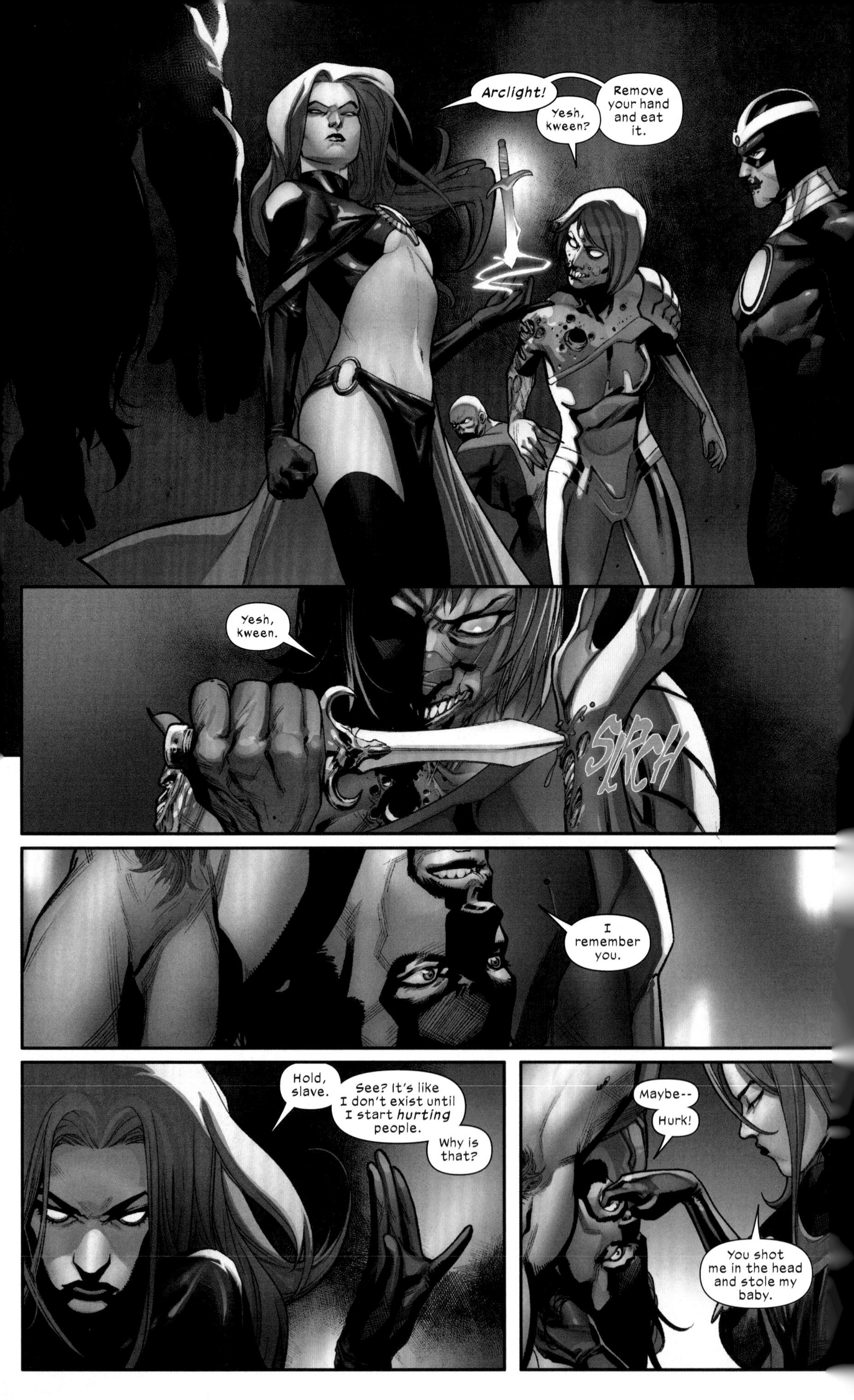
Arclight!
Yesh, kween?
Remove your hand and eat it.
Yesh, kween.
SLRCH
I remember you.
Hold, slave.
See? It's like I don't exist until I start *hurting* people.
Why is that?
Maybe--
Hurk!
You shot me in the head and stole my baby.

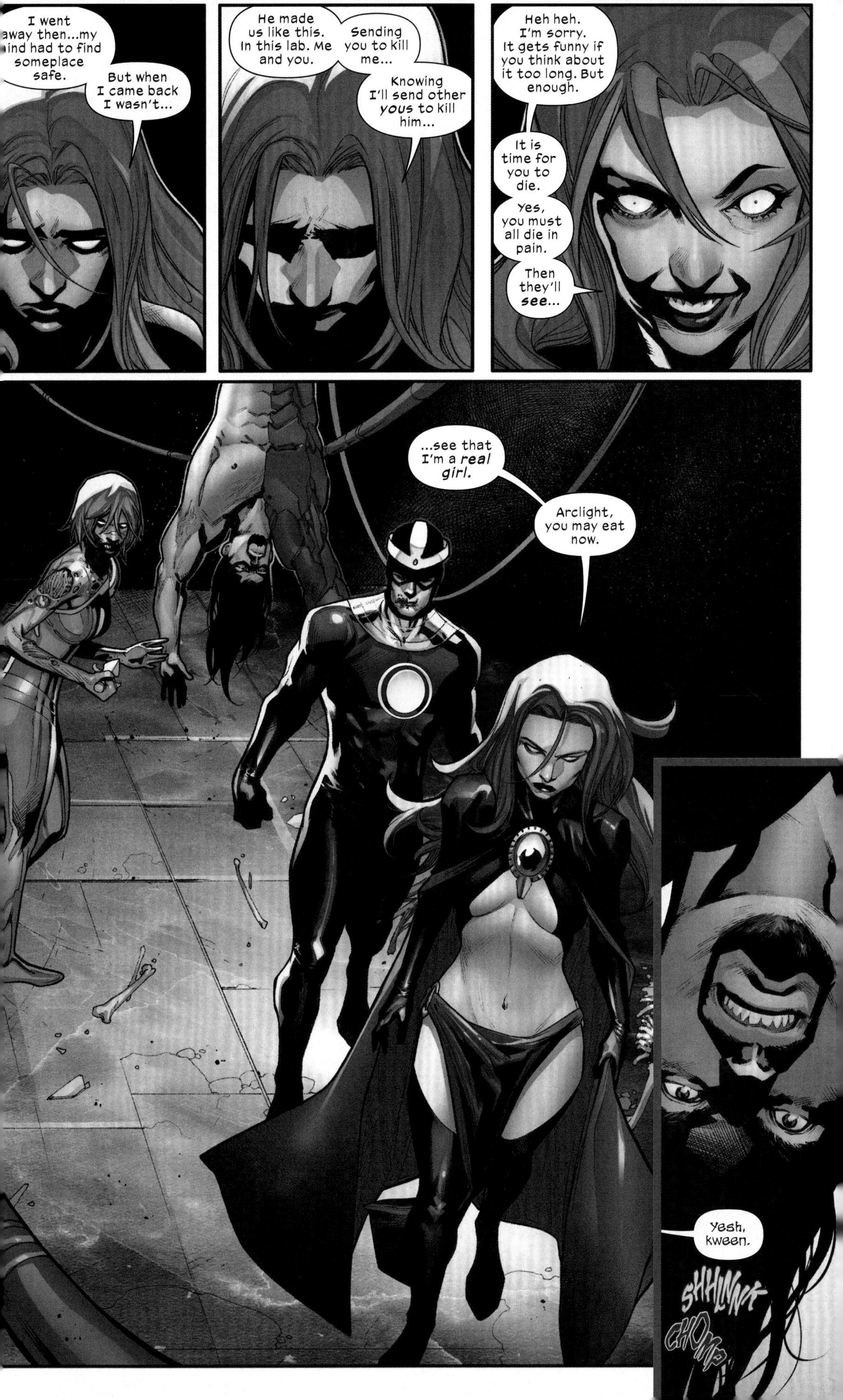

I went away then...my mind had to find someplace safe.
But when I came back I wasn't...
He made us like this. In this lab. Me and you.
Sending you to kill me...
Knowing I'll send other *yous* to kill him...
Heh heh. I'm sorry. It gets funny if you think about it too long. But enough.
It is time for you to die.
Yes, you must all die in pain.
Then they'll *see*...
...see that I'm a *real girl.*
Arclight, you may eat now.
Yesh, kween.
SHHLINNK
CHOMP

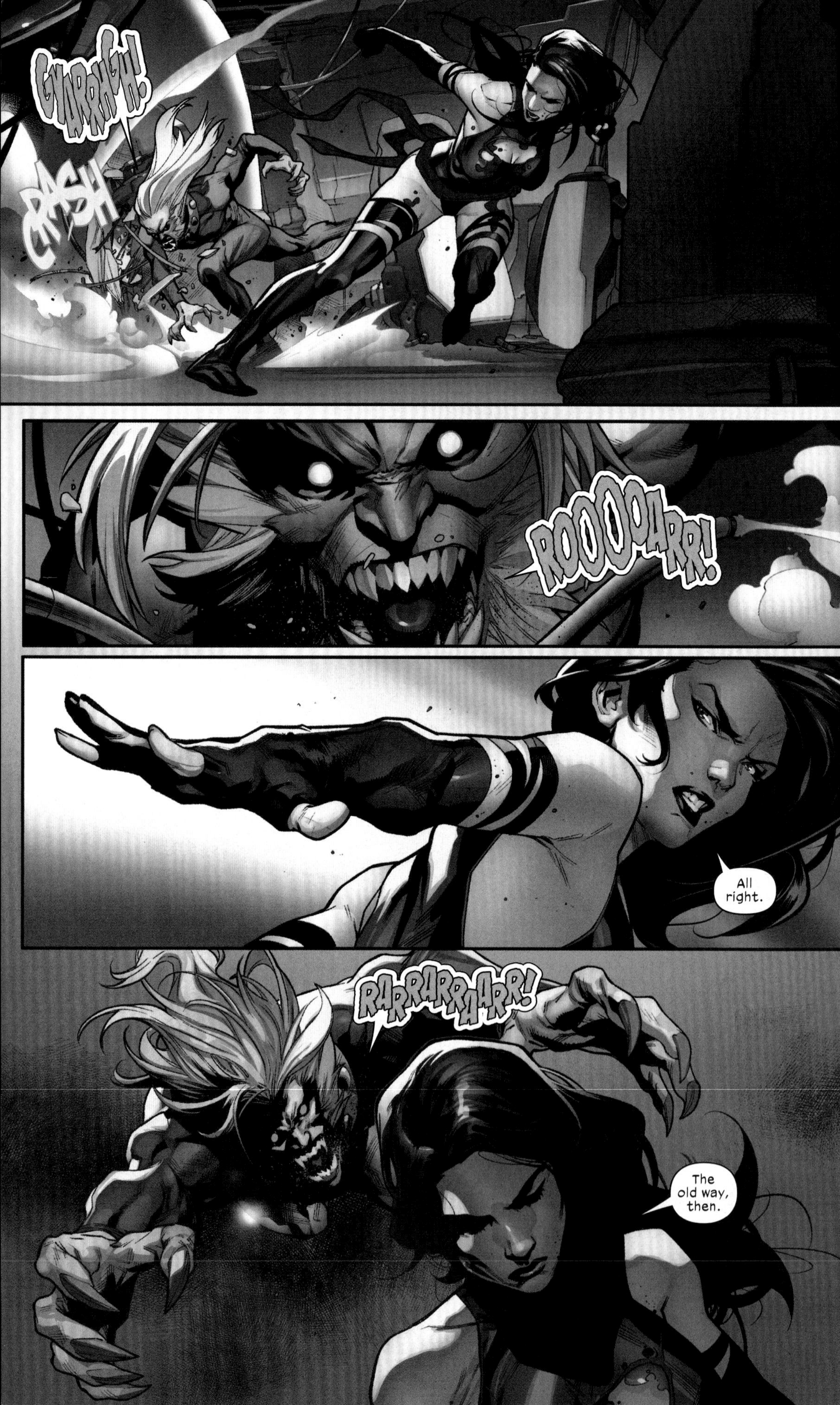

GYARRGH!
CRASH
ROOOOARR!
All right.
RARRARRAARR!
The old way, then.

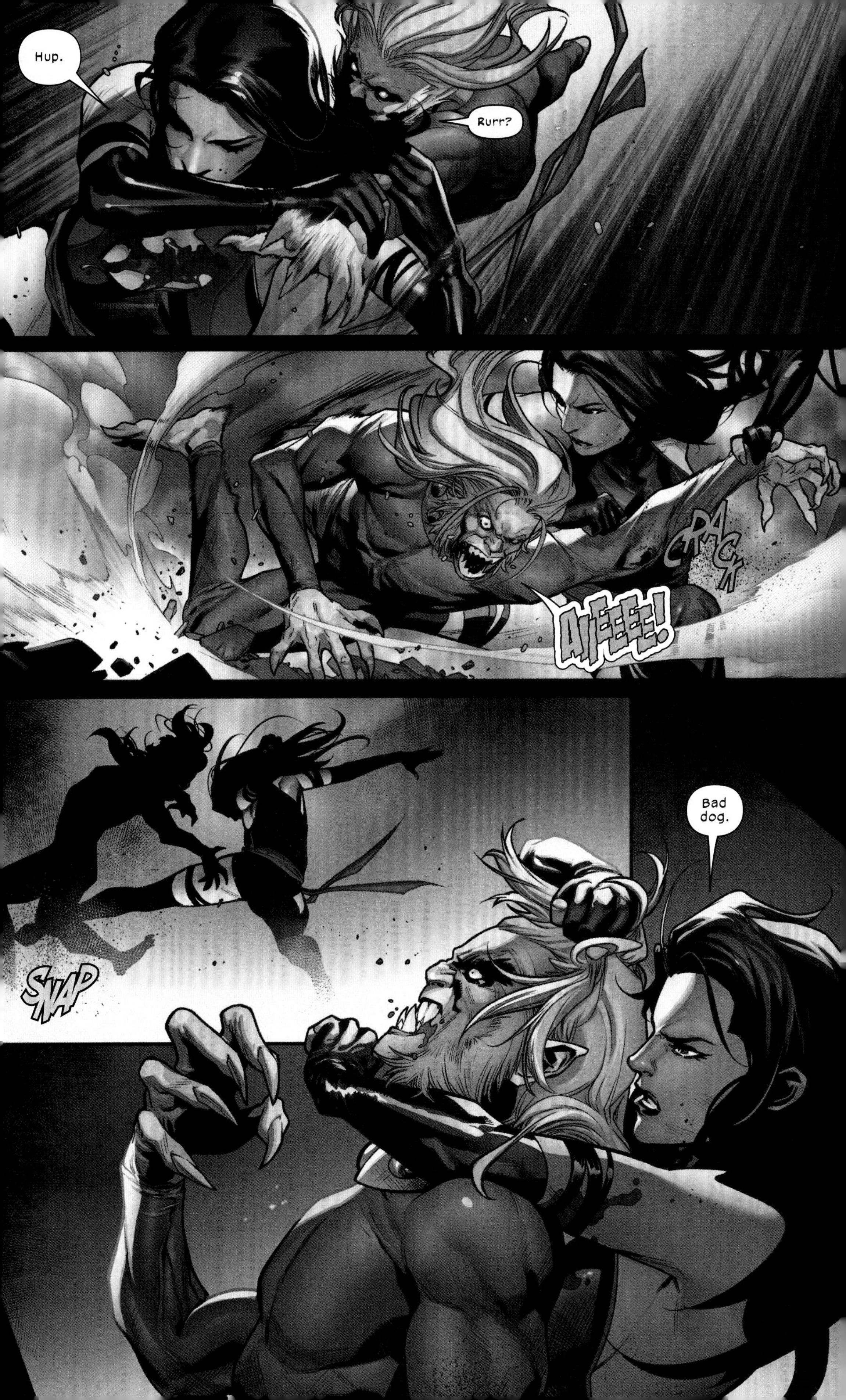
Hup.
Rurr?
CRACK
AIEEEE!
SNAP
Bad dog.

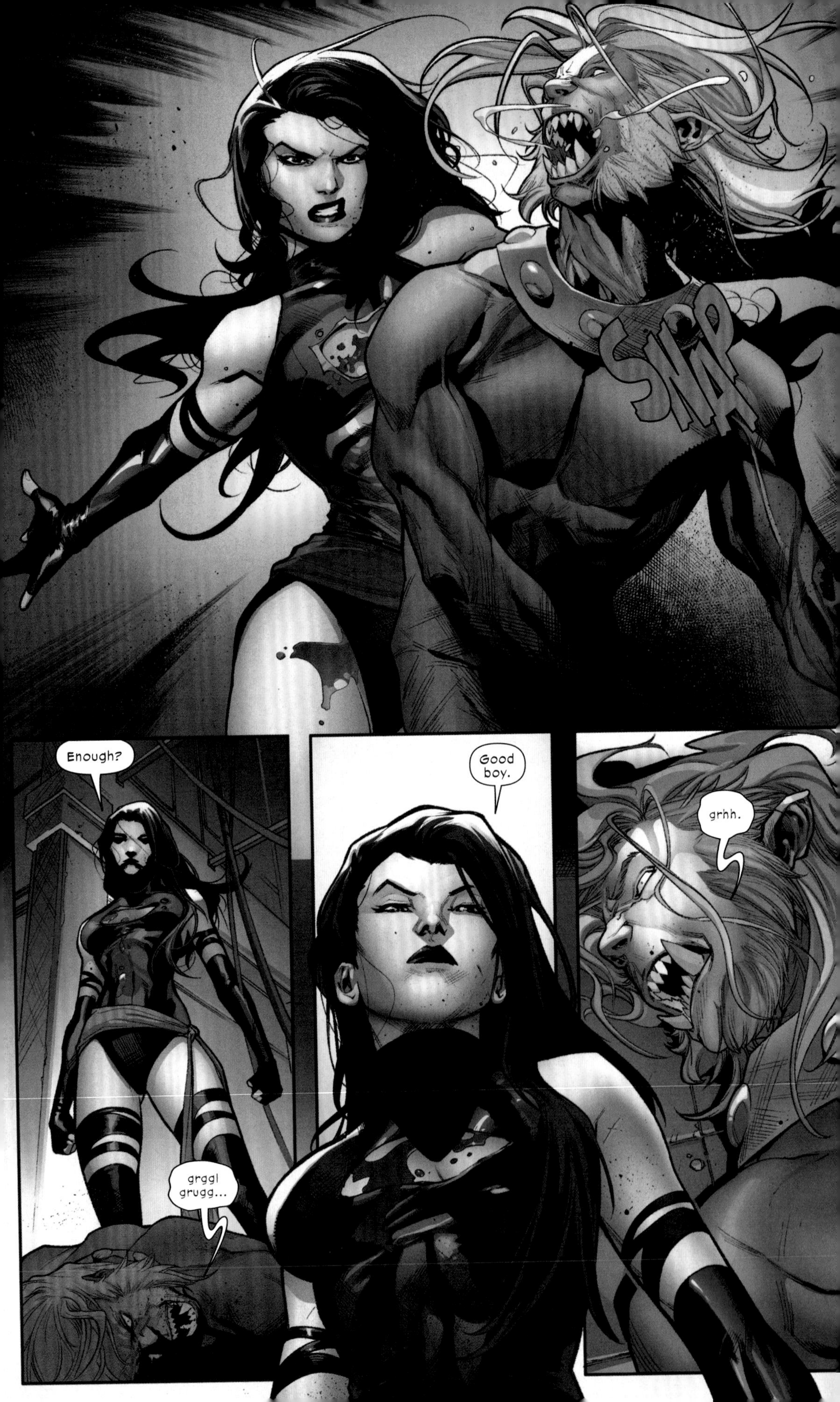
SNAP
Enough?
grggl
grugg...
Good
boy.
grhh.

THAT TIME WE GAVE A TEAM TO A HAND ASSASSIN

Apologies for the dramatic title. But I think it wise, as with all of Mr. Sinister's "Hellions," to examine Psylocke's membership on the team with clear eyes. Scott thinks adding her as a mediating force is a stroke of genius, but Sinister's mawkish protestations to the idea were stunningly transparent. Good luck feigning surprise when it's revealed *it was his plan all along.*

So yes, Sinister has a measure of control over Psylocke, or plans to. But what concerns me, and what Sinister almost certainly underestimates (not that I don't have the *utmost* faith in his faculties), is the bond between warriors at war. Sinister is ostensibly the leader of this ragtag group, but after a few missions whom will they want to follow? The flamboyant clown pulling their strings for his amusement, or the dyed-in-the-wool assassin who's bled for them in battle? We all showed Professor Xavier due reverence in our younger days, but when the big robots with laser-palms came, it was Scott we followed.

All I'm asking is that we keep a watchful eye as Psylocke's influence over her compatriots grows. We must remind ourselves that she is not Betsy. There is much we don't know. And what we do, while not cause for alarm, is certainly reason for caution. Yes, I'm talking about how *she was raised from youth by a mystical ninja murder cult.*

There is no world where Psylocke has found herself under Sinister's thumb unless it serves her in some way. I'm sure she knows a puppet's strings also bind the puppeteer. As Sinister discovers this, will I want to point and laugh? Of course. I'm only mutant. But not if Krakoa burns behind my back.

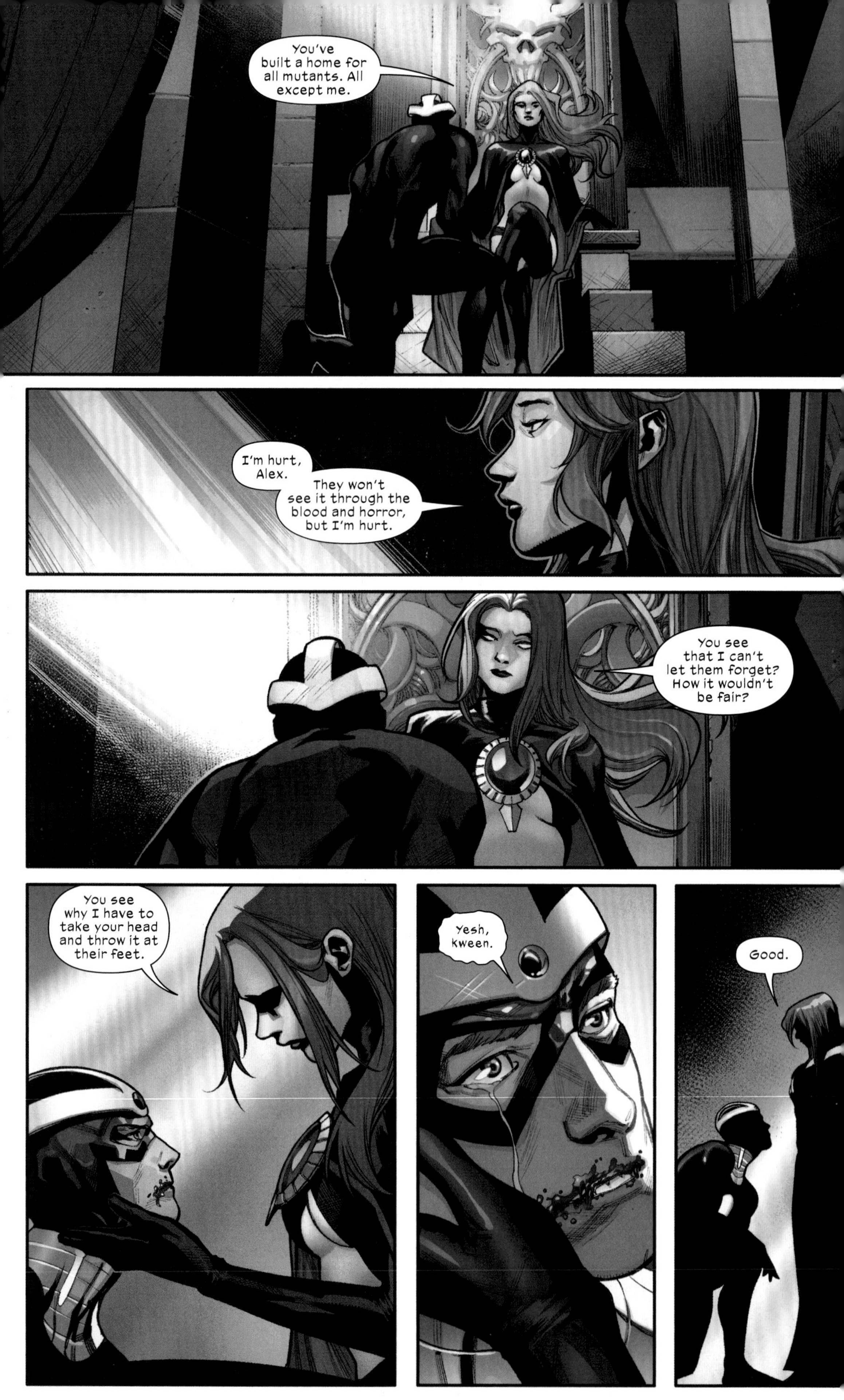
You've built a home for all mutants. All except me.
I'm hurt, Alex.
They won't see it through the blood and horror, but I'm hurt.
You see that I can't let them forget? How it wouldn't be fair?
You see why I have to take your head and throw it at their feet.
Yesh, kween.
Good.

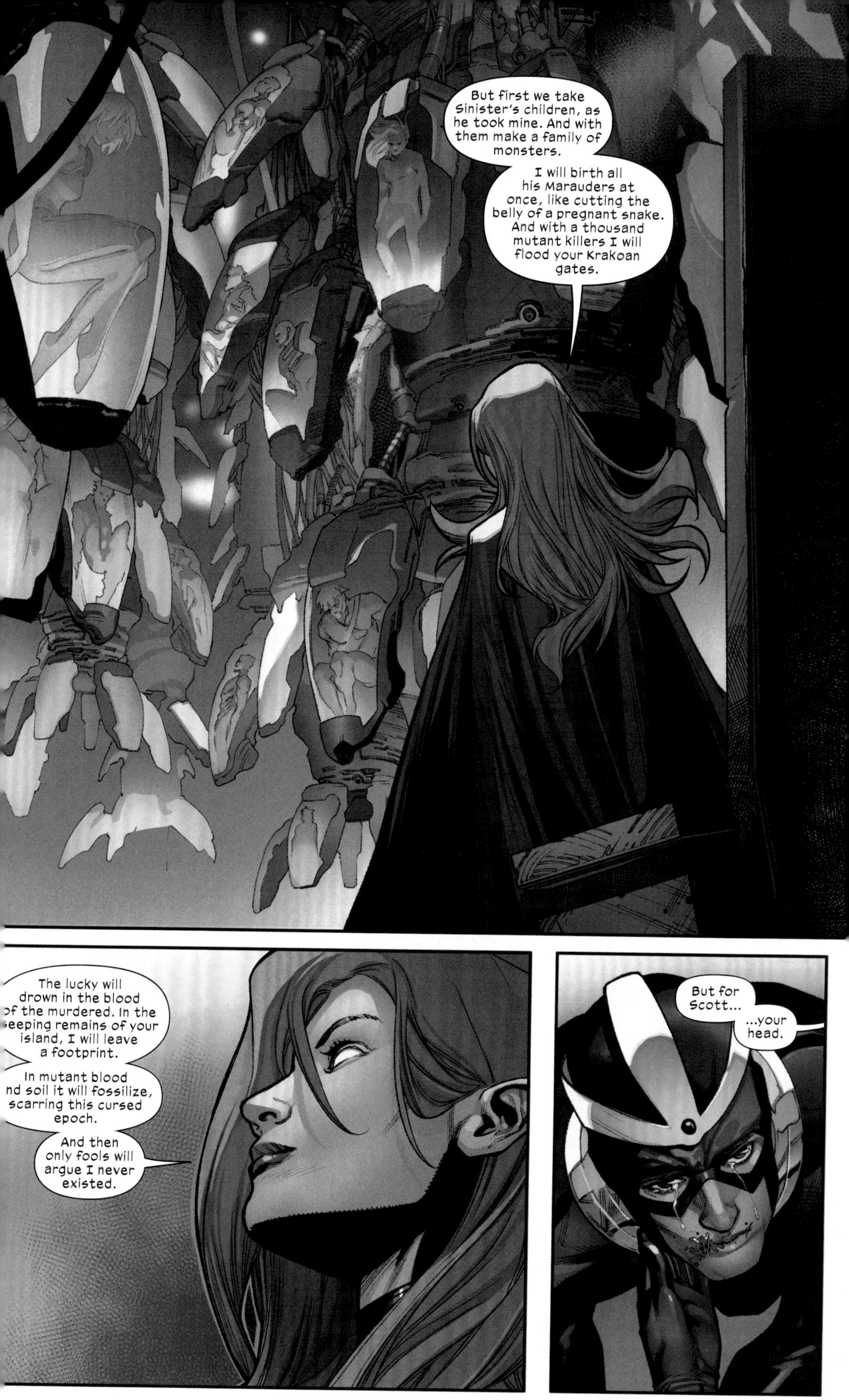
But first we take Sinister's children, as he took mine. And with them make a family of monsters.
I will birth all his Marauders at once, like cutting the belly of a pregnant snake. And with a thousand mutant killers I will flood your Krakoan gates.
The lucky will drown in the blood of the murdered. In the eeping remains of your island, I will leave a footprint.
In mutant blood nd soil it will fossilize, scarring this cursed epoch.
And then only fools will argue I never existed.
But for Scott...
...your head.

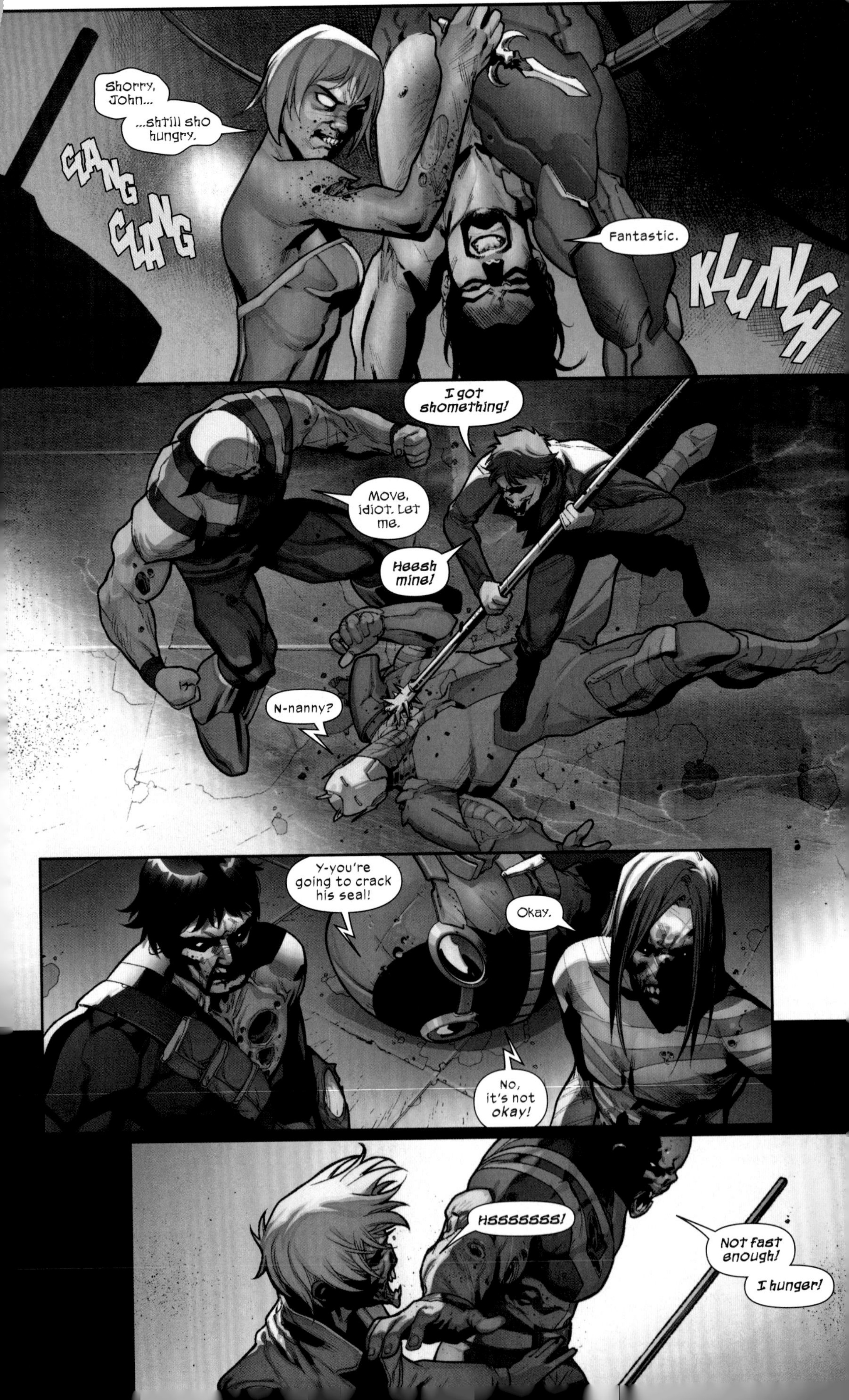
Shorry, John...
...shtill sho hungry.
CLANG
CLANG
Fantastic.
KLUNCH
I got shomething!
Move, idiot. Let me.
Heesh mine!
N-nanny?
Y-you're going to crack his seal!
Okay.
No, it's not okay!
HSSSSSSS!
Not fast enough!
I hunger!

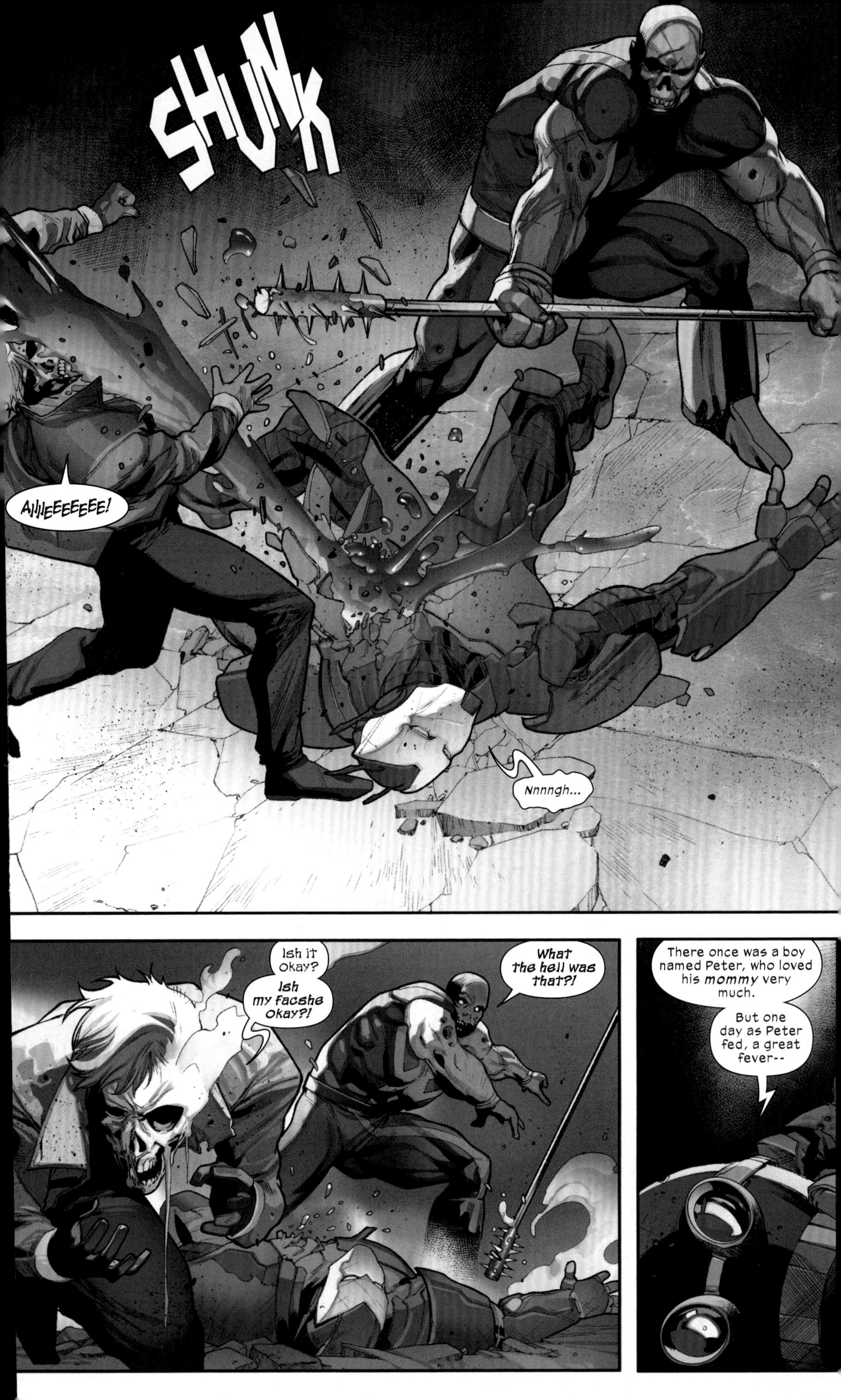
SHUNK
AIIIEEEEEEE!
Nnnngh...
Ish it okay?
Ish my facshe okay?!
What the hell was that?!
There once was a boy named Peter, who loved his *mommy* very much.
But one day as Peter fed, a great fever--

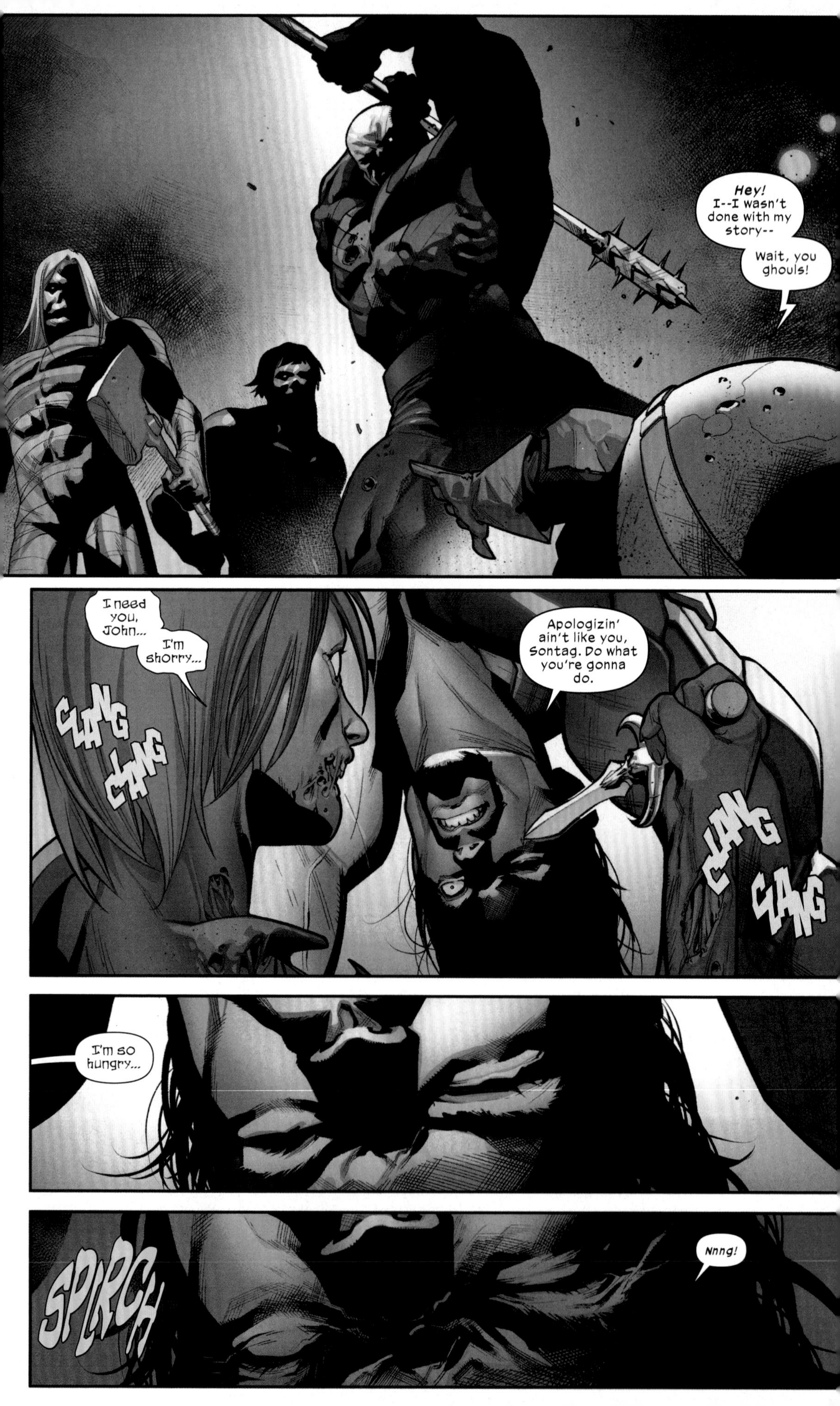
Hey!
I--I wasn't done with my story--
Wait, you ghouls!
I need you, John...
I'm shorry...
CLANG CLANG
Apologizin' ain't like you, Sontag. Do what you're gonna do.
CLANG CLANG
I'm so hungry...
SPLRCH
Nnng!

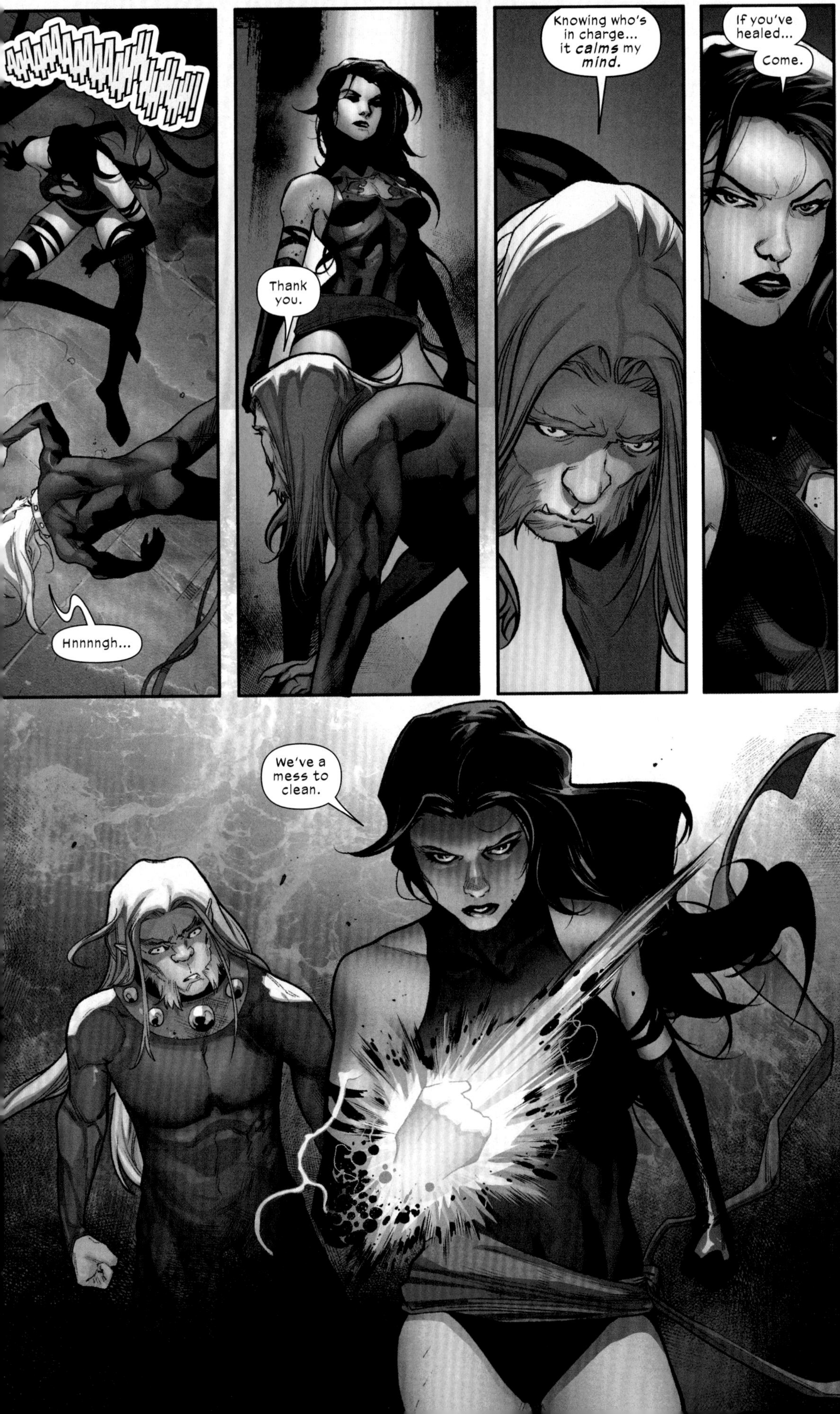
AAAAAAAAAAAHHHHHH!!
Hnnnngh...
Thank you.
Knowing who's in charge... it calms my mind.
If you've healed...
Come.
We've a mess to clean.

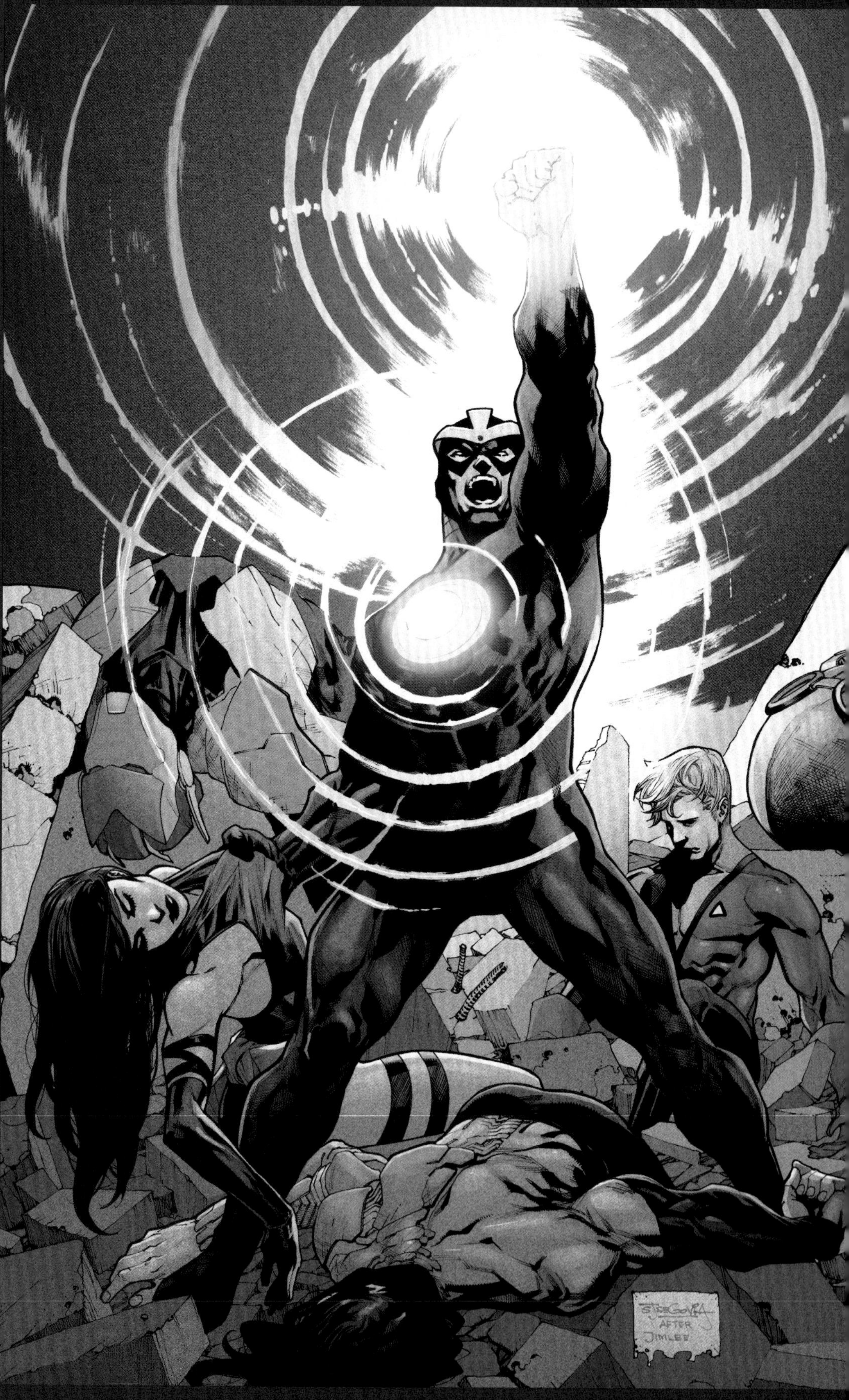
AFTER
JIMLEE

Love Bleeds

[hell_[0.4]
[ions_[0.4]

May I be heard in this: the challenges
of the soul outweigh those of the body.
Either we befriend the sorrows of the
past or they destroy us.

-NIGHTCRAWLER

[hell_[0.X]
[ions_[0.X]

[hell_[0.4].....]
[ions_[0.4].....]

[Hellions_alpha.]

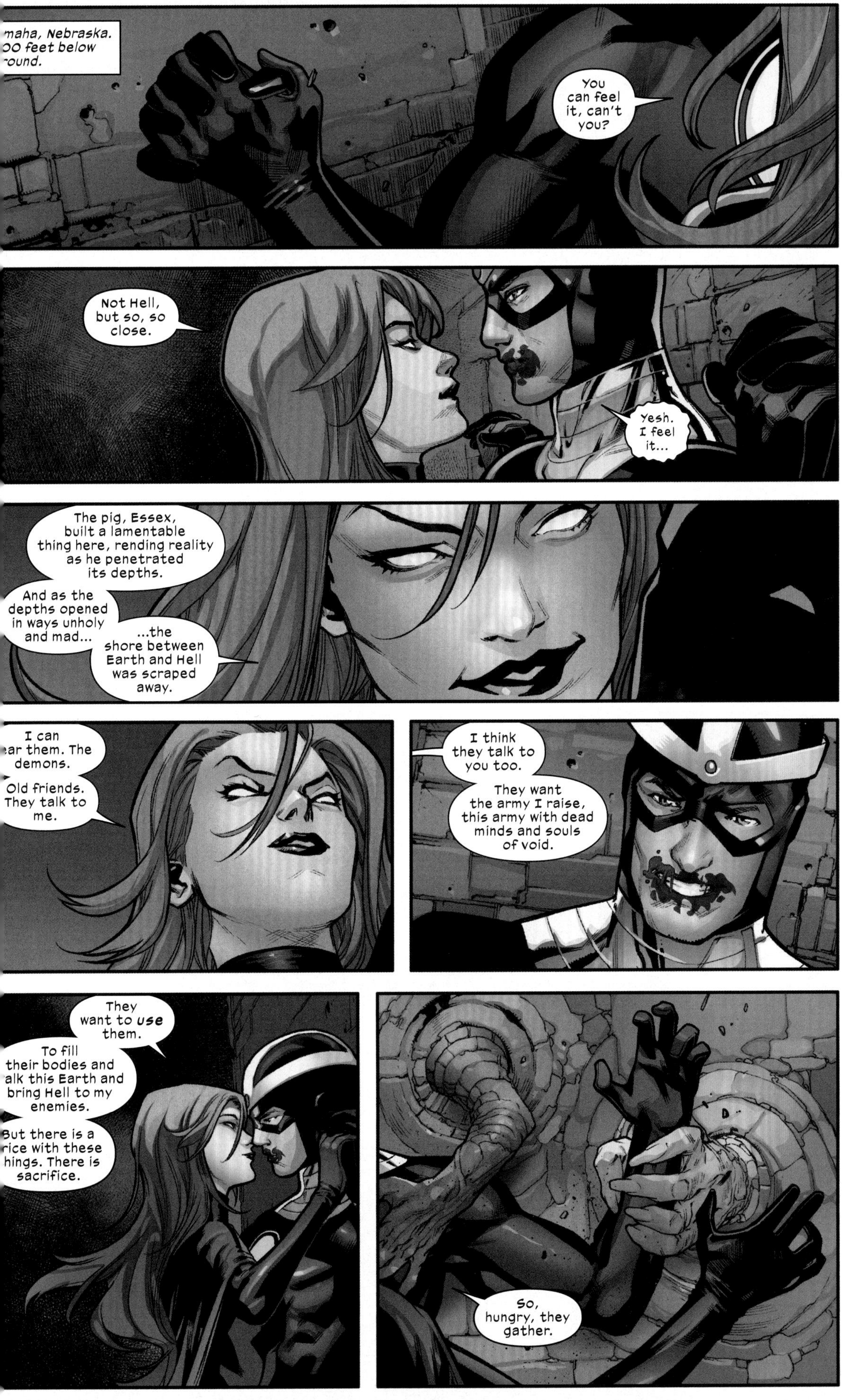

maha, Nebraska. 00 feet below round.
You can feel it, can't you?
Not Hell, but so, so close.
Yesh. I feel it...
The pig, Essex, built a lamentable thing here, rending reality as he penetrated its depths.
And as the depths opened in ways unholy and mad...
...the shore between Earth and Hell was scraped away.
I can ar them. The demons.
Old friends. They talk to me.
I think they talk to you too.
They want the army I raise, this army with dead minds and souls of void.
They want to *use* them.
To fill their bodies and alk this Earth and bring Hell to my enemies.
But there is a rice with these hings. There is sacrifice.
So, hungry, they gather.

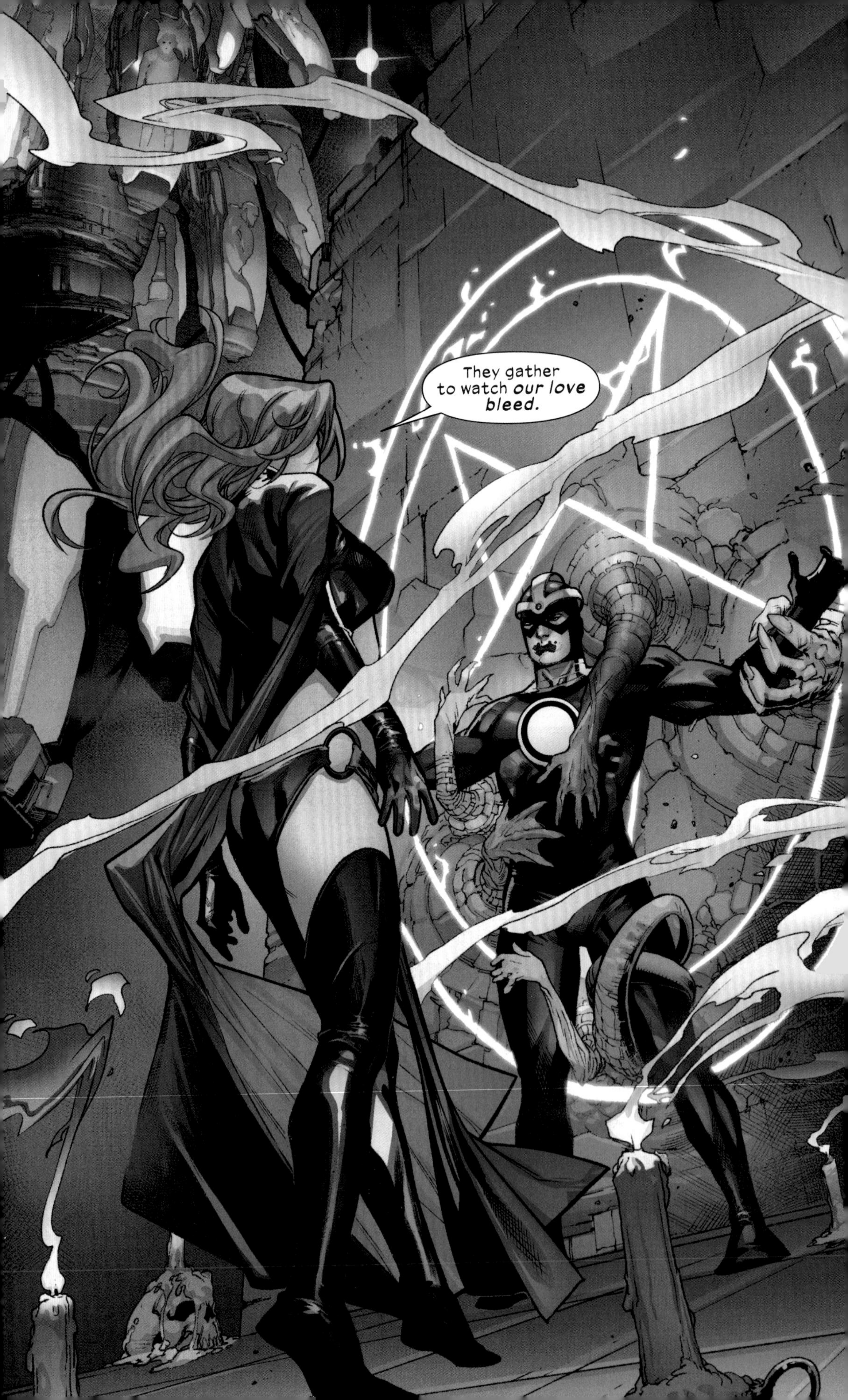
They gather to watch *our love bleed.*

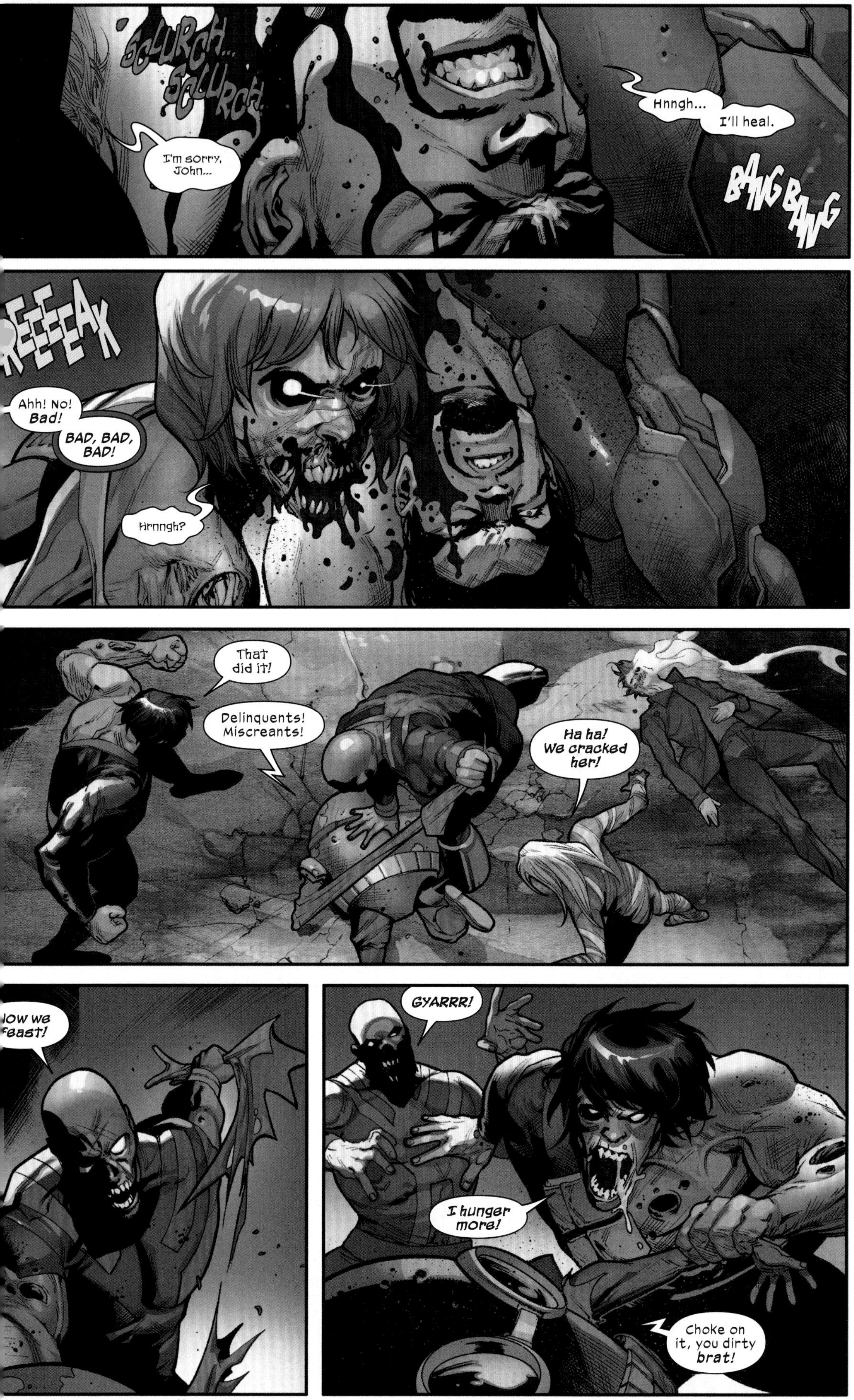
SCLURCH... SCLURCH
I'm sorry, John...
Hnngh... I'll heal.
BANG BANG
REEEEEAK
Ahh! No! Bad!
BAD, BAD, BAD!
Hrnngh?
That did it!
Delinquents! Miscreants!
Ha ha! We cracked her!
GYARRR!
I hunger more!
Choke on it, you dirty brat!

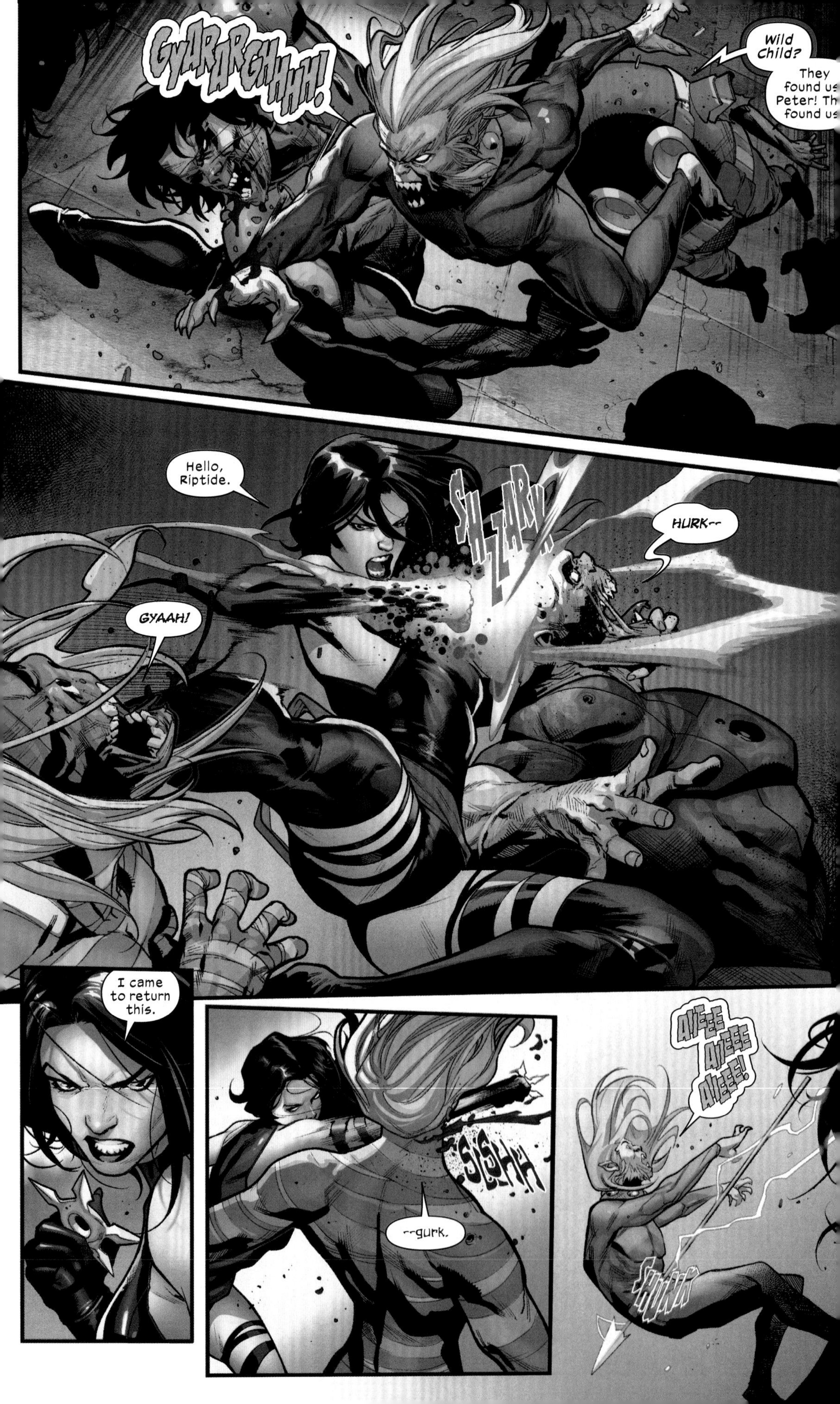
GYARARGHHHH!
Wild Child?
They found us Peter! Th found us
Hello, Riptide.
SHZZARK
HURK--
GYAAH!
I came to return this.
SHSHKK
--gurk.
AIEEE AIEEE AIEEE!
SHUNK

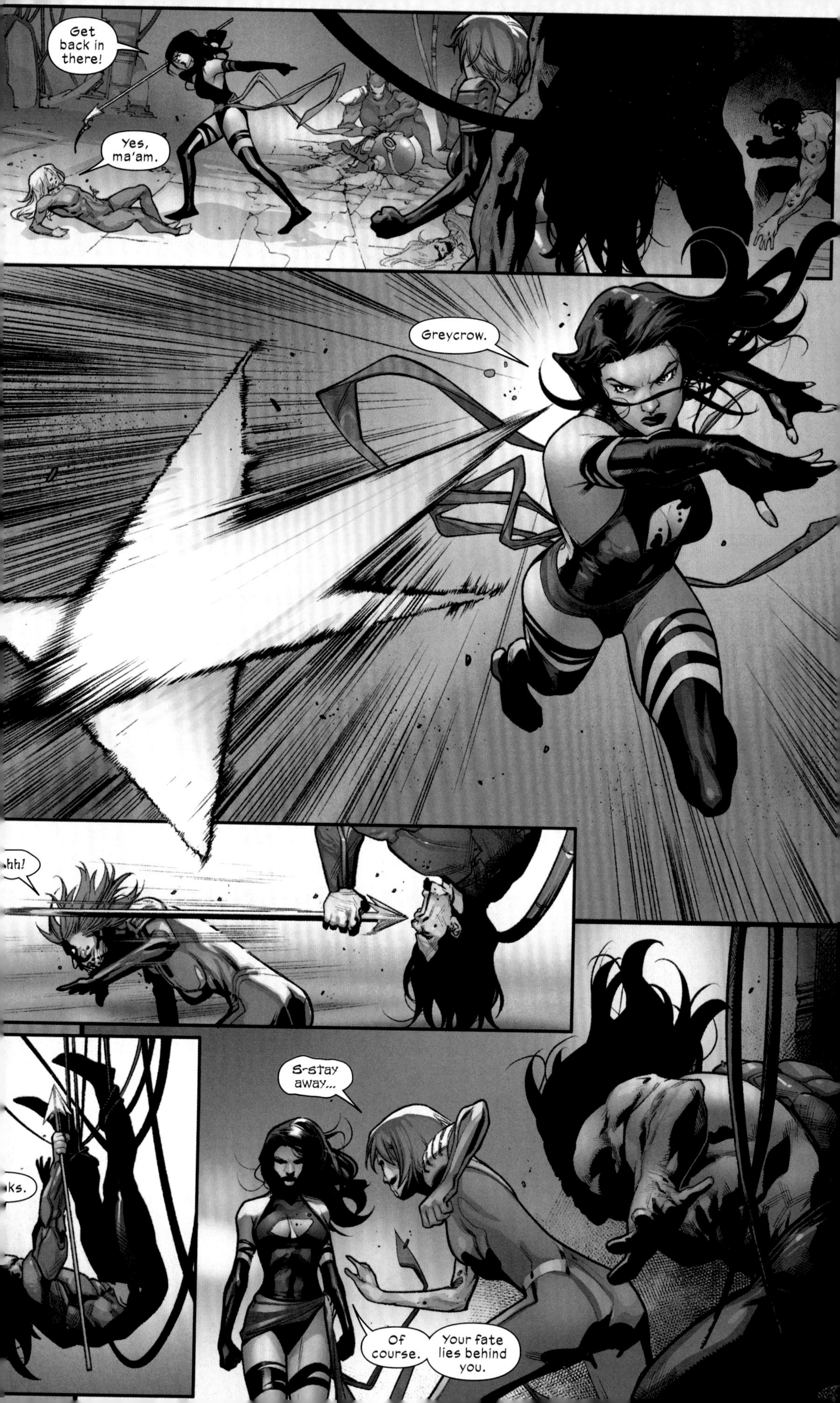
Get back in there!
Yes, ma'am.
Greycrow.
hh!
ks.
S-stay away...
Of course.
Your fate lies behind you.

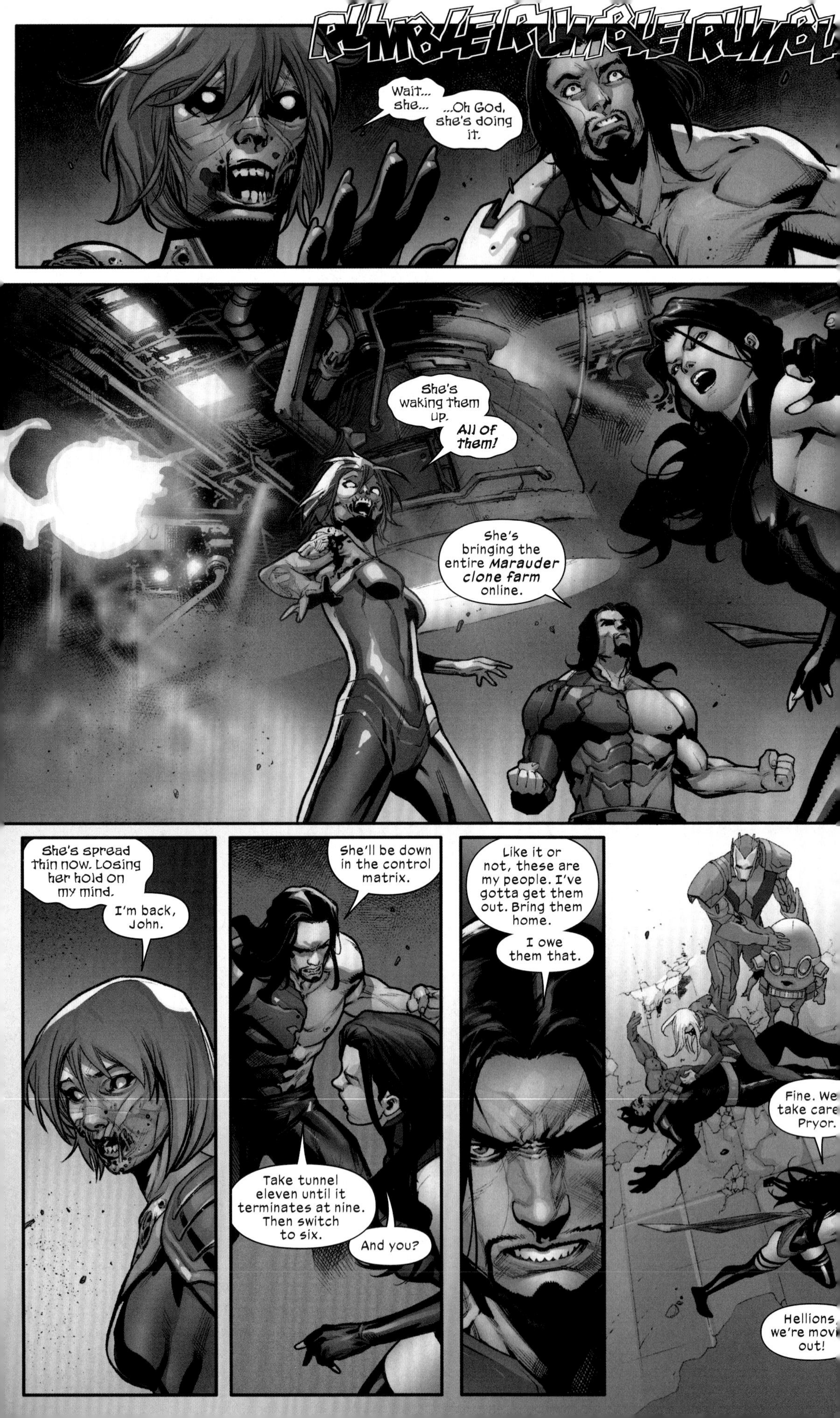

RUMBLE RUMBLE RUMBL
Wait... she...
...Oh God, she's doing it.
She's waking them up.
All of them!
She's bringing the entire Marauder clone farm online.
She's spread thin now. Losing her hold on my mind.
I'm back, John.
She'll be down in the control matrix.
Take tunnel eleven until it terminates at nine. Then switch to six.
And you?
Like it or not, these are my people. I've gotta get them out. Bring them home.
I owe them that.
Fine. We take care Pryor.
Hellions, we're movi out!

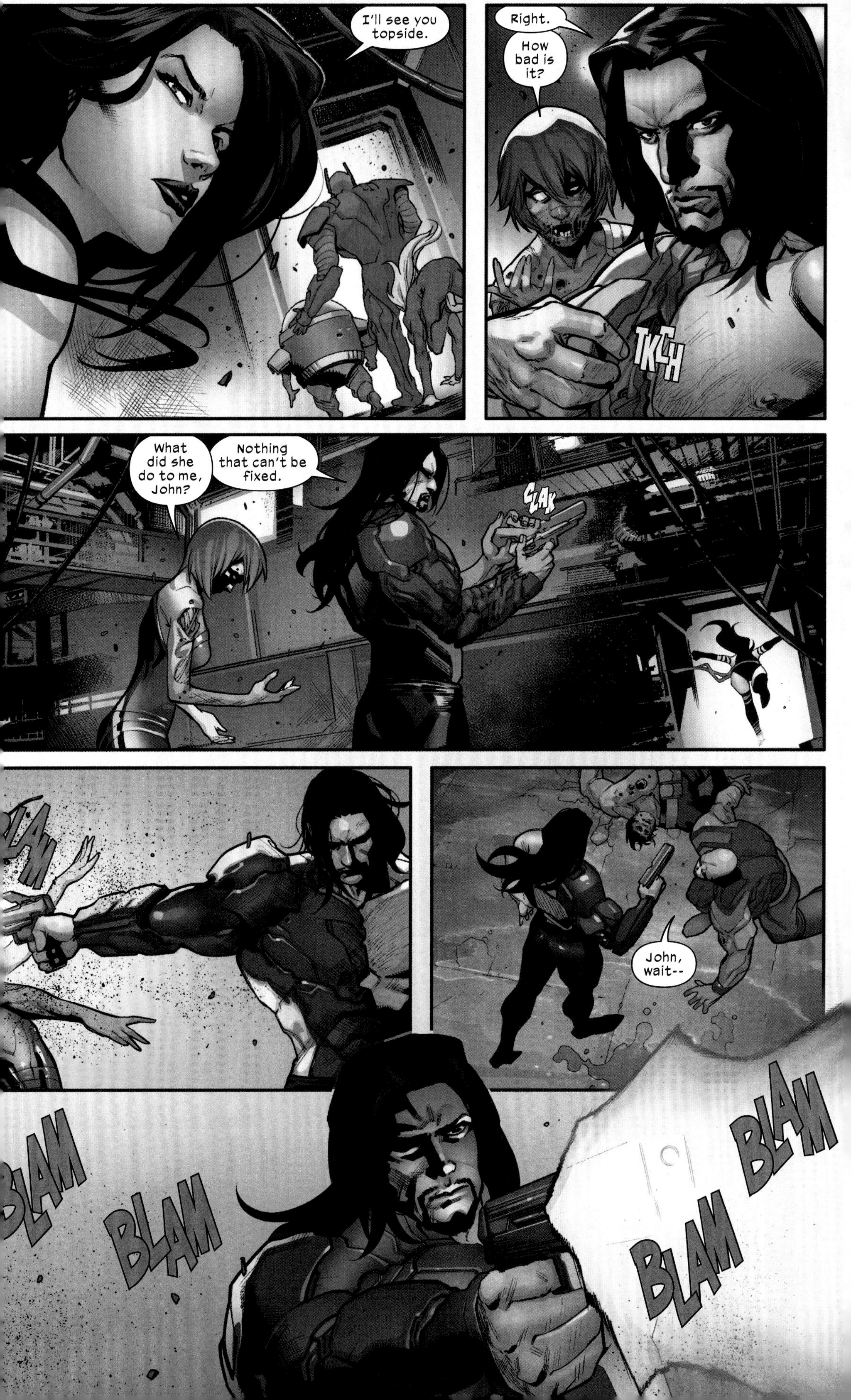
I'll see you topside.
Right.
How bad is it?
TKCH
What did she do to me, John?
Nothing that can't be fixed.
CLAK
BLAM
John, wait--
BLAM
BLAM
BLAM
BLAM

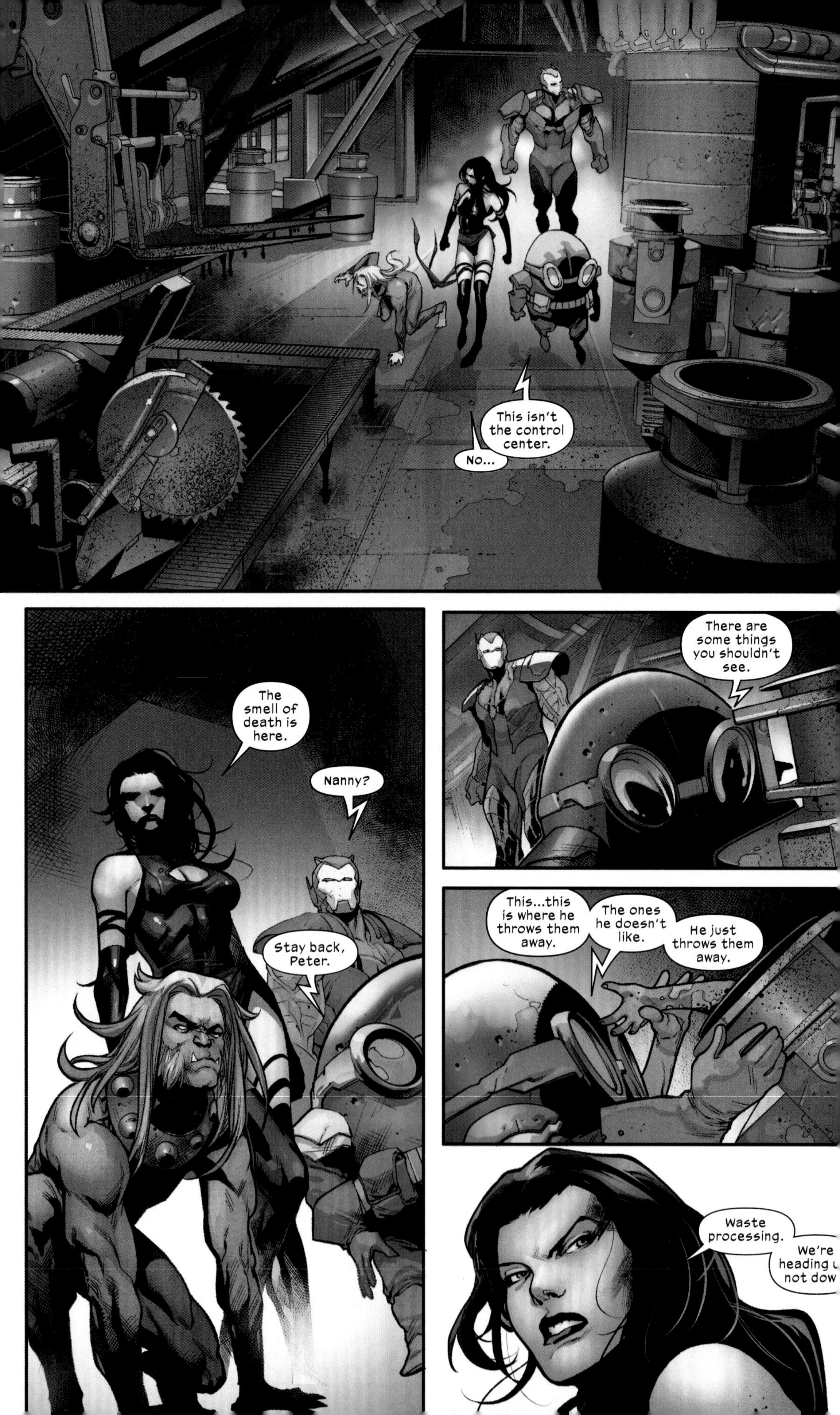

This isn't the control center.
No...
The smell of death is here.
Nanny?
Stay back, Peter.
There are some things you shouldn't see.
This...this is where he throws them away.
The ones he doesn't like.
He just throws them away.
Waste processing.
We're heading
not dow

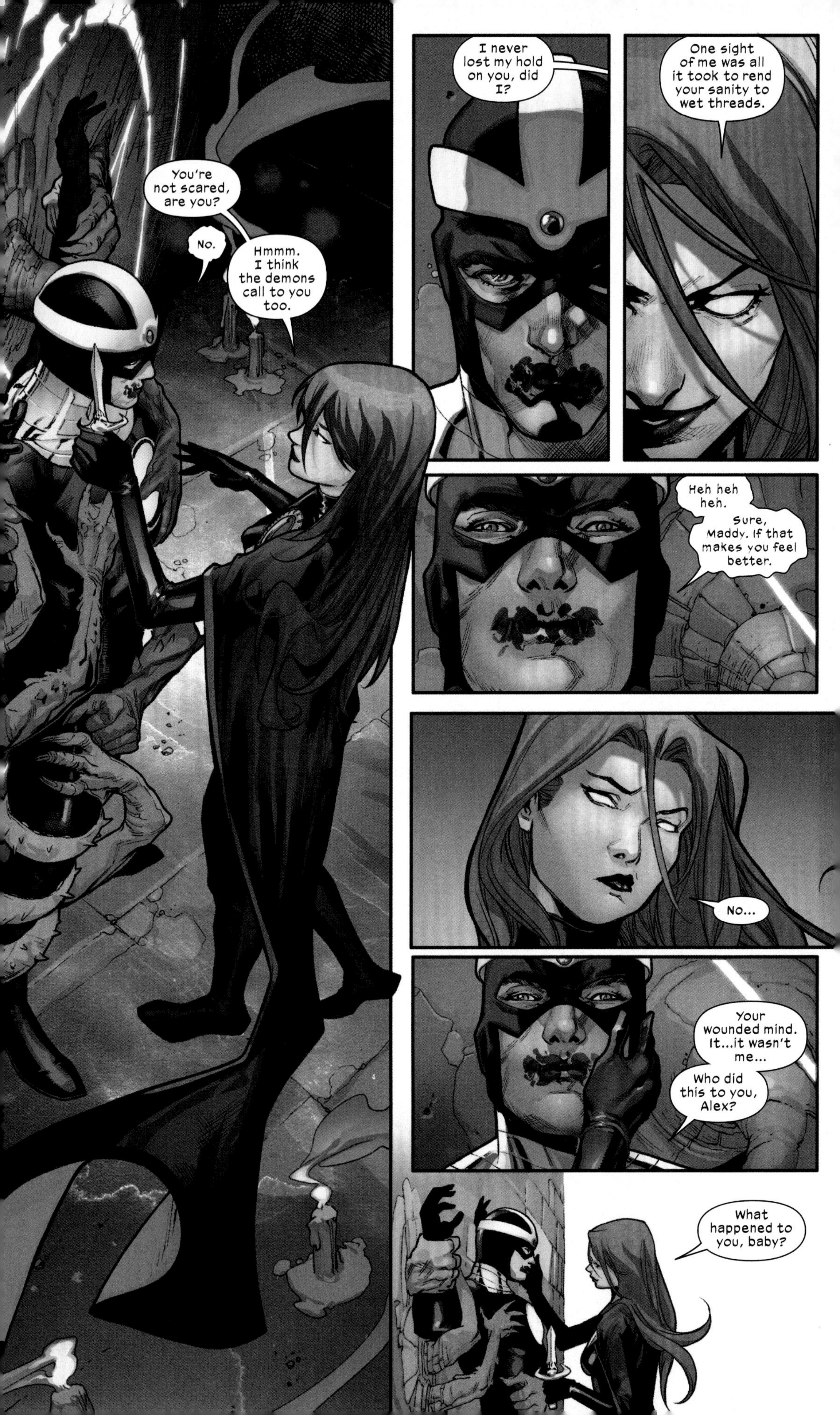
You're not scared, are you?
No.
Hmmm. I think the demons call to you too.
I never lost my hold on you, did I?
One sight of me was all it took to rend your sanity to wet threads.
Heh heh heh.
Sure, Maddy. If that makes you feel better.
No...
Your wounded mind. It...it wasn't me...
Who did this to you, Alex?
What happened to you, baby?

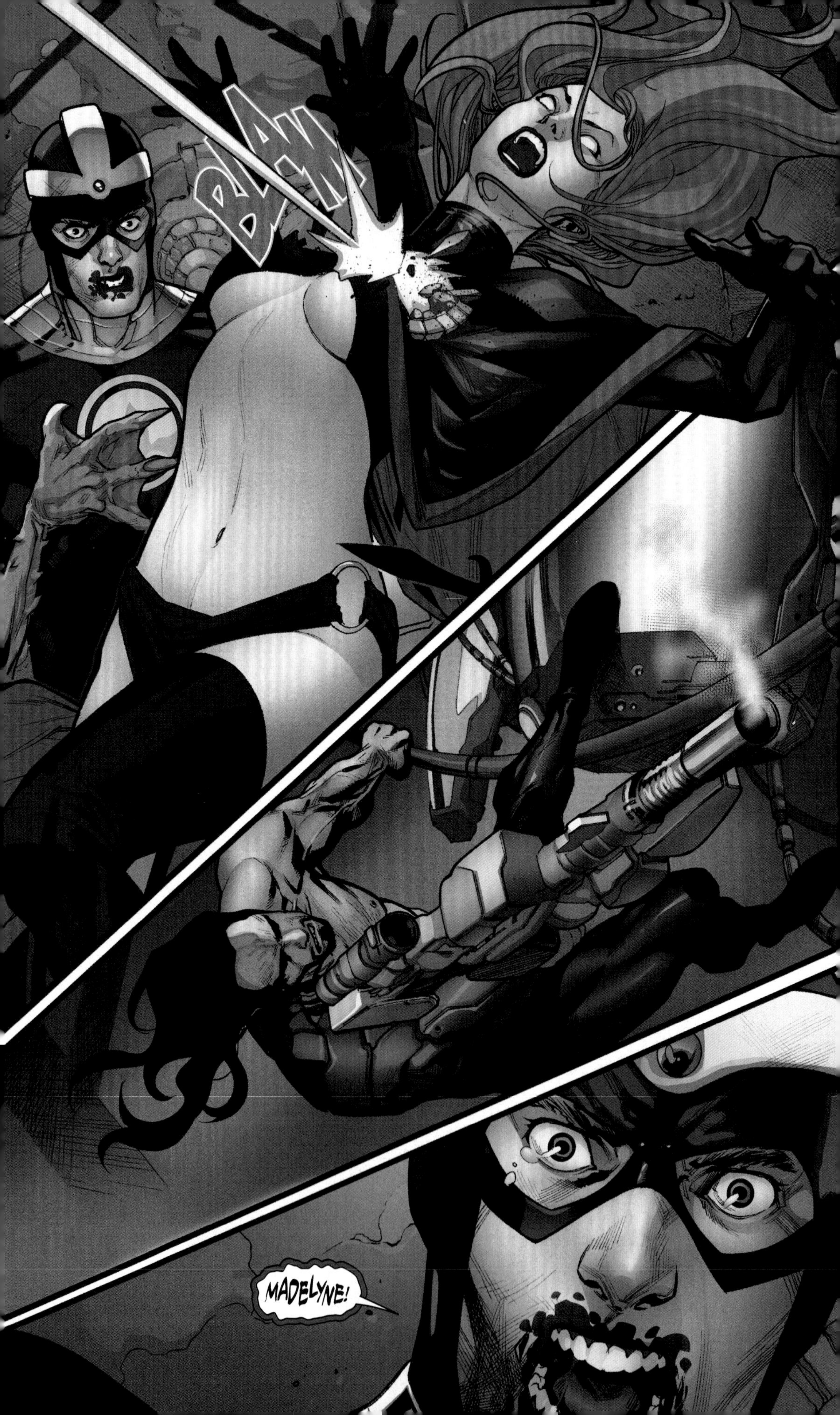
BLAM
MADELYNE!

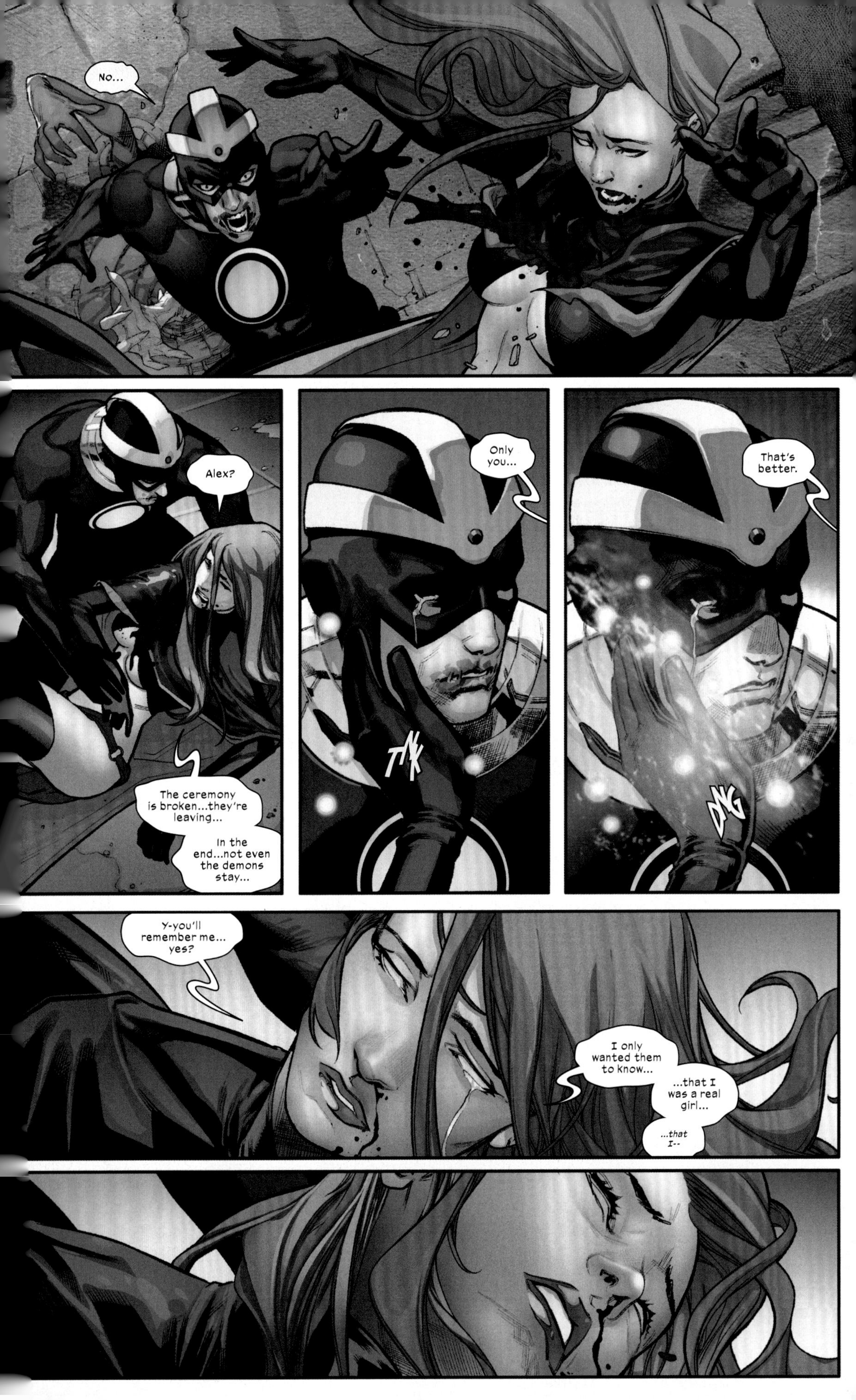
No...
Alex?
The ceremony is broken...they're leaving...
In the end...not even the demons stay...
Only you...
TINK
That's better.
DING
Y-you'll remember me... yes?
I only wanted them to know...
...that I was a real girl...
...that I--

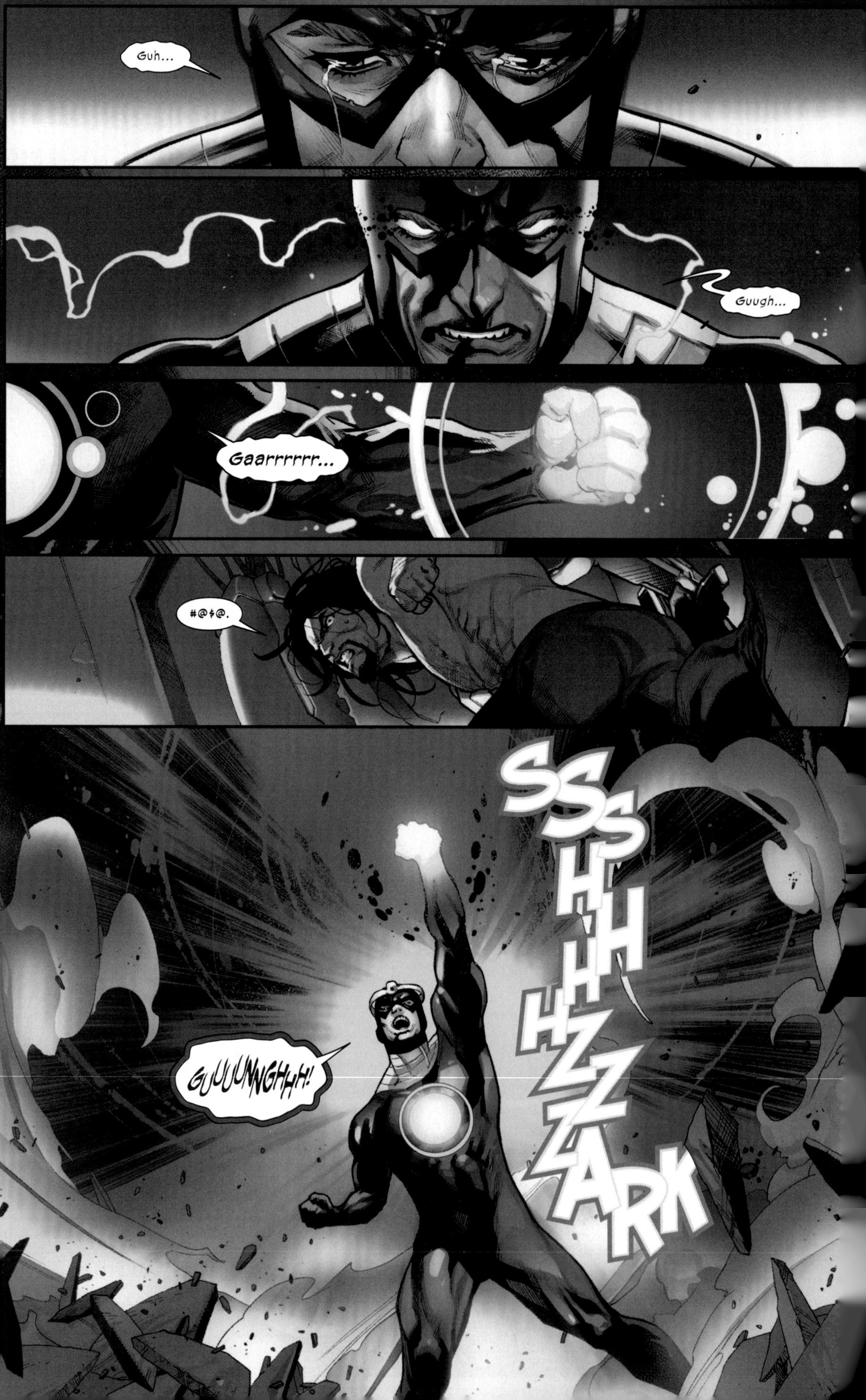
Guh...
Guugh...
Gaarrrrrr...
#@$@.
GUUUUNNGHHH!
SSSHHHHHZZZZARK

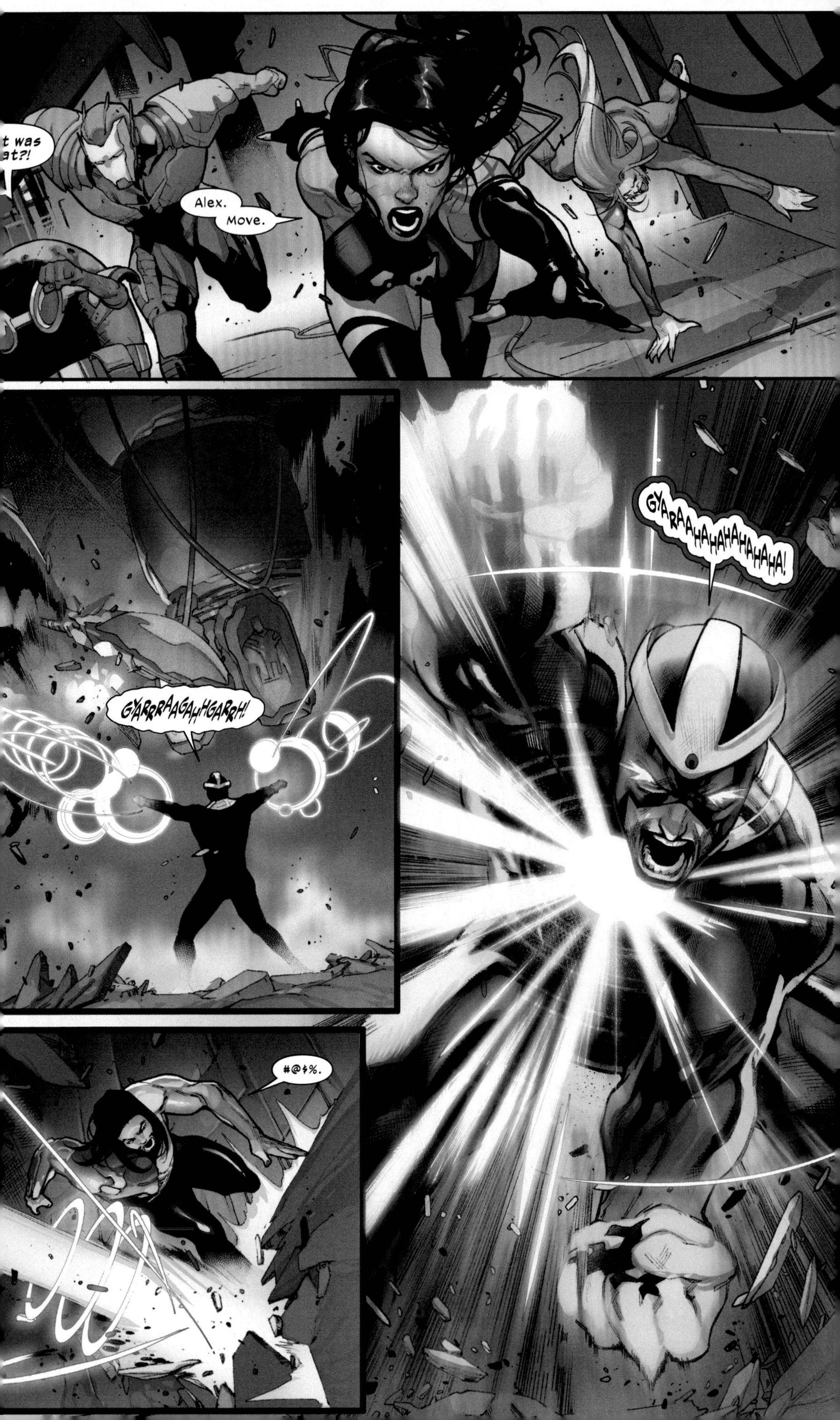
t was
at?!
Alex.
Move.
GYARRRAAGAHHGARRH!
GYARAAHAHAHAHAHAHA!
#@$%.

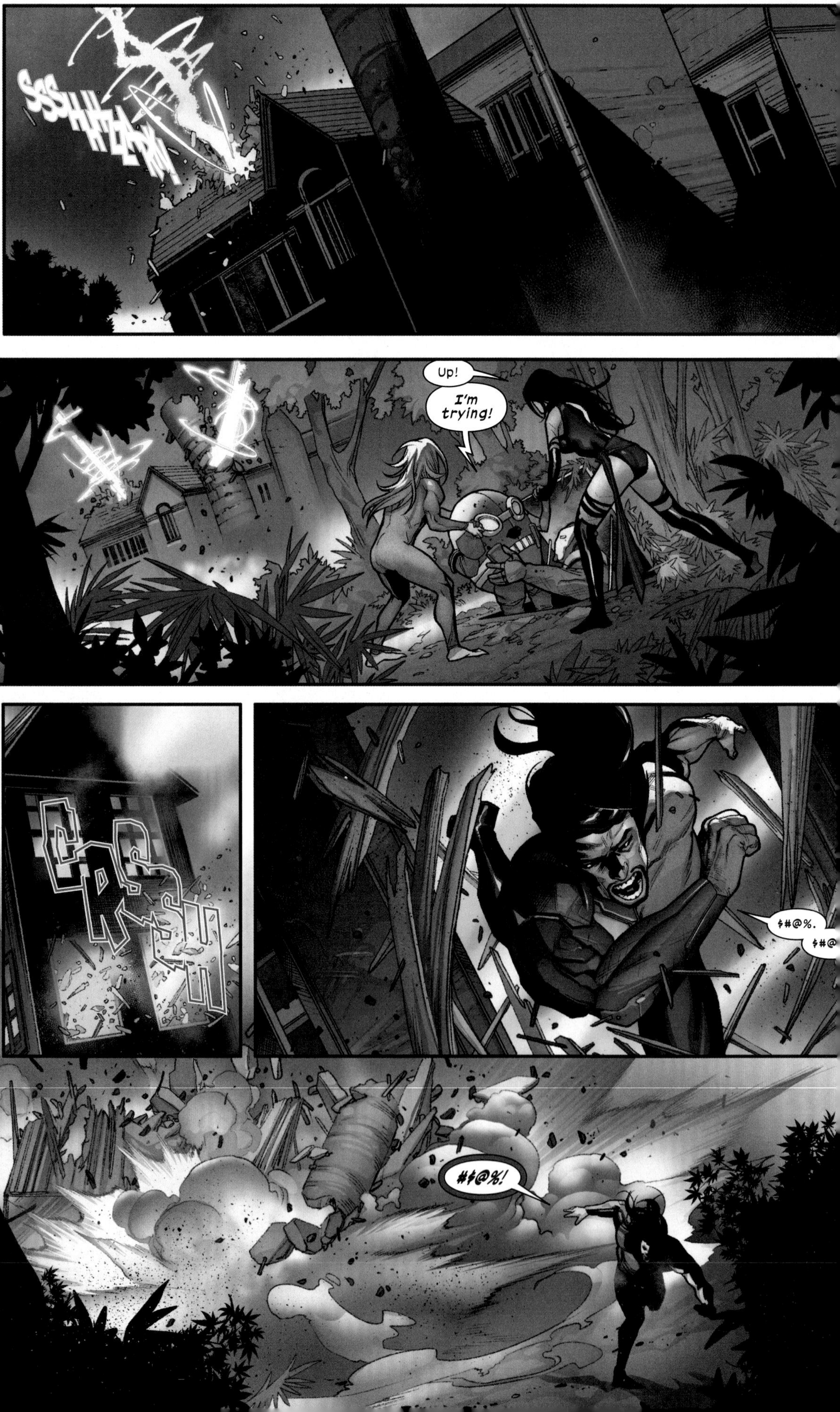
Up!
I'm trying!
CRASH
$#@%.
$#@
#$@%!

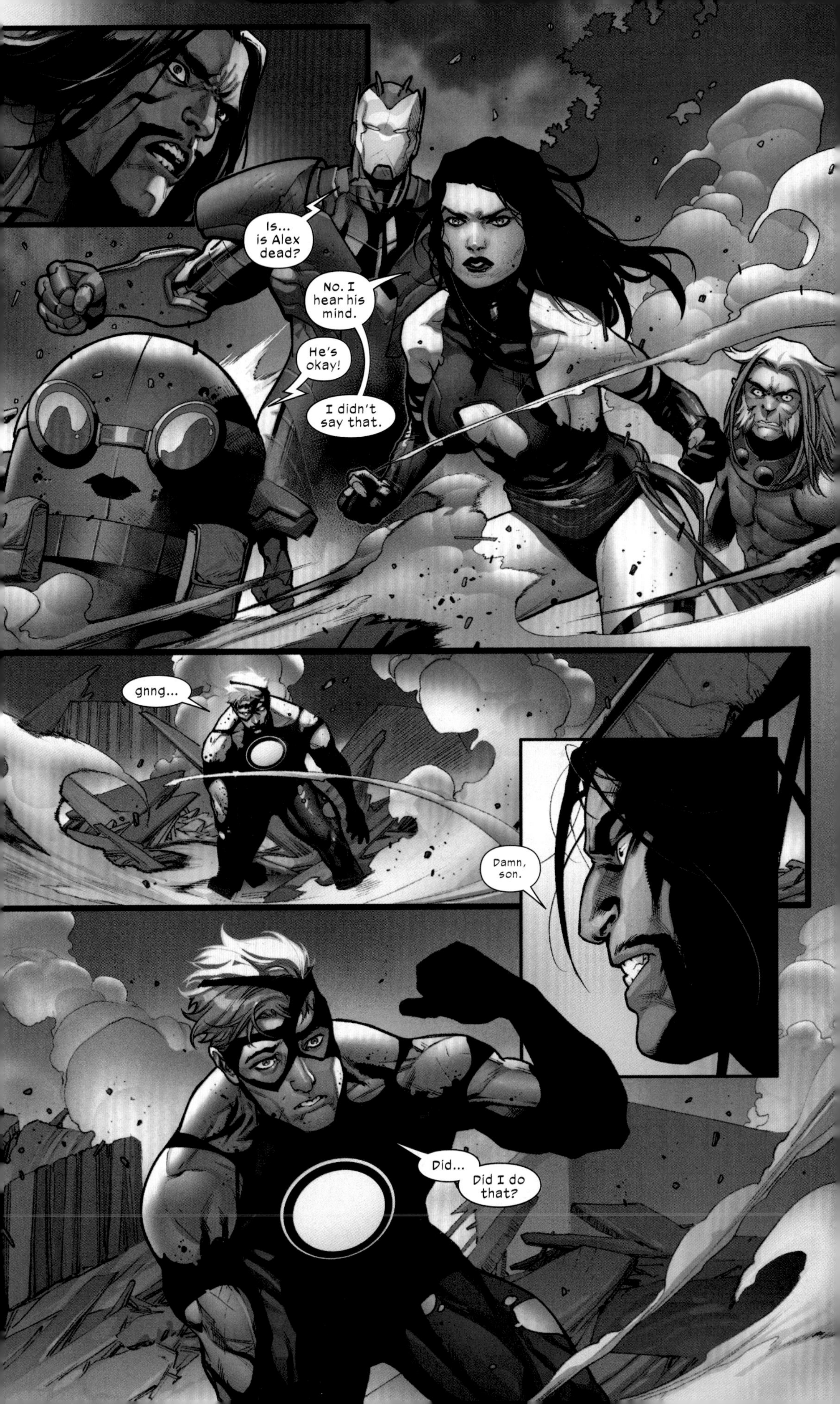
Is... is Alex dead?
No. I hear his mind.
He's okay!
I didn't say that.
gnng...
Damn, son.
Did...
Did I do that?

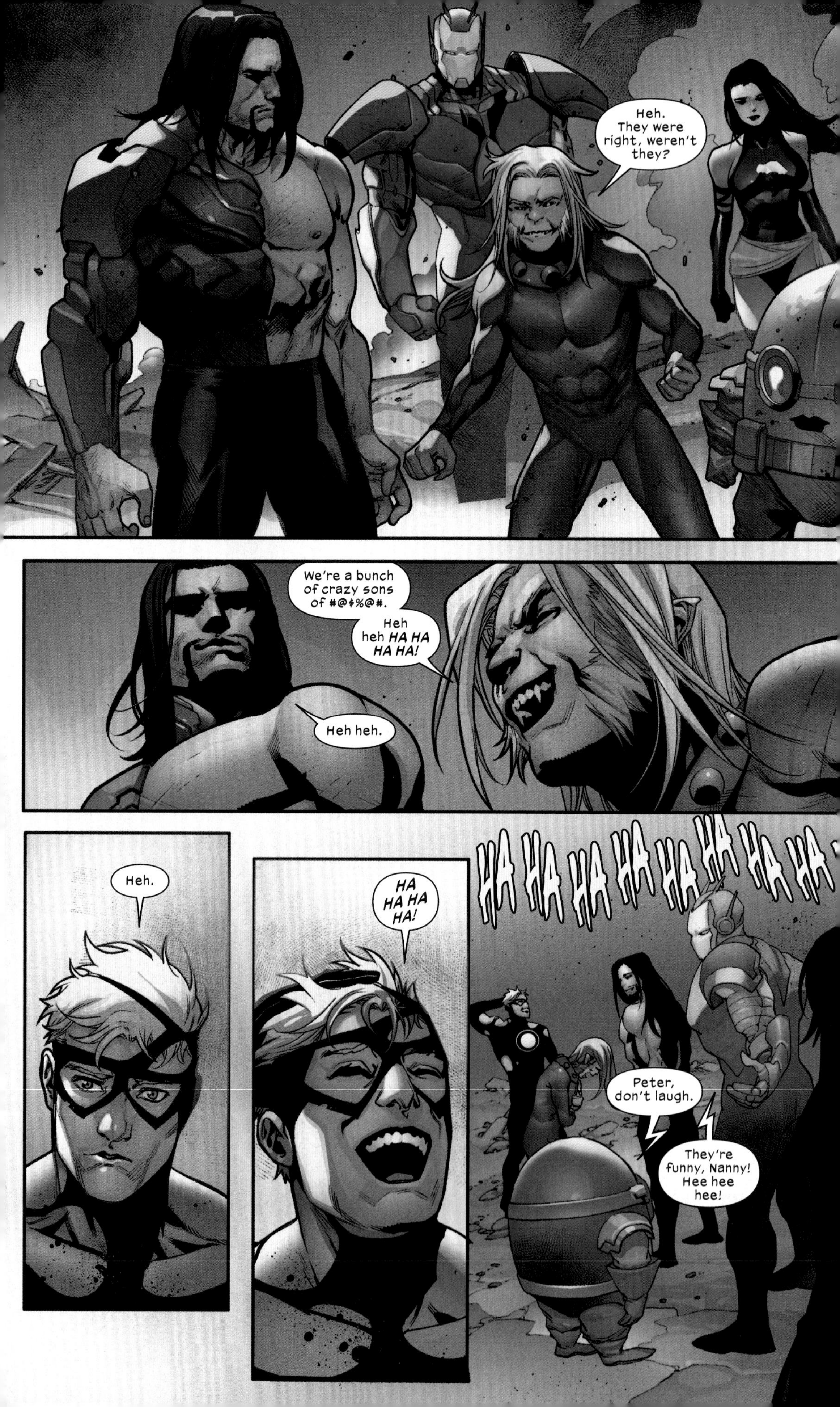
Heh. They were right, weren't they?
We're a bunch of crazy sons of #@$%@#.
Heh heh HA HA HA HA!
Heh heh.
Heh.
HA HA HA HA!
HA HA HA HA HA HA HA HA HA
Peter, don't laugh.
They're funny, Nanny! Hee hee hee!

RE: DEMOLITION OPERATION OF ESSEX STATE HOME FOR FOUNDLINGS

POST MISSION REPORT

As we're a week past the Hellions return from Nebraska, I thought it beneficial to bring you up to speed on the state of our problem children, and in doing so elucidate any benefits they've received from their mission.

Havok remains of utmost concern. By all accounts, he experienced a prolonged episode of disassociation in which the demons that haunt him were very much behind the wheel. Emma provided post-event psy-care and reported sporadic memory loss and a slight detachment from reality. Specifically, Alex remembers Madelyne Pryor being shot but does not remember, or seem that interested in, who shot her. Emma seems hesitant to prod further, citing a lingering guilt from the "bang-up job" she did fixing Alex "last time." I have no reason to doubt her intentions. Yet.

A weight has been lifted from John Greycrow, even as he worries over the resurrection of his former teammates. He very much agrees they should be returned with as few of Mr. Sinister's genetic modifications as feasible, but aside from that refuses to help them assimilate. He feels it's better for everyone if they go their separate ways.

Empath was KIA. Only wry smiles offered as explanation. This was expected and within tolerance.

Wild Child has calmed down considerably, only showing aggression when he perceives a threat to Psylocke, whom he slavishly follows. Psylocke, to her credit, has taken a grin-and-bear-it approach. Well, you'd be hard-pressed to find the "grin," but you understand.

Nanny appears to have brought a trauma home with her, related to seeing the misdeeds of Mr. Sinister's past up close. She had to be reminded to feed Peter yesterday, unthinkable in the weeks prior. Emma assures me that any emotion Nanny lets herself feel is progress and essential to her healing.

So how did we do in hitting our mission parameters?

THERAPEUTIC VALUE

On a whole there seems to have been cathartic value to the mission (Empath notwithstanding, but we knew we'd be taking mulligans on him).

VIOLENT EXPRESSION

The team was able to let loose effectively, as evidenced by the decimated orphanage left in their wake.

HUMAN CASUALTIES

Aside from the corrupted Marauders, Madelyne Pryor was felled as a combatant. This subject is a sensitive one, as you can imagine. It's agreed she wasn't human, so now the Council must decide if she will be considered a clone of Jean or a mutant in her own right. A philosophical debate -- with Madelyne's resurrection hanging in the balance.

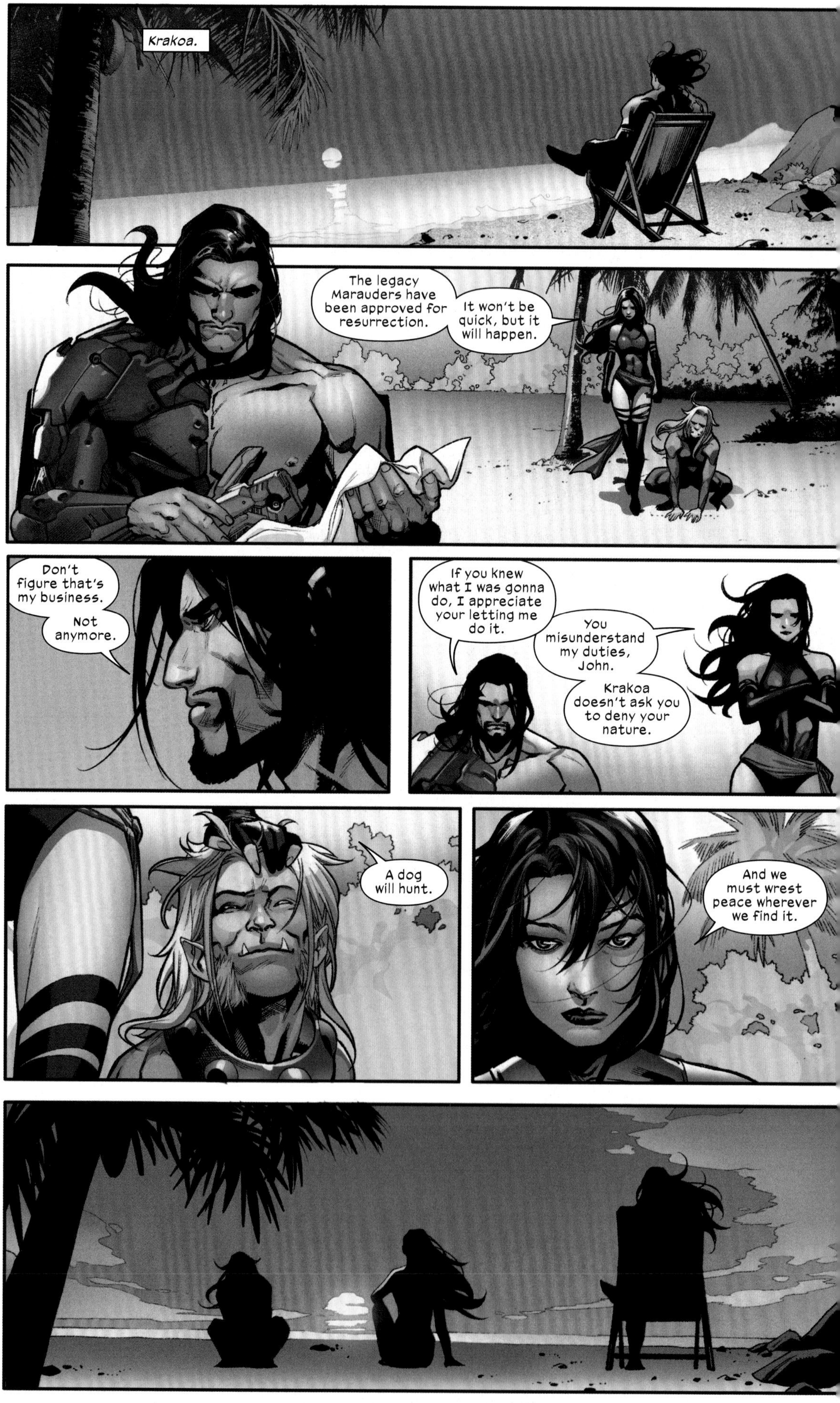
Krakoa.
The legacy Marauders have been approved for resurrection.
It won't be quick, but it will happen.
Don't figure that's my business.
Not anymore.
If you knew what I was gonna do, I appreciate your letting me do it.
You misunderstand my duties, John.
Krakoa doesn't ask you to deny your nature.
A dog will hunt.
And we must wrest peace wherever we find it.

Bar Sinister.

Alex...

...I tried.

It's a "no" then.

There are protocols. She was a clone of Jean. The Council doesn't want--

What do *you* want?

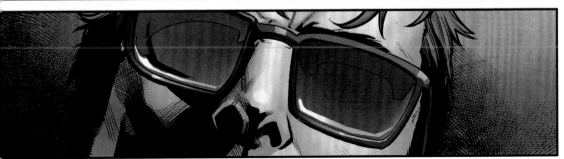

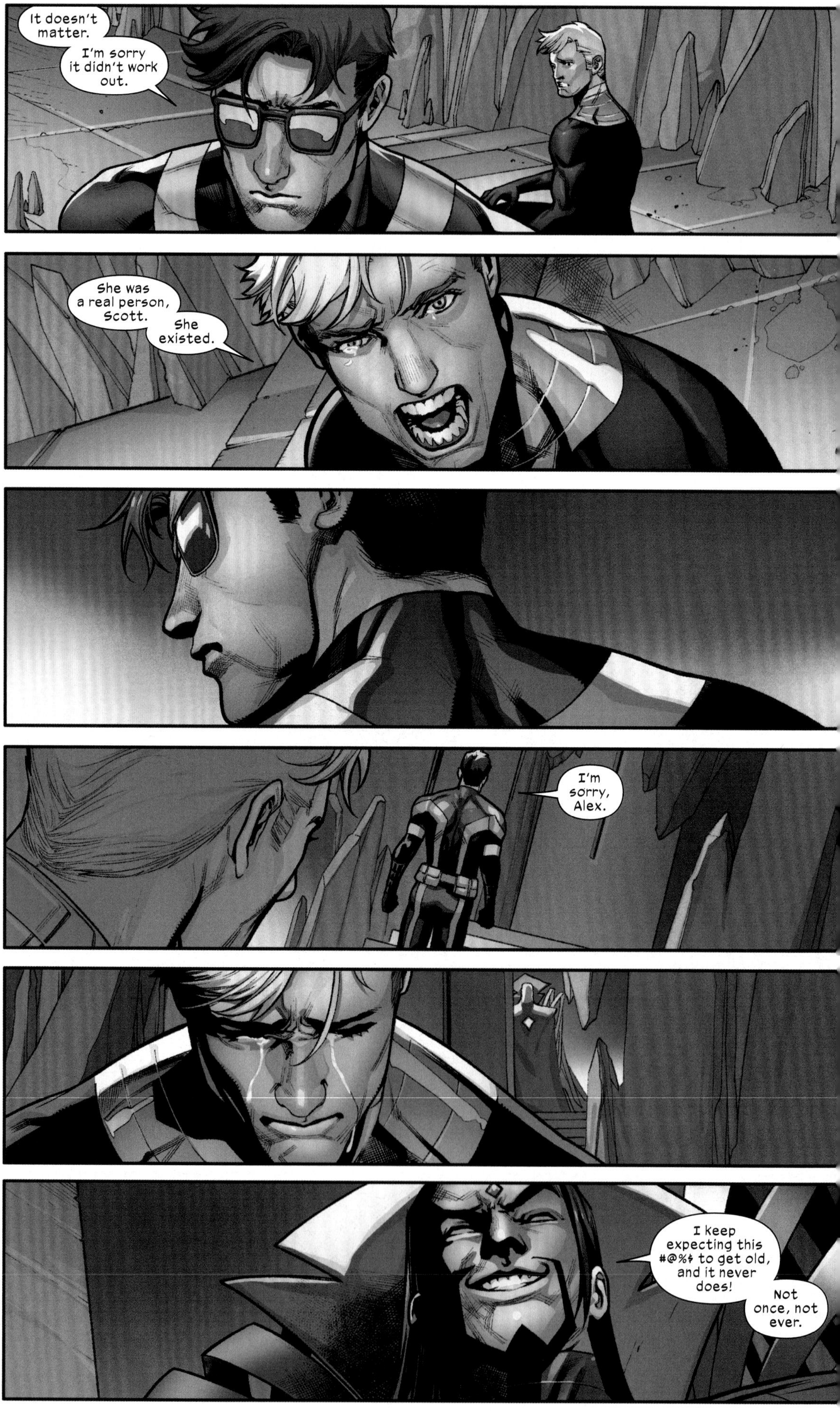

It doesn't matter.
I'm sorry it didn't work out.
She was a real person, Scott.
She existed.
I'm sorry, Alex.
I keep expecting this #@%$ to get old, and it never does!
Not once, not ever.

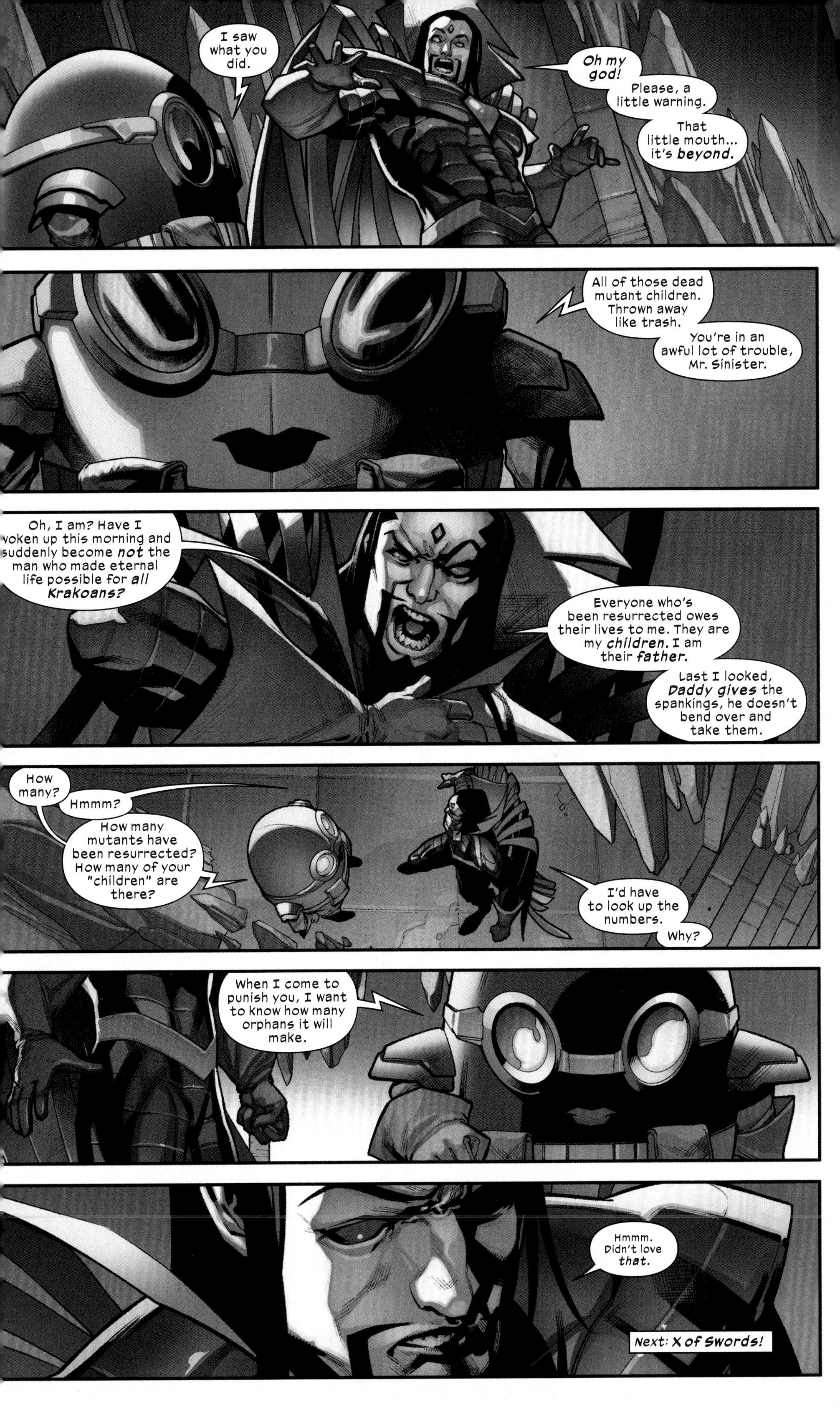

I saw what you did.
Oh my god!
Please, a little warning.
That little mouth... it's beyond.
All of those dead mutant children. Thrown away like trash.
You're in an awful lot of trouble, Mr. Sinister.
Oh, I am? Have I woken up this morning and suddenly become not the man who made eternal life possible for all Krakoans?
Everyone who's been resurrected owes their lives to me. They are my children. I am their father.
Last I looked, Daddy gives the spankings, he doesn't bend over and take them.
How many?
Hmmm?
How many mutants have been resurrected? How many of your "children" are there?
I'd have to look up the numbers.
Why?
When I come to punish you, I want to know how many orphans it will make.
Hmmm. Didn't love that.
Next: X of Swords!

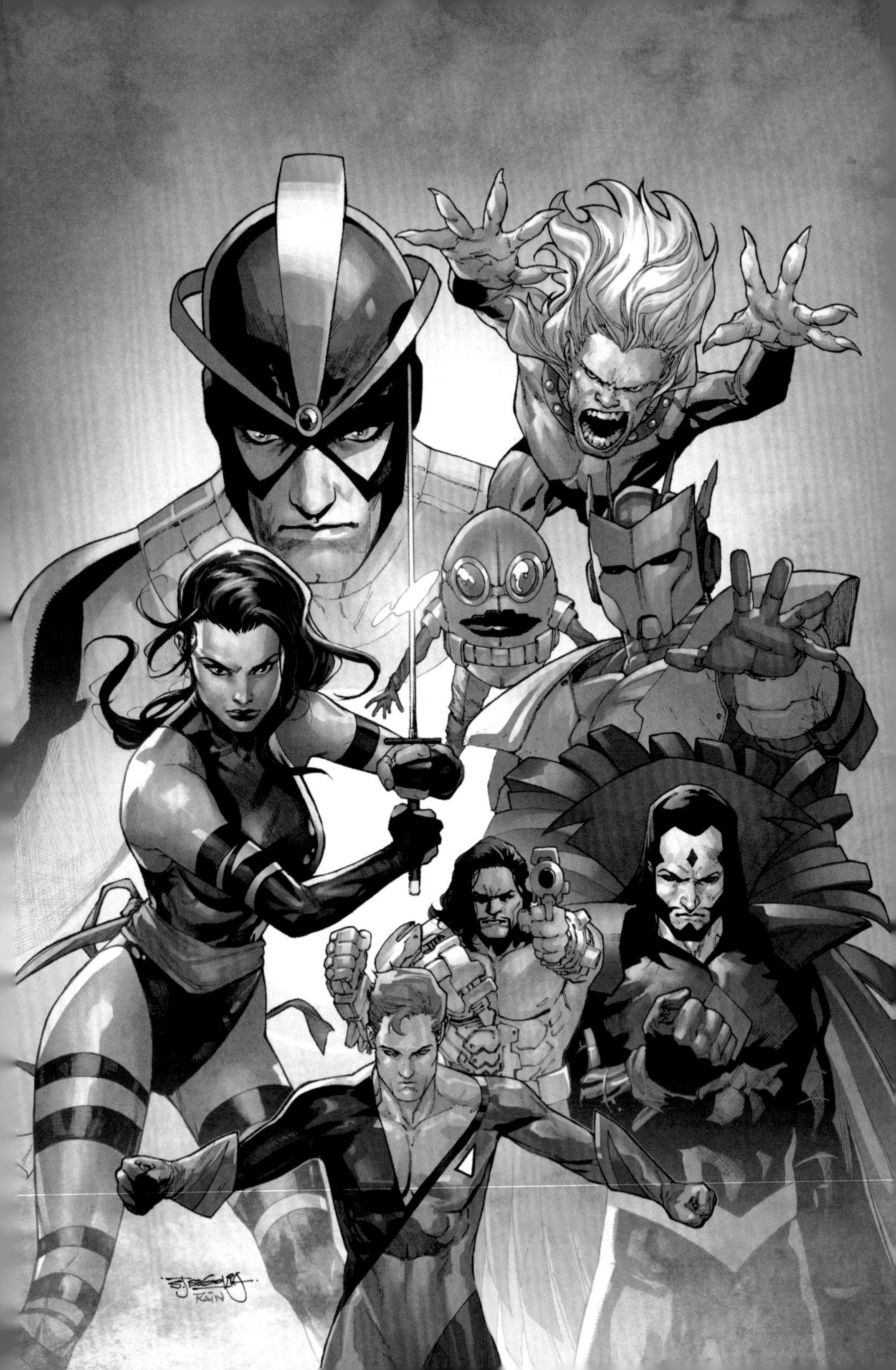

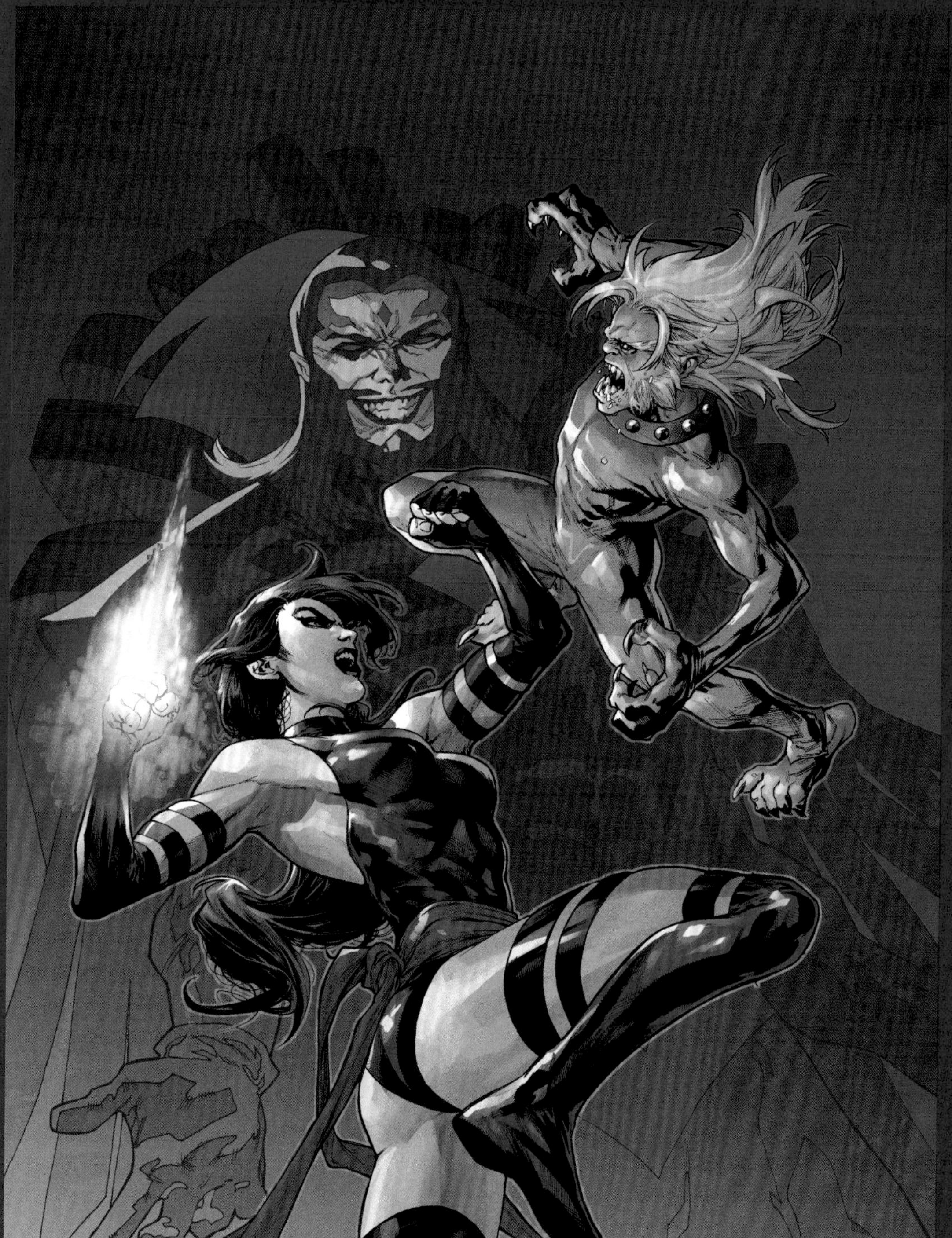

Hellions #2

by Stephen Segovia
& Rain Beredo

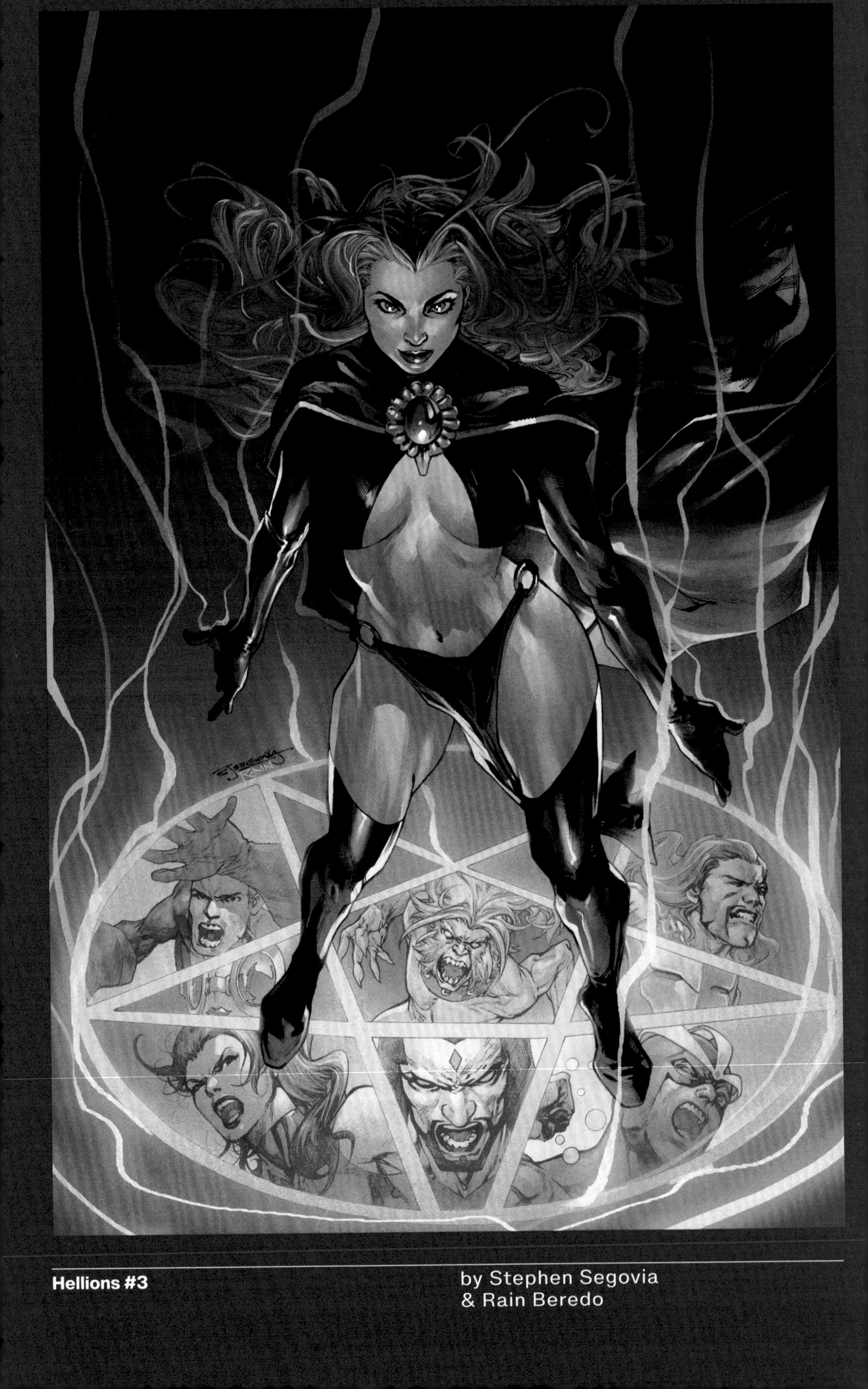

Hellions #3

by Stephen Segovia
& Rain Beredo

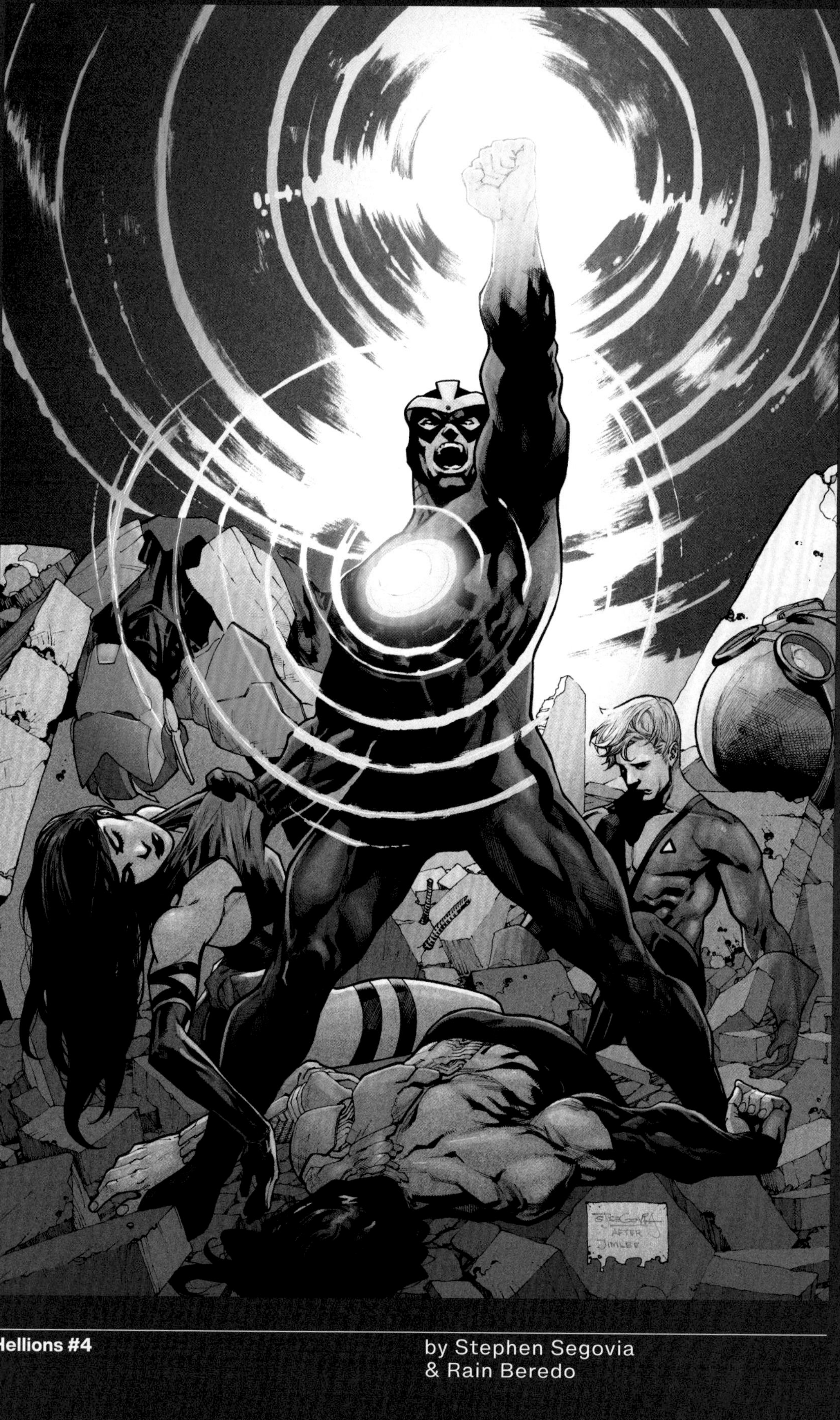

Hellions #4

by Stephen Segovia
& Rain Beredo

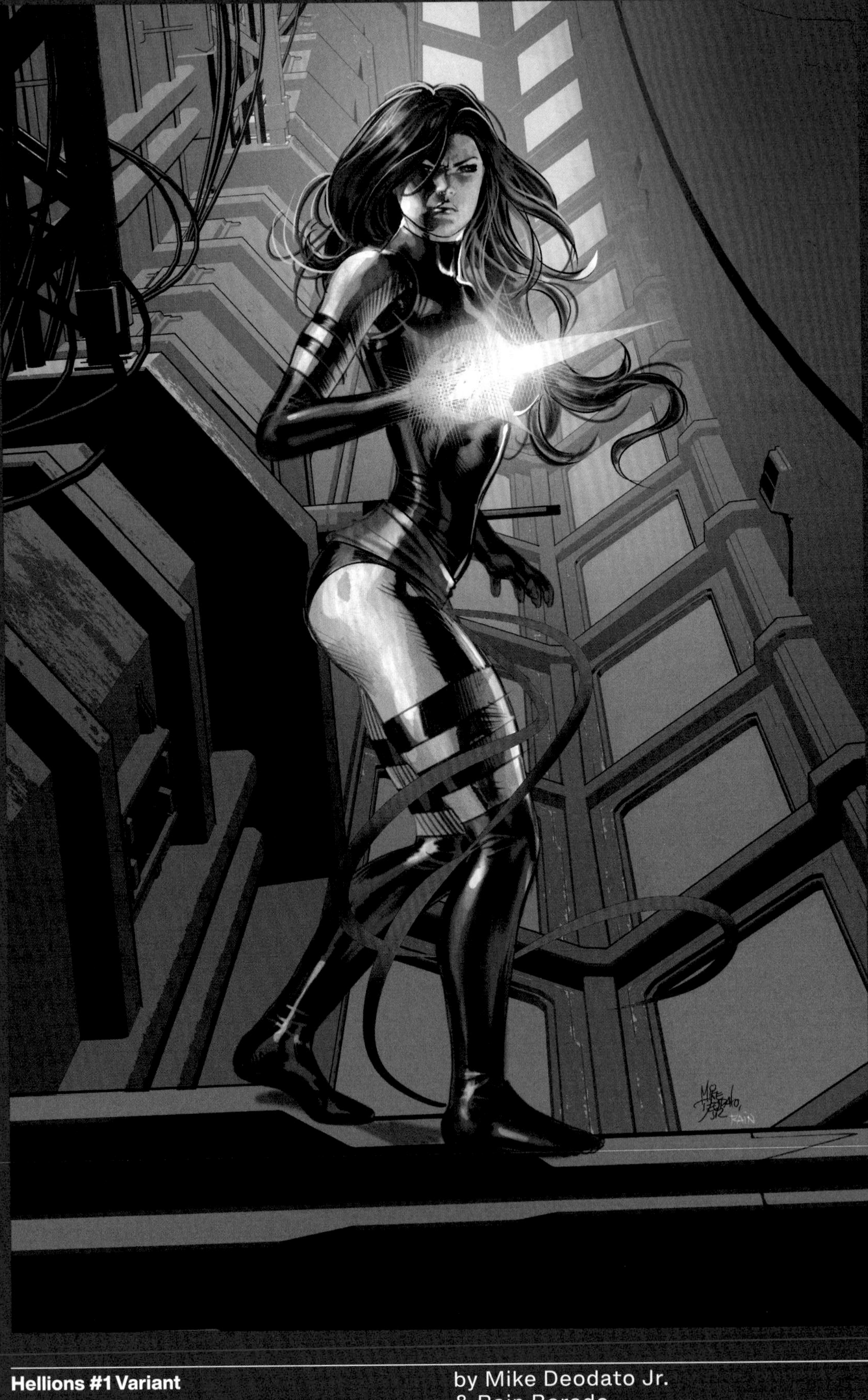

Hellions #1 Variant

by Mike Deodato Jr.
& Rain Beredo

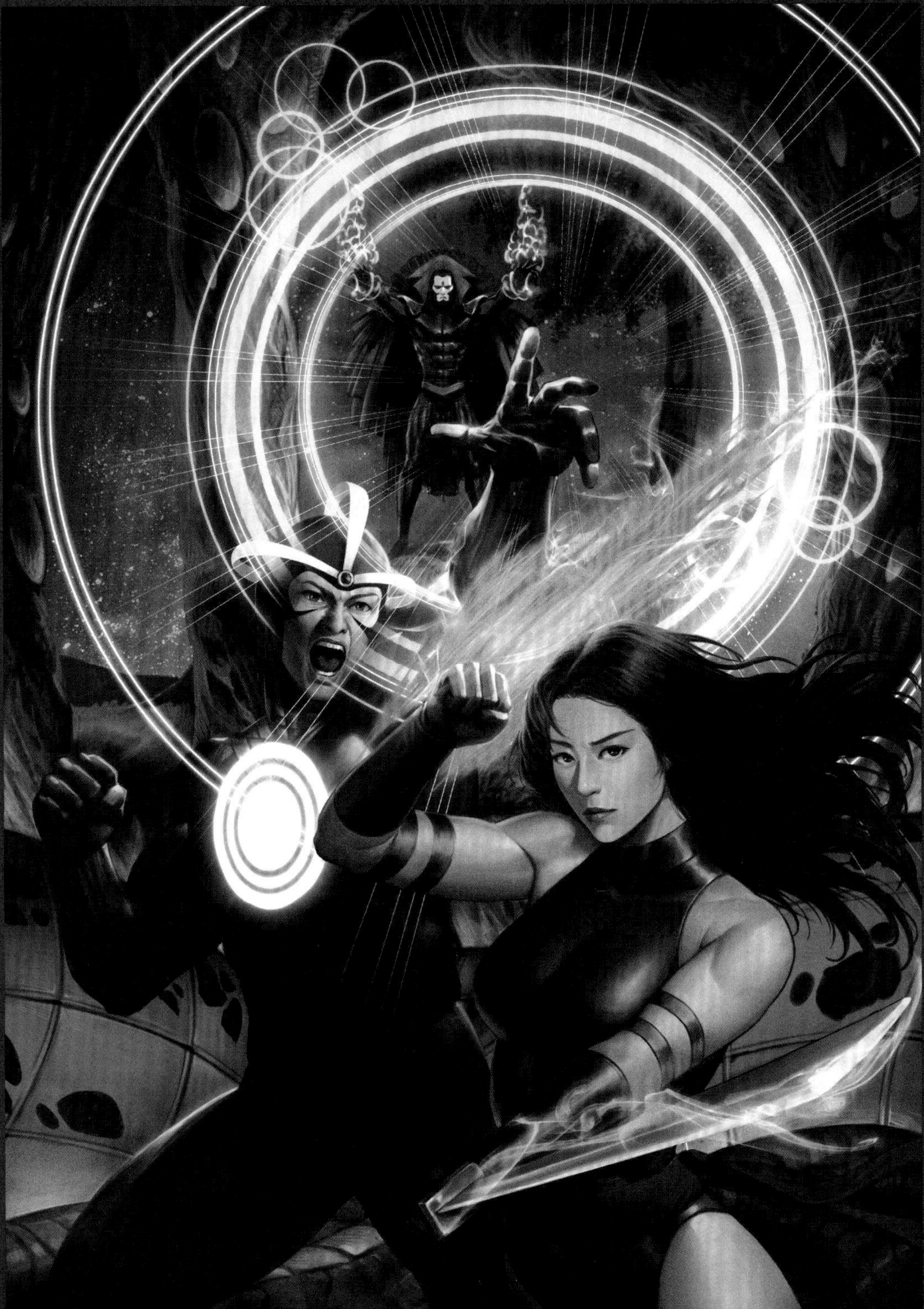

Hellions #1 Variant by Woo Dae Shim

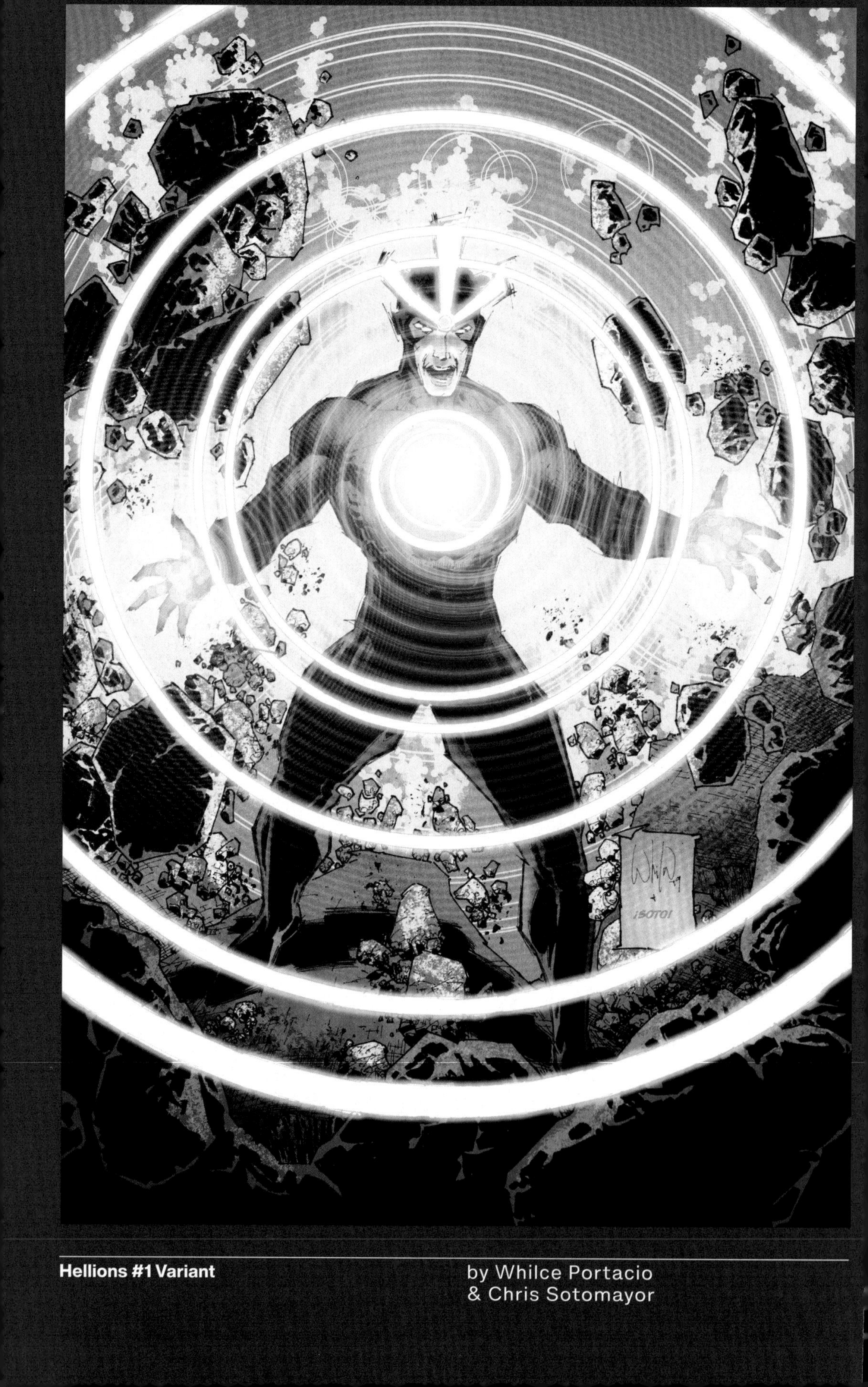

Hellions #1 Variant

by Whilce Portacio
& Chris Sotomayor

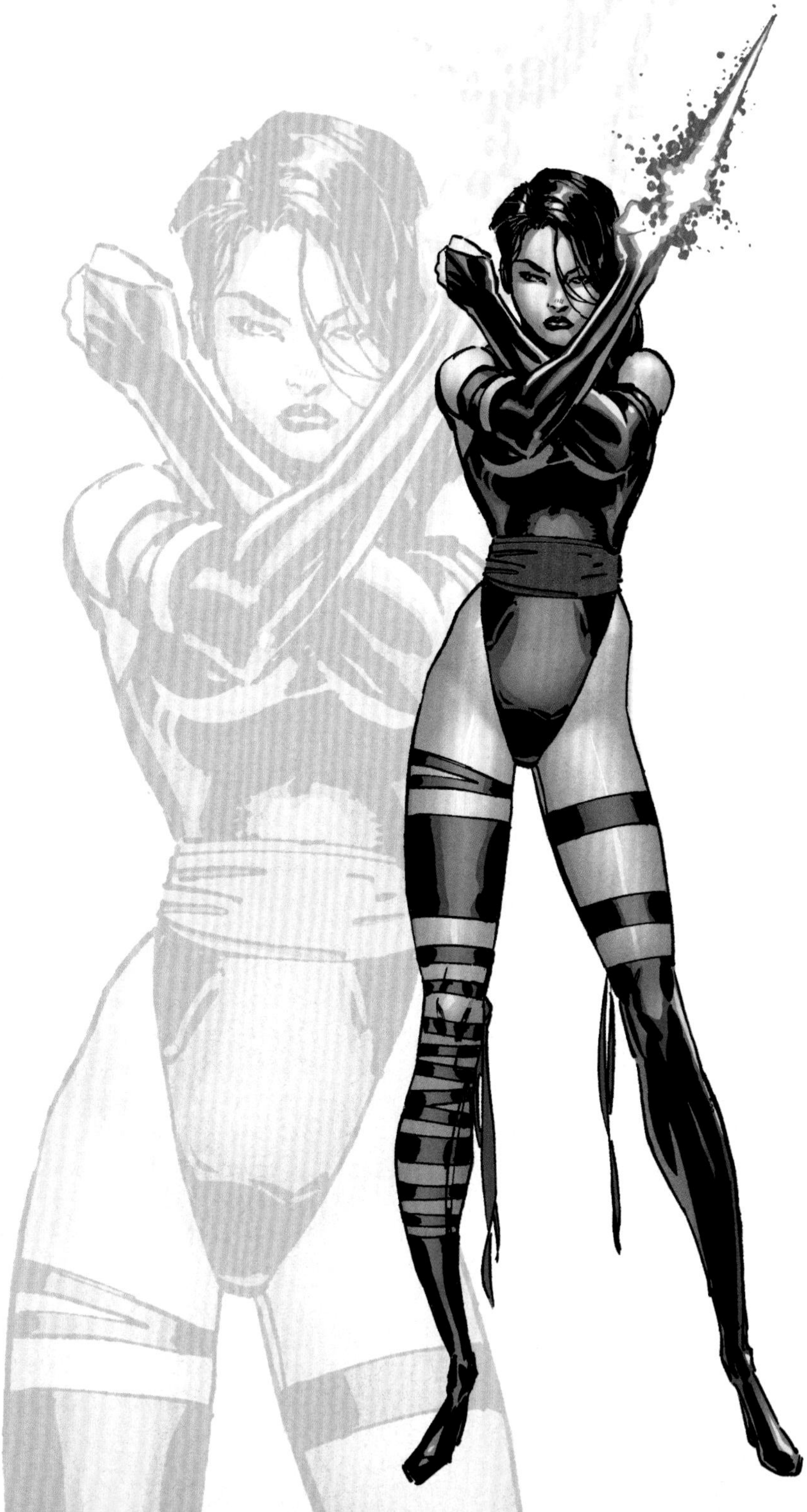

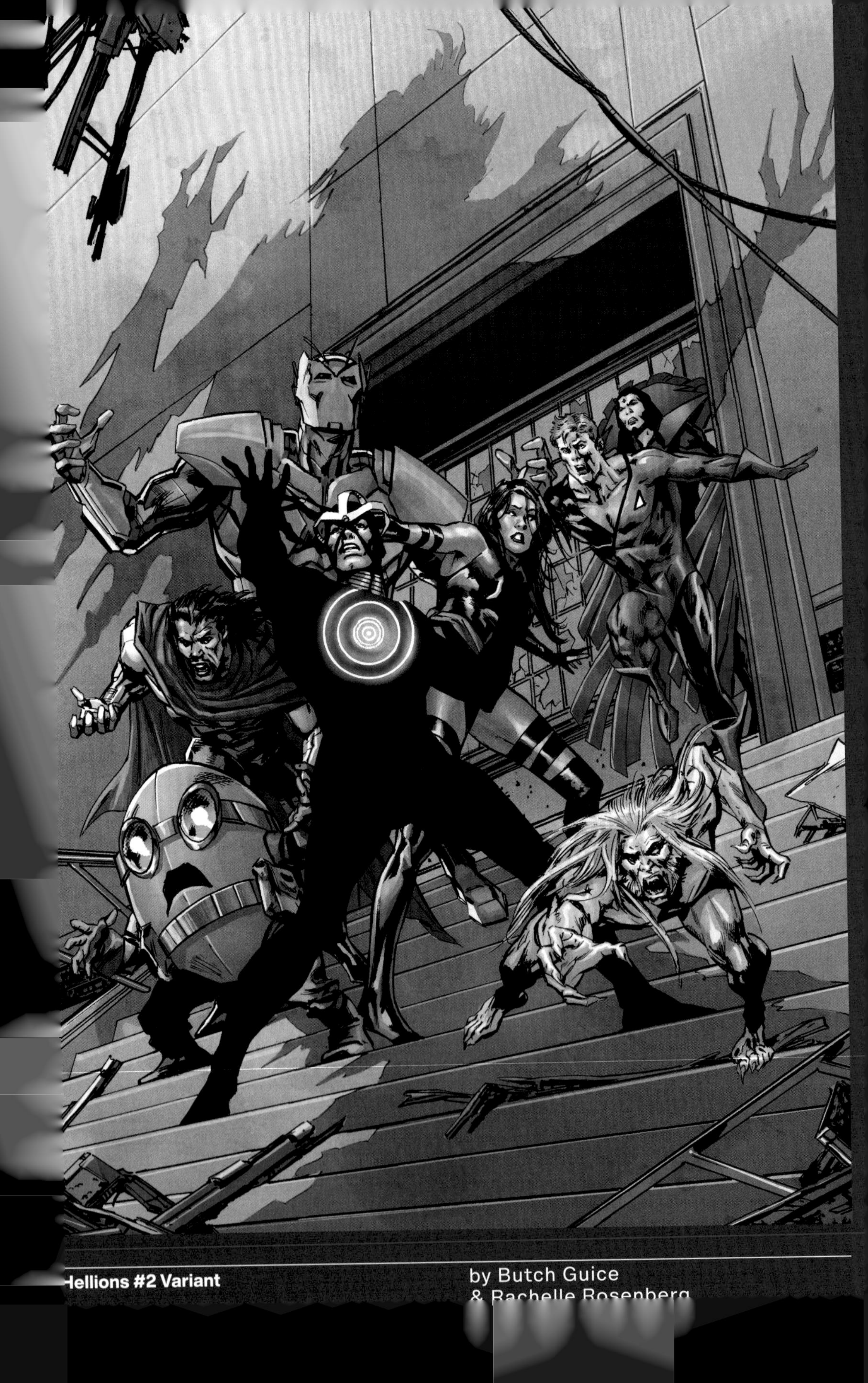

Hellions #2 Variant

by Butch Guice
& Rachelle Rosenberg

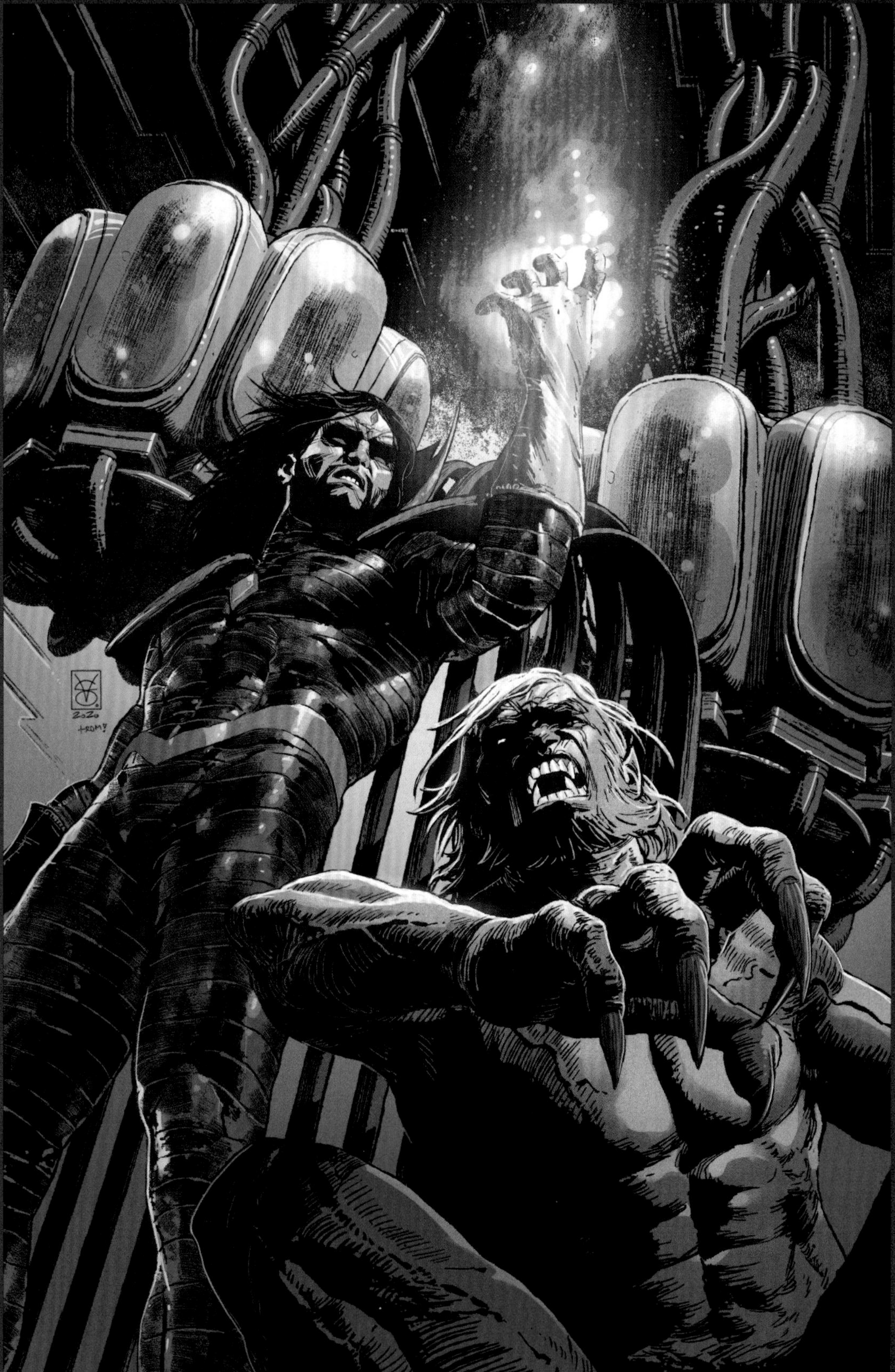

Hellions #3 Variant

by Valerio Giangiordano
& Romulo Fajardo Jr.

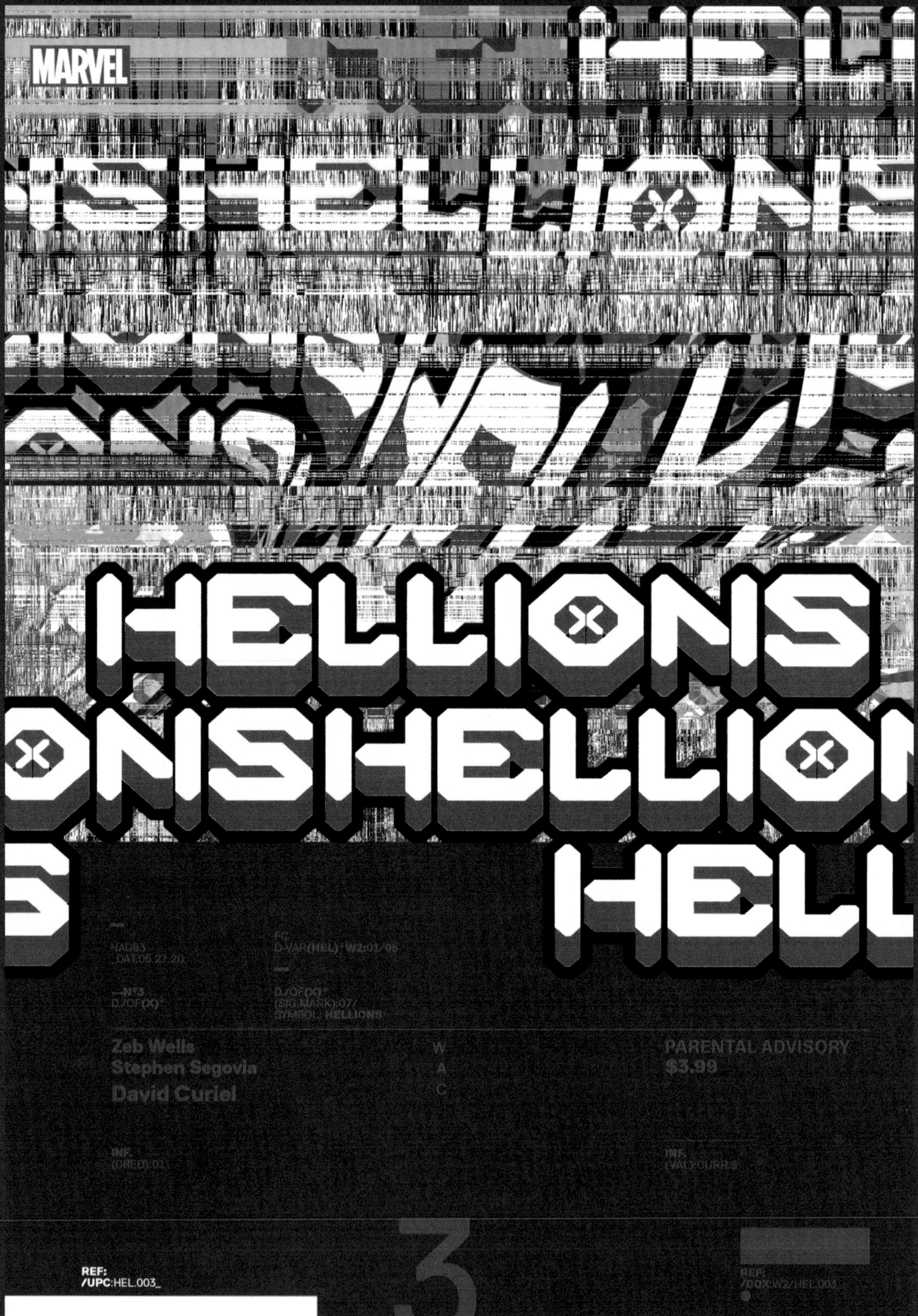

MARVEL
HELLIONS
NAD83
_DAT.05.27.20
FC
D-VAR(HEL)*W2:01/05
—N°3
D./OF(X)*
D./OF(X)*
(SIG.MARK):07/
SYMBOL: HELLIONS
Zeb Wells
Stephen Segovia
David Curiel
W
A
C
PARENTAL ADVISORY
$3.99
INF.
(CRED):01
INF.
(VAL):CURR.$
3
REF:
/UPC:HEL.003_
REF:
/DOX:W2/HEL.003
REF:/TM/MFR:
hello
Muller

Hellions #3 Design Variant by Tom Muller

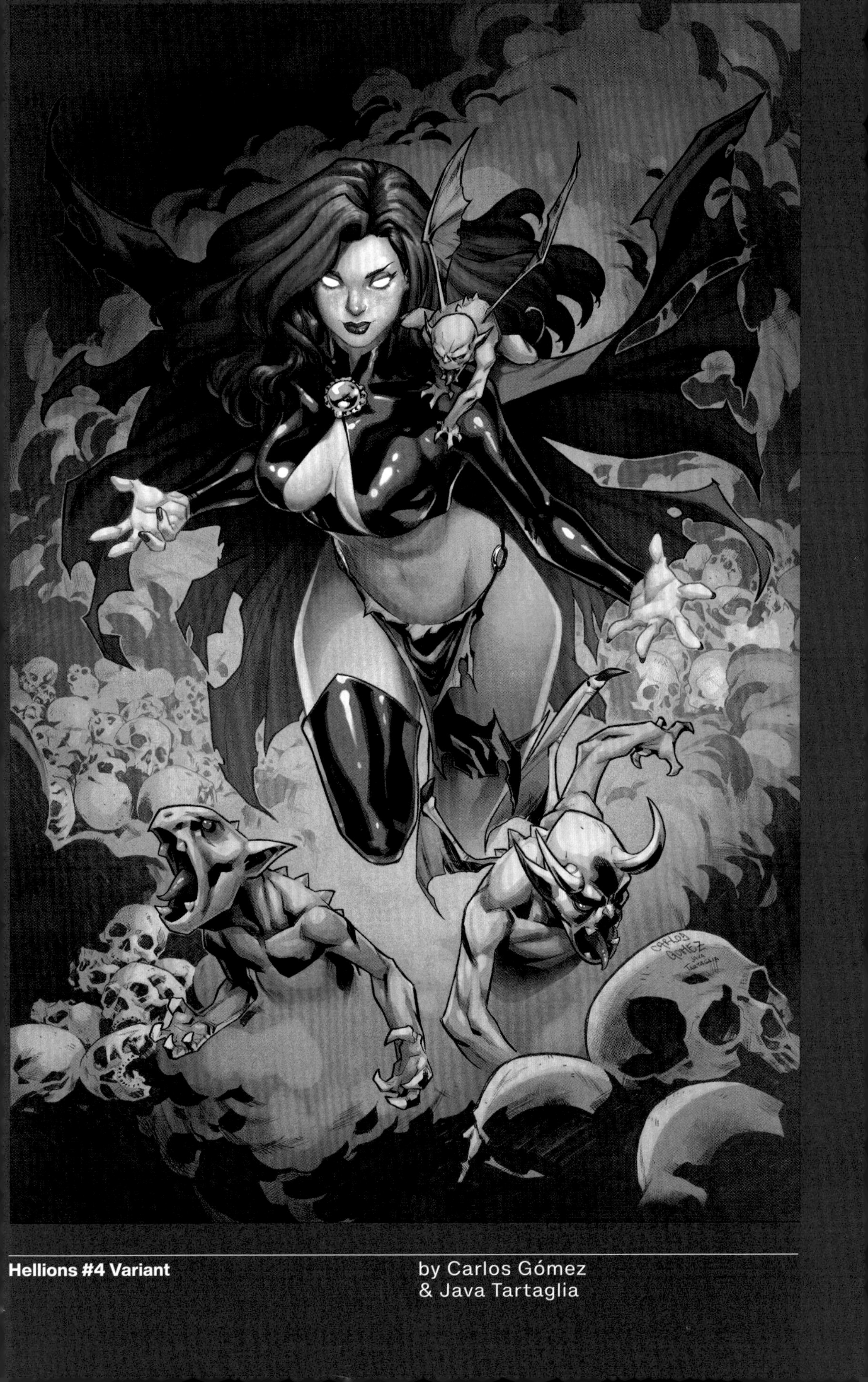

Hellions #4 Variant

by Carlos Gómez
& Java Tartaglia